The Earth Shall Blossom

Shaker Herbs and Gardening

Galen Beale
Mary Rose Boswell

The Countryman Press, Inc.
Woodstock, Vermont

LIBRARY OF CONGRESS CATALOGING-IN-PUBLICATION DATA
    Beale, Galen, 1942-
    The earth shall blossom: Shaker herbs and Gardening /
Galen Beale and Mary Rose Boswell.
        p.   cm.
    Includes bibliographical references and index.
    ISBN 0-88150-183-2
    1. Shakers.   2. Herb gardens–United States.   3. Herbs–
Therapeutic use.   I. Boswell, Mary Rose.   II. Title.
BX9785.H6B43 1991
635'.7'088288—dc20   91-8887
                                                        CIP

Published by The Countryman Press
PO Box 748, Woodstock, Vermont 05091

Distributed by W. W. Norton & Company, Inc.
500 Fifth Avenue, New York, New York 10110

The following have kindly granted permission to allow us to quote from their published works:

Henry Francis du Pont Winterthur Museum, The Edward Deming Andrews Memorial Shaker Collection, Winterthur, Delaware

MacMillan Company: Amy Bess Miller and Persis Wellington Fuller, *The Best of Shaker Cooking,* 1970

Rodale Press Book Division: William H. Hylton, ed., *The Rodale Herb Book,* 1974

Shaker Village, Inc.: Eldress Bertha Lindsay, *Seasoned with Grace,* 1987

Hancock Shaker Village, Inc.: Mary L. Richmond, *Shaker Literature: A Bibliography,* 1974

Cover and text design by Virginia L. Scott
Cover illustration of Mildred Wells' garden at Canterbury Village by Judy Jensen, based on a photograph by Joseph St. Pierre

10 9 8 7 6 5 4 3 2

Printed in the United States of America

This book is dedicated to the memory of
Mildred Wells—gardener, herbalist, and friend.

Behold the Flowers that deck the Field,
The Gentle breeze perfuming,
And Tender Herbs their Fragrance Yield
Are Health and Life Diffusing.

front cover, herb catalog,
Harvard Community, 1843

Contents

Acknowledgments   ix

Who are the Shakers?   xiii

Shaker Timeline   xvii

Shaker Communities   xxiv

1. Creating a "Heaven on Earth"   1

2. The Development of the Shakers' Herb Business   19

3. "If You Want a Splendid Garden, Buy the Shakers' Garden Seeds"   35

4. Shaker Gardens Today   45

5. "Persevering Faithfulness": Creating Your Shaker Herb Garden   63

6. "The Power to Heal": The Shakers' Medical Practices   101

7. The First Herbalists   115

8. The Age of the Cure   133

9. Culinary Herbs 155

10. Domestic Uses of Herbs 177

11. "These Shall Speak with Touching Power": 203
    Shaker Catalogs

    Appendix I: Shaker Catalog 219

    Appendix II: Medicinal Herb Catalogs 223

    Appendix III: Seed Catalogs 229

    Notes 235

    Bibliography 251

    Index 259

Acknowledgments

We had the privilege of working at Shaker Village, Inc., Canterbury, New Hampshire, for a number of years. This was a unique situation where we could study eighteenth- and nineteenth-century documents and, at the same time, consult with living Shakers who would share their views with us.

Eldress Bertha Lindsay always claimed that she was not responsible for any data prior to her arrival at Canterbury in 1905, but she was a phenomenal resource of information about the Canterbury Shakers in the twentieth century. She, Eldress Gertrude Soule, Sister Ethel Hudson, and Mildred Wells were invaluable in identifying Shaker individuals in photographs, documenting artifacts, and directing us to little-known locations on the property. When we felt we had learned all there was to know about a topic, they usually surprised us with a piece of information that we never would have guessed.

One thing we learned from our experience is that it can be dangerous to make assumptions or generalizations about the Shakers. With over two hundred years of history, thousands of members, and a tradition that is evolving even today, this fascinating group of people will always offer something new.

This book focuses on the Shakers' extensive involvement with herbs and provides new information on their business acumen, horticultural skills, resourcefulness, and knowledge as well as the Shaker relations with one another and the World.[1]

We want this book to be a pleasant experience not only for those avidly pursuing all things Shaker but also for gardeners and cooks as well. We have included original recipes, lists, and plans, and, in true Shaker fashion, we have added modern adaptations and suggestions.

This book would not have been possible without the aid and support of many people. We wish to thank the following individuals who helped us in our research: Rita Braskie, Priscilla Brewer, Jerry Grant, Happy Griffith, Marcia Byron Hartwell, Tommy Hines, Dory Hudspeth, Mary Kerwin, Paige Lilly, Bruce Marriott, Mrs. Lawrence W. Miller, Dr. M. Stephen Miller, Bruce Nault, Northwoods Chair Shop, Debbie Larkin Pope, Ann Sindelair, Caroline Smith, Marcheta Sparrow, June Sprigg, David R. Starbuck, Stephen Stein, Martha Vadnais, Dianne Watkins, Tom Weldon, and the staff and members of the United Society of Shakers, Sabbathday Lake, Maine.

We also wish to thank the staff at each of the following institutions for their gracious help and support: the Baker Library, Dartmouth College, Hanover, New Hampshire; Hancock Shaker Village, Pittsfield, Massachusetts; the Museum at Lower Shaker Village, Enfield, New Hampshire; Fruitlands Museums, Harvard, Massachusetts; Mount Lebanon Shaker Village, Mount Lebanon, New York; New Hampshire Historical Society, Concord, New Hampshire; New Hampshire State Library, Concord, New Hampshire; New York State Library, Albany, New York; Shakertown at Pleasant Hill, Kentucky; Shakertown at South Union, Kentucky; The Shaker Museum, Old Chatham, New York; Western Reserve Historical Society, Cleveland, Ohio; Williams College Library, Williamstown, Massachusetts; Winterthur Library, Winterthur, Delaware.

We are indebted to the late Eldress Bertha Lindsay of Canterbury, New Hampshire. As a friend and trustee of Shaker Village, Inc., Eldress Bertha provided us with encouragement for many years while we were employed there and was a source of inspiration to us. We will always be grateful to her for her interest and support.

Finally, we want to thank Tom Boswell, Kenelm Doak, and Roger Gibbs for their expertise and assistance that they gave whenever we asked. We are especially grateful to them for their patience, understanding, and encouragement.

Galen Beale and Mary Rose Boswell

A special note of recognition should be given to the late Louis Wilder, who held the position of production manager at The Countryman Press until his death in August 1990. This book was Lou's last project, and I will always be grateful to him for asking me to work with him on it. Lou and I worked several months together on the book *Seasoned with Grace.* We spent many hours together on the telephone discussing all subjects related to the book, from design to footnotes. I fondly remember those pleasant times. Lou and I did not always agree, and he usually won the arguments. At all times, however, he was gracious, diplomatic, and full of interesting thoughts. It was refreshing that I could be frank with him. For *The Earth Shall Blossom,* Lou had a definite idea about what he wanted this book to be. Galen and I were fortunate to have his wife, Susan, take over during his illness. Because of her abilities as a gardener and an editor, we think this book would have met his expectations.

Mary Rose Boswell

Who are the Shakers?

*T*he members of the United Society of Believers in Christ's Second Appearing, a religious sect commonly known as Shakers, have been of interest to Americans for two centuries. Today their simple furniture sells for seemingly boundless sums of money at auction houses; their medicine bottles, manuscripts, and even their tiny spools of thread are highly prized. Shaker villages, many of which have been preserved as museums in the last few decades, attract thousands of visitors each year. With two remaining active communities, this organization has become the most successful and enduring communal sect in the United States.

Their experiment began humbly with the arrival of nine Believers from Manchester, England, in 1774.[1] Their leader was Ann Lee, a middle-aged factory worker and infirmary cook, whose visions and testimony against sin were so convincing that the members readily acknowledged her as their spiritual mother in Christ. This little society initially had no special creed or order of worship; the purpose of their organization was to increase the work of God and establish the Millennial Church. Later the gospel mission expanded to include the confession of sin, the practice of celibacy, and isolation from all temptations of the

World. Their "holy gifts," manifested in their shaking, singing, and speaking "as the spirit gave utterance," earned them the name of "Shaker." This term was originally given in contempt of their unusual worship practices, but it was never objectionable to the members of the Society and is used by them today.

In time the Believers would develop highly organized, isolated communities that protected the members from persecution and granted them economic security. Converts donated all of their property, including their furniture, buildings, land, and animals, upon entering the Society. Husbands, wives, and children were separated so that all individuals could faithfully devote their lives to creating a more perfect, spiritual "heaven on earth." By 1794 the Believers had established eleven such communities throughout Maine, New Hampshire, Massachusetts, Connecticut, and New York. By 1836 they had formed eleven additional villages, expanding into the midwestern states of Ohio and Indiana. By 1898 they had started two other settlements in Georgia and Florida. At the time of their highest population in the mid-nineteenth century, they had claimed thousands of converts.

Why did this sect attract so many members? Most of the Believers were simple tradespeople and farmers who sought to live a spiritual life on earth. The isolated communities with their mills, factories, meetinghouses, and farms offered men and women a secure home where they could perfect their talents for a higher purpose. The tenets of celibacy, hard work, and perfection gave the members direction and increased their sense of worth.

The Shakers' experiment thrived as long as it did because the members were able to adjust to the World around them. They were entrepreneurs who had an exceptional ability to understand popular trends which they used to their own advantage. As entrepreneurs and artisans, they could readily furnish the World with high-quality goods at competitive prices.

The sect was, for the most part, also blessed with excellent leaders. The elders and eldresses were able to formalize their communities into highly organized social and religious systems. Yet the organization has always been a flexible one; for nearly fifty years, from the time Mother Ann Lee came to America until 1821, the organization existed without any written regulations and relied instead on the guidance and judgment of its leaders as situations arose.

In later years the sect's population declined. The Shakers' mills could not compete with the World's factories; and America's cities, industries, and the western frontier promised men and women adventure and financial success. The communities were left mainly with elderly members and young orphans, none of whom had training in management or were physically able to do much of the work.[2]

Today people may visit the remaining Shakers at Canterbury, New Hampshire, and Sabbathday Lake, Maine. Even in the twentieth century, these Believers have shown remarkable fortitude and resourcefulness in adjusting to the World and keeping the spirit of their religion alive.

Shaker Timeline

1747   Jane and James Wardley, former Quakers living in
Manchester, England, establish a new religious society based on beliefs in the open confession of sins
and taking up the testimony against sin.

1758   Ann Lee, a blacksmith's daughter living in Manchester, England, becomes involved in the Wardley
Society.

1774   Ann Lee and a small band of followers leave the
Wardleys in England and sail to New York to win
new converts. They eventually call themselves Believers in Christ's Second Appearing. Because of their
demonstrated religious fervor, they are also called
Shakers. Ann Lee, whom they acknowledge to be
their spiritual mother in Christ, is called Mother Ann
Lee.

1780-82   Having settled at Niskeyuna, New York (later called
Watervliet), some of the Shakers preach throughout
Massachusetts and Connecticut, urging people to

adopt the ways of Christ, practice celibacy, and forsake the material concerns of the World.

1784   Mother Ann dies, and James Whittaker carries on her mission from New Lebanon, New York.

1787   The Shaker community at Watervliet, New York, is formally established. The Shaker village at New Lebanon, New York, is formed and becomes the home of the Lead Ministry. Joseph Meacham and Lucy Wright become the Lead Ministers.

1790   The Shaker communities at Hancock, Massachusetts, and Enfield, Connecticut, are formed as part of the New Lebanon Bishopric. The seed industry is established at Watervliet.

1791   The Harvard, Massachusetts, Shaker community is formed. Sister Sarah Jewett is the first physician there and is assisted by Tabitha Babbit.

1792   The Canterbury, New Hampshire, and Tyringham, Massachusetts, Shaker communities are established. Tyringham joins the New Lebanon Bishopric.

1793   Communities are formally started at Shirley, Massachusetts; Enfield, New Hampshire; and Alfred, Maine. Shirley forms a bishopric with Harvard; Enfield forms a bishopric with Canterbury.

1794   The community at Sabbathday Lake, Maine, is established and forms a bishopric with the Alfred village. An herb business begins at New Lebanon, New York.

1795   The villages at New Lebanon; Hancock; Canterbury; and Enfield, New Hampshire, have started seed businesses by this time.

1801   The Maine communities begin selling seeds.

1802   The Enfield, Connecticut, Shakers establish a seed business.

1805   The Shirley community starts a seed business.

1806	The Union Village, Ohio, and Pleasant Hill, Kentucky, Shaker communities are formed.
1807	The South Union, Kentucky, Shaker village is founded.
1808	A Shaker settlement is started in Gorham, Maine. In 1819 its members move to Sabbathday Lake and become part of that community.
1810	The West Union (Busro), Indiana, Shaker village is formed.
1812	By this time the New Lebanon Shakers have an herb garden. Eliab Harlow and Isaac Crouch are the first physicians at the village.
1813	Thomas Corbett qualifies himself as a physician at Canterbury.
1815	Benjamin Warren is the first physician at Enfield, New Hampshire.
1816	Thomas Corbett establishes an herb garden at Canterbury. The Union Village Shakers are selling seeds by this time. The South Union members take their first flatboat trip down the river to New Orleans to find new markets for seeds and other products.
1817	The Savoy, Massachusetts, Shaker community is founded.
1820	The Harvard Believers are selling herbs. The Canterbury Shakers start taking trips to resort towns for health reasons.
1821	The Lead Ministry issues the Millennial Laws, which include the first written restrictions on the Shakers' diet. The Order of Physicians and Nurses is established. The South Union members sell their first seeds.
1822	The North Union, Ohio, Shaker village is established.
1824	The Whitewater, Ohio, Shaker community is started.

1826	The Shaker community at Sodus Bay, New York, is founded.
1830	The Watervliet Believers issue the first dated Shaker herb catalog, offering 128 herbs for sale, along with pills, syrups, and two medicinal waters.
1833	The Union Village Shakers establish an herb garden. Abiathar Babbitt and Andrew Houston are the community's physicians.
1835	The Shaker village at Canterbury issues its first herb catalog, listing 180 herbs for sale. The communities of New Lebanon and Enfield, Connecticut, print the *Gardener's Manual*, which contains cultural instructions for seeds.
1836	The Groveland, New York, Shaker village is formed. New Lebanon's first *dated* herb catalog is issued, offering 164 herbs for sale.
1841	The Canterbury Shakers begin making Corbett's Sarsaparilla Syrup. New Lebanon is the first community to sell culinary herbs. The Lead Ministry recommends that Believers refrain from eating pork and drinking tea and coffee.
1845	Harvard issues the first of the community's eleven herb catalogs with 197 herbs for sale. Simon Atherton is in charge of the business.
1847	The Union Village, Ohio, issues its first herb catalog, offering 156 herbs. Peter Boyd is in charge of the trade.
1848	Enfield, New Hampshire, publishes its Extract of English Valerian catalog. The Canterbury Shakers buy an additional 8 1/2 acres on which to grow herbs.
1850	The 19 existing Shaker villages have at least 150 acres under cultivation for medicinal herbs.
1851	Canterbury issues the first *Shakers' Manual*, which advertises both its Corbett's Sarsaparilla Syrup and Enfield's Valerian Extract.

1854   The Enfield, Connecticut, Shakers issue their only herb and seed catalog, listing 220 herbs, 19 extracts, and a large selection of vegetable, flower, and herb seeds.

1859   New Lebanon begins manufacturing Norwood's Tincture of Veratrum Viride. Sales of this product continue into the twentieth century.

1860   The Enfield, New Hampshire, Shakers issue their first herb catalog.

1861   The New Lebanon community changes its name to Mount Lebanon.

1864   The Sabbathday Lake Believers issue their first herb catalog.

1873   The Mount Lebanon Village publishes the last of its large catalogs, "The Druggist Handbook," listing 404 herbs for sale.

1876   Corbett's Shaker's Compound Concentrated Syrup of Sarsaparilla is awarded a medal at the Centennial Exhibition in Philadelphia.

1878   Medals are awarded at the 47th Exhibition of American Institute for Canterbury's Sarsaparilla Syrup and Enfield, New Hampshire's, Valerian Extract.

1881   A. J. White begins publishing the first of many Shaker almanacs. These advertise Mount Lebanon's medicines.

1882   *Mary Whitcher's Shaker House-Keeper* is printed for the Canterbury Shakers. It is a cookbook that includes advertisements for their sarsaparilla syrup and other products that are distributed by their agents, Weeks and Potter.

1886   The Canterbury Shakers register trademarks for their Compound of Wild Cherry Pectoral Syrup and Sarsaparilla Lozenges.

1896   The village at Norcoossee, Florida, is started.

1898   The Shaker community at White Oak, Georgia, is formed.

1906   U.S. Pure Food and Drug Act is enacted.

1913   The Canterbury Shakers distill witch hazel for the last time.

1914   Fruitlands Museums are established.

1931   Sabbathday Lake is incorporated as a museum.

1947   The Mount Lebanon community closes. The Lead Ministry moves to Hancock Shaker Village in Pittsfield, Massachusetts. Members of the Lead Ministry are Francis Hall of Hancock and Josephine Wilson and Emma King of Canterbury.

1957   The Lead Ministry moves to Canterbury. The Lead Eldresses are Gertrude Soule of Sabbathday Lake and Ida Crook and Emma King of Canterbury.

1961   Pleasant Hill and South Union are incorporated as museums. Hancock Shaker Village becomes a museum.

1965   The Lead Ministry vote to close the covenant membership of the Shaker societies.

1969   Canterbury Shaker Village is incorporated as a museum.

1971   Shakertown at South Union, Kentucky, is started as a museum.

1972   Gertrude Soule of Sabbathday Lake visits Canterbury and remains as a resident. Members of the Lead Ministry are Eldress Gertrude Soule and Eldress Bertha Lindsay of Canterbury.

1983   Mount Lebanon is incorporated as a museum.

1986   The Museum at Lower Shaker Village, Enfield, New Hampshire, is established.

1988   Eldress Gertrude Soule, Lead Minister, dies.

1990   Eldress Bertha Lindsay, Lead Minister, dies. The Lead
                  Ministry terminates with the death of Eldress Bertha.
                  Canterbury and Sabbathday Lake remain as active
                  communities.

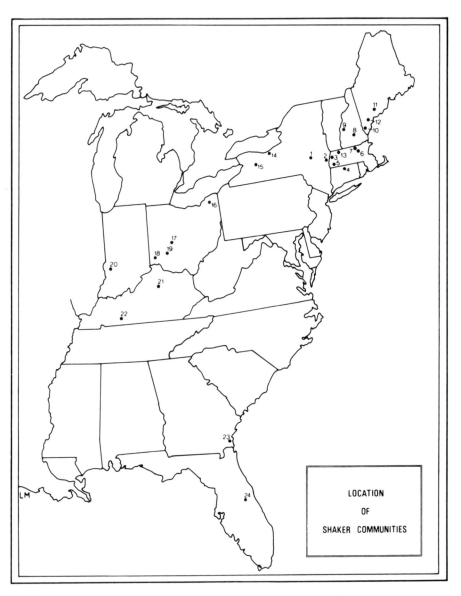

1	Watervliet, New York	(1787-1938)
• 2	New Lebanon, New York	(1787-1947)
• 3	Hancock, Massachusetts	(1790-1960)
4	Enfield, Connecticut	(1790-1917)
5	Tyringham, Massachusetts	(1792-1875)
6	Harvard, Massachusetts	(1791-1918)
7	Shirley, Massachusetts	(1793-1908)
• • 8	Canterbury, New Hampshire	(1792-present)
• 9	Enfield, New Hampshire	(1793-1923)
10	Alfred, Maine	(1793-1931)
• • 11	Sabbathday Lake, Maine	(1794-present)
12	Gorham, Maine	(1808-1819)
13	Savoy, Massachusetts	(1817-1825)
14	Sodus Bay, New York	(1826-1836)
15	Groveland, New York	(1836-1895)
16	North Union, Ohio	(1822-1889)
17	Union Village, Ohio	(1806-1912)
18	Whitewater, Ohio	(1824-1907)
19	Watervliet, Ohio	(1806-1910)
20	West Union(Bustro), Indiana	(1810-1827)
• 21	Pleasant Hill, Kentucky	(1806-1910)
• 22	South Union, Kentucky	(1807-1922)
23	White Oak, Georgia	(1898-1902)
24	Narcoossee, Florida	(1896-1911)

• Museum, open to the public.   • • Active community and museum

This diagram was provided with permission from University Press of New England.

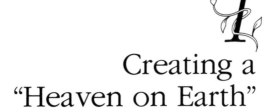

Creating a
"Heaven on Earth"

Go work with ardent courage,
And sow with willing hand
The seed o'er barren deserts,
And o'er the fertile land.

And, lo! earth yet shall blossom,
Though the brighter morn delays;
For God perfects the harvest,
Yea, "after many days."

Quoted in *Mother Ann Lee*, by Elder
Henry Clay Blinn, published by the
Canterbury Shakers, East Canterbury,
New Hampshire, 1901

S hakerism is deeply rooted in an agricultural philosophy.
Traceable to Mother Ann and her followers was the belief in
making a living from the land. Frederick Evans, a Shaker from the
New Lebanon village, summarized the concept in this way:

> Every commune, to prosper, must be founded, so far as its
> industry goes, on agriculture. Only the simple labors and
> manners of a farming people can hold a community together.[1]

Throughout their history, the Shakers amassed large tracts of land
which they used to their fullest capacity. In trying to create a
"heaven on earth," they applied their ideals to all of their tasks. This
pursuit of perfectionism soon became evident in their products,
work-saving devices, and new branches of business, including the
highly successful herb industry.

When John Hocknell, one of Mother Ann's followers and the financier for the early Shakers, searched for a place in which to establish the Society in 1774, he had many criteria for their new home. In order for the Shakers to live separately from the World and be self-sufficient, he had to find a spot that suited their particular needs. The site had to have an adequate supply of pure water, good drainage for crops, and sufficient woodlands to provide timber for their dwellings and shops. It was this dual requirement to be isolated and self-sufficient that set the Shakers' pattern of land acquisition, which was to continue in the settlement of all their communities.

The Societies were naturally similar as they shared a common belief system; and when an enterprise such as the herb industry proved to be profitable at one community, it was adopted by others. Yet each village had its own distinct characteristics, depending on the abilities of its members and the nature of the land on which they settled. These early settlement patterns provide an understanding of how the herb trade developed and why it became one of the most successful financial endeavors of the Shakers.

The usual pattern in forming a new community was to enlist converts, who, upon following the advice of their leaders, would surrender their houses, barns, acreage, money, and tools to the common cause. Neighboring lands given to the Society were incorporated into a single farm. Contributed property located far from the central site was either traded for adjacent land or maintained as an outlying farm by Shakers or hired labor.

At each Society members were organized into Families, to which they owed their allegiance. Each Family had its own shops, dwellings, and gardens. These units were usually located within a mile or so of one another and were named according to their geographic location relative to the main, or Church, Family (such as the West Family), or according to their importance in the Society (such as the Second Family). Each was governed by two Elders and two Eldresses, who looked after the governmental and spiritual concerns. Two Deacons and two Deaconesses supervised the day-to-day activities. Two Trustees and two Office Sisters managed transactions with the World. All of the Families were under the control of the Church Family Ministry. Each community looked to the Lead Ministry at New Lebanon, New York, as the final authority.

To keep harmony within the neighboring villages, a common Ministry was given charge of two or more Societies. This territorial jurisdiction was known as a bishopric. The Elders and Eldresses of the bishoprics were selected by the Lead Ministry at New Lebanon for their managerial abilities and practical experience and were well schooled by the Ministry. Once appointed as Elders and Eldresses, they had their own quarters, dining room, workshop, and horses.[2]

The New Lebanon and Watervliet communities were united in the first bishopric under the direct supervision of the Lead Ministry. The members of this Ministry lived in a building attached to the meetinghouse and dined in a room isolated from their Brothers and Sisters. They made baskets in a shop designed exclusively for this purpose. Because of their relative seclusion and the fact that they often served for many years, these men and women looked to other bishopric leaders for friendship and moral support.

All bishopric Elders and Eldresses were required to visit New Lebanon each year to keep in touch with the Lead Ministry, and they took this opportunity to stop at other communities on the way. They traveled from village to village and frequently communicated in writing to one another.

Although the Families were geographically and economically autonomous, all the members of a community would join together during Sunday worship services and at other important occasions. Despite their separateness, there was a great deal of cooperation among them. When necessary, one Family would help the other by supplying materials, labor, technology, and often money.

As trade with the World increased, the Trustees upheld their belief in creating a "heaven on earth." Everything made or sold by Believers always had to be perfect.

> We were to exceed the World in all our temporal management and workmanship. We were to do what ever we did faithfully, especially articles manufactured for sale. All such articles were to be made in a neat and substantial manner, without unnecessary ornament or blemish. . . .The Trustees were not permitted to sell any article whatever manufactured in the Church, at any price unless it was entirely free from blemish. Such articles might be used at home, or given to the poor. We often received specimens of the various kinds of manufacture as samples from New Lebanon, made in the most substantial and perfect manner. . . .[3]

The Trustees also set up a system whereby the Believers rotated their jobs in order to distribute the work evenly, relieve monotony, and educate the members so that substitutes were always available in times of illness or crisis. Natural ability and initiative were fostered. If a member entered the Society with a trade, he was allowed to devote the majority of his time to it. Everyone, regardless of age or sex, was busily employed in some activity. When there were

Elder Henry Blinn (1824-1905) helped oversee the Canterbury and Enfield Shaker communities in New Hampshire. During his sixty-seven years as a Canterbury Shaker, he held many jobs, including beekeeping. The bees were used to pollinate the orchards. (Private collection)

seasonal needs for labor, such as haying, sugaring, planting, or gathering, all hands would be called upon to help; at times, some shops were closed until the rush work was completed.

The Ministry appointed the Trustees, who were chosen in recognition of their integrity, leadership, and interpersonal and financial skills. Once selected, Elders and Trustees often remained in the same position for many years.

Henry Blinn was a good example of such a leader. Born in Providence, Rhode Island in 1824, he entered the Canterbury community when he was fourteen, already having apprenticed as a tailor and a jeweler. His first job at Canterbury was sawing staves for pails. Later he worked on the farm, and in the winter he helped out in the blacksmith shop. Recognizing that he did not have the strength to succeed at blacksmithing, he apprenticed as a wool carder, and, in his spare time, worked as a tinsmith and night watchman. By 1842 Blinn was given the charge of the carding mill. At nineteen he became a schoolteacher, and he taught the young boys some of the trades as well as academic subjects. He studied printing and binding and became a typesetter and editor when Canterbury became the Society's printing center. Blinn is chiefly recognized as an Elder and historian, spending most of his life in those positions; nevertheless, he continued working in other occupations such as dentistry, beekeeping, and cabinet-making. Over his lifetime, Blinn had thirteen different jobs at the village.

With the Order of Trustees established, the Shakers began their commerce with the World; and their successful ventures grew. Because the Believers were recruited from surrounding settlements, their initial endeavors were based on agricultural practices and typical New England trades. Subsistence agriculture was the rule in these rural areas; potatoes, flax, wheat, rye, and oats were the predominate crops, with large portions of land used for hay crops.

The first village to organize was called Niskeyuna (later called Watervliet), located a short distance from Albany, New York. The early Shakers struggled to clear their land, construct their buildings, and become self-sufficient. They raised sheep and cattle, made brooms, grew fruits and vegetables, and carried on simple trades. Whatever surplus they had, they sold to the World to buy essentials that they could not supply themselves. For several years the Watervliet Shakers lived in poverty, but the community eventually grew to house 350 members and four Families, with 2,500 acres at the home site. They owned an additional two thousand acres elsewhere in the state; they had a thirty thousand acre farm in Kentucky and land in Illinois and Virginia.[4]

As the Shakers' missionary efforts expanded in the 1780s, many converts continued to live in various houses scattered throughout New England. They may have had difficulty selling their land, joining as a family with children, or settling their business affairs. Elder Henry Blinn, the renowned and respected Elder, described these people in this way:

> At the time of the organization of the Society [they] were not in a condition to become consecrated members as their business and marital relations could not be so adjusted as to allow them to exercise the freedom which the case demanded. They were not, however, excluded from the privileges of the body of Believers as far as they could enjoy them in their isolated conditions. Some of this class were gathered into smaller families and allowed to conduct their affairs very much as they did before they had accepted the faith.[5]

To help these members form new communities, Joseph Meacham, Lead Minister, sent Shaker leaders to guide them. Meacham had great organizational skills, and, under his strong leadership, the Shaker movement spread throughout New England. Before he died, Meacham managed to oversee the establishment of eleven

*The New Lebanon Shaker community's Second Family, looking
from the East. (Private collection)*

Societies: four in Massachusetts, one in Connecticut, and two each
in New York, New Hampshire, and Maine.

The community of New Lebanon (called Mount Lebanon
beginning in 1861) was founded under the guidance of Joseph
Meacham in 1787. Its location followed Hocknell's land criteria
precisely, as described by Charles Nordhoff, who visited New
Lebanon nearly a century after it was settled:

> Mount Lebanon lies beautifully among the hills of Berkshire,
> two and a half miles from Lebanon Springs, and seven miles
> from Pittsfield. The settlement is admirably placed on the
> hillside to which it clings, securing it good drainage, abundant
> water, sunshine, and the easy command of water power.
> Whoever selected the spot had an excellent eye for beauty
> and utility in a country site.[6]

Many travelers of the early nineteenth century noted the
precision with which the village was planned.

> We were indeed not clear of the mountain, before we found
> ourselves in the midst of their singular community. Their
> buildings are thickly planted, along a street a mile in length. All

of them are comfortable and a considerable proportion are large. They are, almost without an exception, painted of an ochre yellow, and, although plain, they make a handsome appearance. The utmost neatness is conspicuous in their fields, gardens, courtyards outhouses, and in the very road; not a weed, not a spot of filth, or any nuisance is suffered to exist. Their wood is cut and piled, in the most exact order; their fences are perfect; even their stone walls are constructed with great regularity, and of materials so massive and so well arranged, that unless overthrown by force, they may stand for centuries; instead of wooden posts for their gates, they have pillars of stone of one solid piece, and everything bears the impress of labour, vigilance, and skill, with such a share of taste, as is consistent with the austerities of their sect. Their orchards are beautiful, and probably no part of our country presents finer examples of agricultural excellence.[7]

Years later another visitor, a journalist, observed:

Mt. Lebanon strikes you as a place where it is always Sunday. The walls appear as though they had been built only yesterday; a perfume, as from many unguents, floats down the land; and the curtains and window blinds are of spotless white. Everything in the hamlet looks and smells like household things which have long been laid up in lavender and rose leaves.[8]

This village became the first fully organized community in the Society. Its proximity to Mother Ann's home community of Watervliet and its excellent leaders caused this Society to grow rapidly. For many decades it was the seat of the Lead Ministry, and for more than a century, the rules and regulations governing all aspects of Shaker life, spiritual and material, emanated from this source. At its peak in 1870, New Lebanon had the largest population and the most land—600 members in eight Families, and 6,000 acres located in several states.

Calvin Harlow, a member of the Ministry at Watervliet, was sent east to oversee the establishment of many of the other communities. Under his guidance, the second bishopric was formed in 1790 with the villages at Hancock and Tyringham, Massachusetts, and Enfield, Connecticut.

Hancock was the largest of these settlements. On the border of Massachusetts and New York, not far from New Lebanon, it grew to hold 300 members in six Families. In 1847 Hancock owned about 5,000 acres which included several outlying farms. The central, or Church, Family was situated on a mountainside with cold and wet soil that made most of their agricultural ventures difficult. Aside from the sale of sage, which they produced in great quantities, their seed business was their most successful undertaking.

The Enfield, Connecticut Shakers made their living on 3,300 acres of excellent farmland on the east side of the Connecticut River. At its peak, the village had five Families and more than two hundred members. For many years the members of this prosperous community raised seeds, leaf tobacco, and herbs. The Believers also made lead pipe. When Enfield closed in 1917, many of the members moved to Hancock.

The Tyringham, Massachusetts, community was located eighteen miles southeast of Hancock. This beautifully situated site was a short-lived village, attracting one hundred members and two Families. Their primary source of income was the sale of garden seeds. When the community dissolved in 1875, the members moved to the other societies in the bishopric.

The eastern Massachusetts villages of Harvard and Shirley formed a bishopric under the ministerial care of Eleazer Rand and Hannah Kendall in 1793. These two communities each had a maximum membership of about two hundred. Harvard grew to hold four Families with eight hundred acres at the home site, an outlying farm, and a tract of land in Michigan totaling two thousand acres. The Harvard Shakers had good orchards and a nursery business, and they preserved and sold fruit, made brooms, and marketed dry sweet corn and maple syrup. Their herb business grew to be very important. Mother Ann and the Elders spent two years at Harvard, making it their headquarters while attracting converts and visiting nearby villages. A large portion of the Shirley Shakers' income came from raising seeds. Among the community's landholdings was a farm in southern New Hampshire where they raised cattle. These two villages survived until the first decade of the twentieth century.

The establishment of the Canterbury Society north of Concord, New Hampshire, began with the gathering of converts at Benjamin Whitcher's farm, which later became the site of the Church Family. Whitcher owned one thousand acres on which he cleared a large tract of land and built a house and barn. Before the Shaker village was formally established there, as many as forty Believers lived in his house. Whitcher served as Elder from 1794 until his death in 1827.

The Second Family, which was located on Chase Wiggins' farm on land adjacent to Whitcher's, already had twenty members at the time of the founding of the Church Family, but it was not officially established until 1800. Chase Wiggins, who had been living in Hopkinton when he became a Believer, exchanged his land with John Thompson of Canterbury when he learned that the community would be founded in that vicinity. The Second Family prospered until 1871 when most of its members merged with the Church Family. In 1891 the remaining Shakers joined the Church Family.

The North Family, originally known as the Sanborn Family, was organized in 1801. Unlike the Second Family, which was closely tied with the Church Family, the North Family was designed to house novitiates, people who had not yet committed to a lifetime of Shakerism. Once they made the decision and signed the covenant, they moved either to the Church or Second Family.

Believers lived at this site as early as 1792. When the North Family closed in 1894, the remaining seven Brothers and twenty-two Sisters moved to the abandoned Second Family where the office building, laundry, and two brick structures were renovated for them. After 1894 this Family became known as the Branch. When it closed in 1916, the remaining residents—all Sisters—moved to the Church.

With several buildings already in place by 1800, Canterbury's West Family was gathered in 1805, under the control of the North Family. The West Family had their own school, washhouse, and water-powered mill. The members also had a shoemaker and blacksmith shop and a good stock of cows, sheep, and hogs. As did the other Families, the West Family raised a sizable portion of their own food and manufactured most of their woolen cloth and some linen. Their dwelling house was small—there were never more than forty members—and they cooked over a fireplace. When the West Family closed in 1818, the remaining ten members moved to the North Family. Eight years later the dwelling house was also moved to the North Family.

Canterbury's early industries were typical of many New England communities. In a history of the village, Canterbury Shaker John Whitcher listed the various income-producing activities:

> As our soil, (though productive) was very stoney and hard to cultivate, it was deemed more economical and even indispensable to get our support mostly by trades. Accordingly several trades for manufacturing various and useful articles for sale, were set up and carried on by members severally appointed for that purpose; among which were the following: blacksmithing, manufacturing cut and wrought nails, brass clocks, skimmers and ladles; candlesticks, hats, tanning & currying leather; shoemaking, sieves, wool and linen wheels; wool and cotton cards; cart wheels & waggons completely ironed; wooden shovels shod with iron and steel; whips, raising garden seeds &c[9]

The Canterbury Society grew to house three hundred members, with three thousand acres. By 1810 they had accumulated almost all the cultivable land they would own. Later the community would jointly possess, with their sister village in Enfield, a farm in western New York, where they maintained eight hundred head of sheep and grew broom corn.

Enfield, in west-central New Hampshire, had been a gathering place for Believers ever since the early Shaker missionaries were sent from New Lebanon to travel throughout New England. From the time Ebenezer Cooley and Israel Chauncey were sent by Mother Ann in 1782, until the founding of the bishopric, missionaries came to the Enfield area as often as every six weeks in an effort to hold the group together before a village was established. In 1787 eleven families from Bradford, New Hampshire moved to the area to await the establishment of the community. The converts gathered at a place known as Shaker Hill, James Jewett's farm, which was the center of the Shaker movement in the area. During those early days Father James Whittaker and Elder Joseph Meacham came to New Hampshire. When these visits occurred, the meetings were held eight or ten days in a row with only short intermissions. The meetings produced many converts. In Jewett's house "Some powerful revival meetings were held and the singing & shouting was heard for several miles."[10] Among the Believers who lived in the area were some who owned farms on the other side of Mascoma Lake. This land was, for the most part, level and free of stones and had a never-failing water supply from a lake 1,500 feet above. Because this area was considered more suitable for settlement, Shaker Hill was subsequently sold, and the Believers moved across the lake on March 25, 1793. Since most of the land had not been cleared, the Enfield Shakers spent much of their time in the beginning cutting timber and diverting a brook around the village. In July the community began its permanent organization with the formal appointment of officers. At the time seventeen Brothers and twenty Sisters were living at the Church Family, and about five families who wanted to join resided in nearby houses and farms.

During the first six years after the two New Hampshire communities were established, the Canterbury and Enfield Shakers closed their doors to their neighbors, and, indeed, to all who wished to visit them. Their most frequent visitors were the Ministry who traveled to the villages.

While most of this time was spent clearing land, farming, and building, the members also developed trades to manufacture products for sale, providing themselves with income to purchase other items they needed but could not make. Caleb Dyer, a village historian, recounted that in 1793 the Enfield Shakers were manufacturing several kinds of leather, cutting and heading nails,

Nineteenth-century view of a New Lebanon barn and two Brothers. (Private collection)

making and setting card teeth. Two years later they began to raise and package garden seeds for sale.[11] The Believers were also manufacturing spinning wheels, snaths, rakes, pails, and measures.[12] The Sisters made few, if any, items for sale at this time, but they did produce their own cloth (cotton, linen, wool, and satin); "in fact, all but the cambric and muslin for [their] caps and kerchiefs and the silk of which but little was worn." [13] Because these Shakers had already been living and planning together for ten years, they were able to undertake these small businesses rapidly.

With farms on the western shore of the lake donated to the Society, an outlying farm twelve miles away, and additional purchases, the Enfield Shakers eventually acquired three thousand acres. Enfield grew to be a prosperous village with a wide variety of industries to keep it going. In the years to follow, the members made medicines; sewed shirts for Boston; knitted goods; made flannel shirts, drawers, and socks; and operated a woolen mill and a grist mill. About 1850 they erected a bedstead factory.[14] Eventually Enfield grew to house three hundred members living in three Families. When the community closed in 1923, the remaining Brothers and Sisters moved to Canterbury.

In the same year that Enfield was founded, the Parent Ministry was also organizing a bishopric in Maine. The village of Alfred was established in 1793 under the guidance of John Barnes and Sarah Kendall. The Alfred Shakers manufactured and sold garden seeds, brooms, sieves, and tanned leather, and leased out several mills. Their soil was not very fertile or easily cultivated, and by the early 1870s they decided to sell their property and move to a milder climate. Because they had no offers for the entire tract, they judiciously sold their unprofitable land. Income from the sale of much of their property, which had grown to 1,200 acres, provided a nice income for the members, and they continued to live on the site. At one time their membership grew to be two hundred. In 1932 the village was dissolved, and the remaining Shakers moved to Sabbathday Lake.

Originally called New Gloucester, then West Gloucester, the second Maine community was named Sabbathday Lake after 1890. In 1794 it was nearly the last of the eastern communities to be organized. In 1808 a group was formed in Gorham, quite a distance away from New Gloucester. In 1819 its members moved to a new location a mile from the Sabbathday Lake's Church Family on a site known as Poland Hill. This group then became known as the Gathering Family.

At its peak Sabbathday Lake owned two thousand acres and had 150 members living in three Families. In the beginning these Shakers supported themselves by selling garden seeds, brooms, woodenware, and spinning wheels. At one time their most profitable industry was the manufacture of oak staves for molasses hogsheads that were sent to the West Indies.

After the first eleven villages were established in the east, seventeen years passed before the Parent Ministry reached out to the west and south to establish other communities. The founding of the western Shaker Societies took place between 1811 and 1826, during which time two villages were founded in Kentucky and four in Ohio. As were the eastern Societies, the western communities were formed during a regional religious revival. Although they were founded later, the western villages did not lag behind but maintained a steady growth comparable to those in New York and New England.

The Parent Ministry saw the Kentucky religious revival in 1807 as an opportune time to gather more converts. In 1810 the first of the new settlements began with the establishment of a short-lived community in Busro, Indiana. Known as West Union, it was located on the frontier where the Shakers faced the threat of Indian wars. While the converts were setting up their new home, armies were marching into the area, and local residents retreated to the forts for protection. Eventually the Shakers also deserted their settlement until the danger had passed. Unfortunately when they returned, they had to face another enemy—malaria. In 1827 the community was abandoned, and the three hundred members moved to the Ohio Societies.

The year after Busro was established, Shakers began gathering at South Union, the first of the two Kentucky villages. Although their early dwellings were log cabins, they were constructing beautiful stone buildings by 1827. These Shakers became famous for their fine cattle and garden seeds; they also sold canned preserves throughout the southern states. In 1875 they began operating a hotel by a railroad station in a nearby summer resort. When the Civil War erupted, they fed both Union and Confederate troops; at times they were called upon to feed entire units with only a few hours' notice, and as many as 1,200 soldiers camped on their property.[15] In addition, their medicinal herb business flourished during this time. Despite the horrors of the war, which caused them the loss of their crops, stock, and two mills, the South Union Village survived until 1922. During its peak, it had 349 members, 4 Families, and 6,000 acres, of which 3,500 were located on the home farm; and the rest, four miles away.

The village at Pleasant Hill, Kentucky, which was referred to as "the topmost bough upon the Tree," was gathered in 1809.[16] Established in the bluegrass region, this community acquired 4,200 acres of rich farmland. John Meacham, one of three missionaries sent from New Lebanon, became the Society's first Elder, with Lucy Smith as Eldress.[17] The organization grew from 128 covenantal members in 1814 to eight families and 490 members by 1820. Its sales goods were similar to South Union's: garden seeds, preserves, brooms, and fine stock. The community's Shorthorn cattle were famous and were often exhibited at county fairs.

The Pleasant Hill Shakers sold their produce throughout the South. The steamboat *Blue Wing*, which ran between Louisville and the Shaker wharf, provided a means of travel along the Ohio and Mississippi rivers. Both South Union and Pleasant Hill Believers also built wooden boats that they loaded with their sales products. They floated these downriver; and when they reached the end of their trip, they dismantled the boat, sold the planks, and returned home by steamboat.

As did the South Union Shakers, the members of Pleasant Hill saw the profitability of catering to the public. In 1817 they converted one of their buildings into a tavern and gave the Family Deacon the charge of innkeeper. By 1836, however, this enterprise was met with disapproval and was temporarily abandoned. In the 1870s it was revived and remained active until the Society closed in 1910.

Broadside advertising Sabbathday Lake, Maine Shaker horse-drawn bar mower. The success of many of the Shaker villages was due to their ability to manufacture a broad range of products, including stoves, washing machines, mowing machines, furniture, and agricultural products. (Private collection)

Less affected by the war than South Union, the Pleasant Hill members did, nevertheless, experience military operations on their land. Fortunately, Confederate General John Morgan, who was a native of the area and was sympathetic to the Shakers, protected them from his own troops.

Union Village, Ohio, founded in 1812, became the largest of the western villages. Gathering six hundred members into six Families, it compared in size and population to New Lebanon. Its prestige grew to such an extent that the Ministry was given the authority of overseeing all the western Shaker villages. This responsibility helped the Lead Ministry at New Lebanon, who supervised all the communities but, due to geographic limitations, focused its attention on the eleven eastern Societies.

Union Village was gathered between 1805 and 1810 and was among the most prosperous in the order. These Shakers owned 4,500 acres of fertile river bottomland as well as outlying farms. One of their most profitable businesses was raising thoroughbred Durham cattle. According to their records, they also made steel, leather, holloware, pipes, and woolen yarn in addition to the usual industries. The village prospered for many years but eventually fell into debt due to mismanagement. It was sold in 1912.

Three other villages were established in Ohio. The first, Watervliet, grew to only one hundred members. When it closed in 1910, its 1,300 acres were sold, and the remaining members moved to Union Village. The community of Whitewater originally began in Darby in 1823 on the plantation of Samuel Rice. The forty converts met hardships similar to those found at Busro; they were beset with fevers and legal claims against their land. In 1824 they moved to Whitewater where they were also plagued by sickness and poverty. Joined by the majority of Believers from the closed Busro community in 1827, their numbers grew to 150 members in three Families, living on 1,500 acres. The smallest of the Ohio villages, Whitewater merged with Union Village in 1907.

North Union, founded in 1822, was a larger, more successful Society. Starting out in log cabins, the membership grew to three hundred by 1840. The community owned 1,355 acres on which they conducted a large dairy business. In the 1870s they capitalized on the growth of nearby Cleveland and supplied the city with milk and vegetables. With good and energetic leadership, they prospered. When the village closed in 1889, the remaining members moved to Watervliet, Ohio. When that village closed in 1910, the remaining Believers moved to Union Village.

The Shakers continued their expansion, establishing more missions and branches; but no major communities resulted in these efforts, and the endeavors were short-lived. The last large Shaker village to be founded was Groveland, New York, established in 1836. This Society had begun ten years earlier at Sodus Point, where the Shakers owned 1,300 acres. The Sodus Point community grew to have two Families and a dwelling house, but in 1834 they received an offer they could not refuse. The Sodus Canal Company, anticipating a new line which terminated on the Shakers' land, bought out the village; and its 150 members moved to a 1,670-acre site in Livingston County, where they established the Groveland community. There, they amassed two hundred members, two thousand acres on the home farm, and outfarms totaling two hundred acres. The Groveland Shakers worked at many of the same industries as the other villages and raised high-priced cattle. The village closed and was sold in 1895, and the remaining Shakers moved to Watervliet, New York.

As these communities grew, they became an available source of many products for their neighbors. The Shakers' mills provided flour, wood, textiles, leather, brooms, and furniture, among other items, for themselves and for the World. In addition to manufacturing these necessities, many communities also specialized in industries new to the area. The Canterbury Shakers, for example, made industrial washing machines, and Hancock Shakers made table swifts for holding skeins of wool or silk. These industries contributed greatly to their income, but the foundation of all the villages, with their large land holdings, was agriculture. Their maple syrup, seeds, herbs, barks, animals, cider, fruits, and vegetables were all provided by the land. The Shakers were looked upon as leaders in these endeavors, as explained by one admiring neighbor:

> When the farmers in the vicinity want to buy new implements or machinery, they usually... see what the Shakers are using, and what they think will serve best for the purpose. To have gained the endorcement of the Shakers for his wares is a great care for a manufacturer or dealer, and one man remarked that he would rather do a piece of work for them for nothing than make a bad job of it, as their good will was not to be despised.[18]

The Shakers' seeds and herbs gave the members a reputation as excellent horticulturists. Eventually they mass-produced these products for sale throughout the World, and their businesses evolved and lasted into the twentieth century.

Shaker Bishoprics

The Shaker communities were organized into geographic groupings called bishoprics. Each bishopric was supervised by a local Ministry accountable to the Central Ministry at New Lebanon. The Ministers were nominally residents in the seats of the bishoprics, shown below. In performing their duties the Ministers traveled within their bishoprics, often staying in one village for periods as long as six months.

Central Ministry-New Lebanon, New York

Bishopric Communities

New Lebanon, New York*
Watervliet, New York
Savoy, Massachusetts
Groveland, New York (formerly Sodus Bay)
Narcoossee, Florida

Hancock, Massachusetts*
Enfield, Connecticut
Tyringham, Massachusetts

Harvard, Massachusetts*
Shirley, Massachusetts

Canterbury, New Hampshire*
Enfield, New Hampshire

Sabbathday Lake, Maine*
Alfred, Maine
Gorham, Maine

Union Village, Ohio*
Watervliet, Ohio
Pleasant Hill, Kentucky
South Union, Kentucky
West Union (Busro), Indiana
North Union, Ohio
Whitewater, Ohio
White Oak, Georgia

* Seat of Bishopric

During the Shakers' two hundred years of existence, the Bishopric Order changed. At times, the Central Ministry directed a bishopric to supervise one that was faltering. For many years, the Maine communities were supervised by the New Hampshire Bishopric. Beginning in October 1868, a new bishopric, formed by South Union and Pleasant Hill, Kentucky, existed with South Union as the seat. After June 1872 the supervision of the Kentucky villages was returned to Union Village, Ohio.

This list was compiled with information provided by Priscilla Brewer, Dale Covington, Larrie Curry, Jerry Grant, Robert F.W. Meader, June Sprigg, Steven Stein, and Dianne Watkins.

The Development of the Shakers' Herb Business

About the year 1820 there was some beginning at preparing roots and herbs for sale, by drying, pressing and papering them, in nice compact form.[1]

*T*he Shakers were one of the first in this country to establish an herb business, but their endeavor began modestly. The early Shakers had no routine for finding the herbs they needed; they gathered the plants in surrounding fields and woods—wherever they could find them. In 1830 Benjamin Gates, a gardener from New Lebanon, recorded the process:

> July 14, 15th. Working in physic garden, here a little, and there a little, but don't fret. August gathering herbs here and there—go on west hills after lobelia. 26 and 27th work in medical garden, 30 and 31st gathering bugle here and there. Sept 1830 spend this month gathering herbs and roots here and there, up hill and down. 22nd, 23, 24th, down to Sheffield after blue cohosh, 28th on the mountain after maidenhair.[2]

Children, whose numbers at times swelled the populations of the Shaker communities, often bore the responsibility of collecting the herbs. The Shakers also enlisted the help of local Indians who were experts at identifying indigenous plants. When necessary, the Brethren would sometimes travel great distances to gather the plants.[3]

Eventually the Shakers developed procedures for collecting the

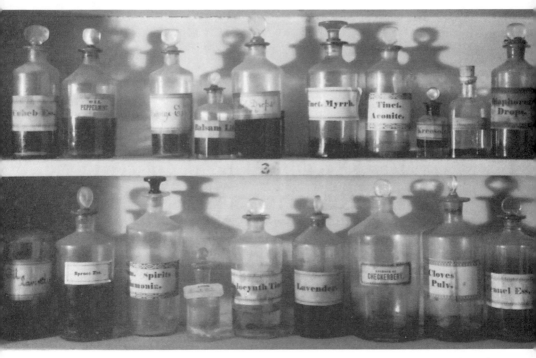

Infirmary cupboard, Canterbury Shaker Village. The Shakers purchased hand-blown bottles to hold their herbal extracts and tinctures. (Collection of Linda Butler)

wild herbs; this form of quality control helped make their products desirable.

> . . . there were . . . herbs of many kinds. Lobelia, pennyroyal, spearmint, peppermint, catnip, wintergreen, thoroughwort, sarsaparilla and dandelion grew wild in the surrounding fields. When it was time to harvest them, an elderly Brother would take a great wagonload of children, armed with tow sheets, to the pastures. Here they would pick the appointed herb—each one had its own day, that there might be no danger of mixing—and, when their sheets were full, drive solemnly home again.[4]

The Shaker physicians had to be excellent botanists in order to select the correct plants for their medical needs. They were knowledgeable in many factors that affected the potency of their herbs, including soil identification, weather, and pest conditions. William Tripure, assistant to physician Thomas Corbett, was responsible for maintaining the herb garden at Canterbury. When Isaac Hill visited the village in 1840, he made the following glowing report:

> William Tripure [is] the botanist who has the personal charge of the Botanic Garden, and who at the same time practices physic in the Shaker Families . . . . Probably there is not the second individual in the United States of his age who has so extensive a practical knowledge of botany as this young man. There is not a plant in the herbiary that he cannot give both the common and its botanical name with a description of its peculiar qualities.[5]

The physicians determined not only what was to be harvested, but also when it was to be done. The Shakers collected one variety of a plant at a time, at the peak of its growth, and only the part that was needed. This portion was either the leaves, flowers, roots, or seeds. A single plant could have several different medical purposes. The bark of the hemlock tree, for example, was used to treat gangrene, diarrhea, leucorrhea, and prolapsed uterus; the oil from the leaves was added to liniments; and the gum was saved for making plasters.[6]

In the fall, the heavy roots were gathered in baskets and brought indoors to be cleaned, split, and thoroughly dried with artificial heat.

The more fragile parts of the herbs were collected on tow sheets, usually fifteen feet square. Flowers, the most valuable part of the plant, were taken at their first opening and were quickly dried to retain their colors. The leaves were removed when the flowers bloomed. The Shakers gathered them in the morning, after the dew had evaporated, and before the day grew too hot. They took them back to the village, carefully removed any dead or yellow pieces and spread them out to dry. Leaves of biennial plants, such as foxglove (digitalis), were picked in their second year.

Bark was taken in the fall or spring when the sap was rising and when the bark could be peeled or shaved with a drawknife more easily. The Believers usually cut down large branches to remove the bark and took care not to harm the tree.

The timing of the seed harvest required vigilance since the gardeners had to compete with the birds and other wildlife. The Shakers ripened the seeds in the sun until the leaves turned yellow. Fully ripened seeds were obtained by winnowing out the lighter seeds.

The quality of their herbs earned the Shakers a reputation as fine horticulturists. As the demand for their products increased, the Believers expanded their sales beyond the local area. One of their most important targeted markets was the medical com-

"Crushing the Roots for the Shaker Extract." This image and the ones following in this chapter are from a series that documents the process of the manufacture of an extract of roots made at the New Lebanon community. This extract, known to help treat dyspepsia, was called Seigel's Syrup. (Collection of New Hampshire Historical Society, Concord, New Hampshire)

munity, whose members apparently were dissatisfied with their imported plants.

> . . . [the Shakers'] physic grounds (which embrace the largest portion in the States), cover about one hundred and fifty acres of cultivated plants and within a few years has been largely increased, as the demand for such medicines as they raise and collect doubled within a short time. This is partly owing the frequent importation of spurious and adulterated drugs, which had led intelligent physicians to seek among our own genuine medical substances new remedies and suitable equivalents . . . most of the native remedies offered in the market were collected by persons destitute of necessary botanical information . . . [and]were generally worthless . . . [So] the Society . . . commenced improvements in this line, . . . which, from its convenience and manifold advantages, met the approbation of the public.[7]

As their businesses developed, the Shaker physicians used many methods to supply their clients. They capitalized on the need for large quantities of pure and conveniently packaged herbs for the pharmaceutical trade. They bought in bulk from one another and organized their orders so that the herbs could be harvested and carefully dried at the correct time. They advised their clientele to send in their orders early, preferably between October and December, or from March to June. Eventually, the demand outstripped their ability to gather all the herbs themselves so the Shakers bought herbs from simplers, or peddlers, who traveled throughout the countryside, as well as from the Indians. One simpler, Horace Jennings of Searsburg, Vermont made the following offer to the Shakers:

> I learnt by a man gathering herbs for you, you bought Balmony [Snakeroot], Skullcap, Wake, Robin, etc. I am gathering some of these kinds. I have of Balmony 300 pounds well sorted & dried in house on racks. What do you pay for it? Some was gathered in bud, some in blow. I cannot make it look as well as Skullcap. What is Evens Root worth? . . . Dwarf Elder is plenty on my route with Latice [Lettuce], Pipsisaway, Mountain Ash, Sassafras etc. . . . my Balmony is Dry . . . .[8]

Out of necessity, the Shakers began planting gardens to ensure a steady supply of non-native or scarce plants. In order to meet the increasing demand for their herbs and grow certain plants under carefully controlled conditions, they created scientifically organized "physic" or botanical gardens. These plots of land required relatively little acreage since many herbs continued to be harvested in the wild. At the peak of the business, the Shakers had about 150 acres of herbs under cultivation. The rest of their fields were devoted to such crops as hay and wheat, or pasturage.

The first known mention of the Shakers growing herbs in an organized fashion is recorded in a diary by a New Lebanon Brother called Jethro, who wrote that in June 1812 "a violent storm did much damage in herb garden."[9]

The New Lebanon Shakers were selling herbs on a small scale between 1812 and 1821. Edward Fowler, head of New Lebanon's herb industry, years later reported that by 1822, the Believers gave this endeavor their full attention:

> Drs. E. Harlow and G.K. Lawrence of Mt Lebanon . . . introduced a more systematic arrangement and scientific manner of conducting [the herb business] especially as to the seasons for collection, varieties and methods of preparation.[10]

The Shakers' physicians were initially responsible for these

"Shakers boiling the Roots for the Shaker Extract of Roots, or Seigel's Syrup."
(Collection of New Hampshire Historical Society, Concord, New Hampshire.)

gardens. They transplanted the herbs from the wild and grew them from seed. Their acreage was kept separate from the Shakers' other plots that supplied the communities' vegetables and seed businesses. To identify their plants and ensure a steady and pure supply for the market, the doctors referred to botanical books from the World, such as *A Manual of Botany for the Northern States* and *Medical Flora.*[11]

Although the physicians and their assistants oversaw the content and cultivation of the physic gardens, other Brothers occasionally helped them. Seth Bradford, head horticulturist who tended the Enfield, New Hampshire, seed business for many years, recorded in his diary in 1840 that he performed many chores for the doctors. Early in the year he filled the hotbeds with dung; and in March, as the spring planting commenced, he planted thyme, low balm, solomon seal, and rue. In April he helped the physicians set rue again as well as valerian root. A month later he sowed sweet lavender, summer savory, and saffron.[12]

The herb business at New Lebanon, being considerably larger than those at the other communities, acted as the trade model for for all the villages. In the mid-nineteenth century ten to twenty people picked the plants, cleaned the roots, and dried, pressed, and packaged the herbs.[13] Several buildings and facilities were devoted to various aspects of the industry; garden barns, pressing and printing machines, and packaging and storing areas were scattered throughout the New Lebanon Society. The sites of these operations shifted over the years, but in 1857 the herb house was the headquarters for the trade.

... visited Herb House with [gardener Edward Fowler] where the various botanical preparations are put up for market. [It] is a frame building in the centre of the village one hundred and twenty feet in length and forty feet in width, and two stories and an attic in height . . . . The lower part is used for the business office, store-rooms, and for pressing and packing the herbs and roots. The second story and attic are the drying rooms, where the green herbs are laid upon sheets of canvas, about fourteen inches apart supported by cords.[14]

Once the herbs were dried, they were put in "large and tight bins" on the second floor. They were then pressed into small packages.[15]

The herb presses were home built or commissioned in the World and customized at home. They used a variety of systems to achieve the pressure needed. Some had simple cranking devices; others used hydraulic, water, steam, or horsepower to operate them. In the 1850s New Lebanon's press was located in the second story and was operated by horsepower in the basement.

That press... has a power of three hundred tons, and turns out each day about two hundred and fifty pounds of herbs, or six hundred pounds of roots, pressed for use. This performance will be doubled when steam shall be applied to the press. The herbs and roots come out in solid cakes, an inch thick and seven and a quarter inches square, weighing a pound each. These are then taken into another room, where they are kept in small presses, arranged in a row, so as to preserve their form until placed in papers and labeled. During the year 1855 about seventy-five tons of roots and herbs were pressed. . . . [16]

In 1853 the Harvard community commissioned a new herb press; and Elisha Myrick's herb diary recounted its manufacture, arrival, adaptation, and success. Myrick, as did many of the other Shaker herbalists, worked happily at his trade for many years, and his diary is an intimate look at the daily workings of the herb department.

It will be Twenty one years next April since I began to work in this department spending the most thus far & I fear the happier part of my life in one occupation; I have not been instructed in so great a variety of experience as many others, still I have been taught steady habits which are not without value. [17]

In May Myrick's assistant George B. Whiting went to oversee the construction of the new herb press in Holyoke, Massachusetts. Whiting returned to the village five weeks later, but the press did not arrive until July 8. Expectantly, the herbalists went to the depot to pick up the press.

> July 8. George Whiting and I go to the depot & bring home the long expected press—get it into the House and set up & it would have been ready for trial but for a leg that was not sent which will have to be made before the press can be put into operation.

> July 9. George and I get the press ready for the operation & press a few pounds to gratify the anxiety of some of the Folk.[18]

The press was soon up and running and was a successful labor-saving device for the Harvard Shakers; they finished the year pressing 5,500 pounds of herbs, and the following year they pressed over eighteen tons.[19]

By the end of 1854, Myrick hailed the horsepowered herb press as a valuable labor-saving device:

> Dec 31, 1854 . . . . It has proved to be a useful and excellent machine saving labor and doing the work effectively. With the improvement of machinery the most laborious part of our work in doors is performed without requiring so much hard labor from human hands.

> We hail with delight every improvement relieving human toil or facilitating labor thus giving time and opportunity for moral, mechanical, scientific and intellect improvement and the cultivation of the finer and higher qualities of the human mind."[20]

By 1860 many improvements had also been made to New Lebanon's system.

> The Machinery [in the Herb Shop] is driven by an oscillating Engine, the exhaust steam being used for drying herbs, warming the house and heating water &c. [The Shakers] use coal for fuel and have a patent drying kiln for drying herbs, and a hydraulic press for pressing them.[21]

It was inevitable that the machinery did not always operate smoothly. Sometimes kilns overheated, and herb shipments were returned because of unacceptable quality. At Enfield, New Hampshire the following was reported:

> The fire [was caused] by friction in a machine shop, where a mill was kept slowly in operation for the grinding of Indigo.[22]

Because Harvard's press was in constant use, pressing about 274 pounds of herbs a day, it was also in need of continual repair. George Whiting spent many hours hanging shafts from the first floor to the cellar so the press could be run by horsepower. He was also continually fixing its pulleys, belts, and springs as well as building other machinery to receive the pressed herbs and to cut these bricks into ounces.[23]

The public, who had previously purchased their herbs loose, were not accustomed to the pressed bricks of herbs, and it was a struggle for the Shakers to have this new system accepted. Isaac Hill, a friend of the Shakers, noted the difficulty Canterbury physician Thomas Corbett experienced in selling his pressed herbs, even in Boston.

> The vegetable preparations have grown gradually into an establishment probably more extensive than any other in the United States. The vegetables were introduced in the shape of dried leaves pressed into a solid cake weighing a specific quantity, in shape like a brick. When those articles of different kinds, such as chamomile, coltsfoot, elecampane, goldthread, horehound, johnswort, rose flowers, saffron, sage, summer savory, and the like, were first introduced and left at the apothecary stores in Boston, they were the food of merriment to some of the regular physicians. Gradually, however, Dr. Corbett has succeeded in their introduction until the prejudice of the doctors has been so far conquered that many of the faculty are constantly applying for them.[24]

The herbs, once pressed and wrapped, were packed in tin boxes, which were then put in wooden boxes, and shipped to the customers.

> Pack 5 Tin Boxes holding about 200 lbs. each & have them soldered, nailed up in wooden Boxes & marked. . . .[25]

Packaging was an important sales tool. In addition to marketing the medicinal herbs in pressed bricks, the culinary herbs were sold in tin canisters. By 1853 Harvard's Elisha Myrick was experimenting with putting herbs in glass bottles.

> I prepare the Specimens of herbs in Glass Bottles for the Mass. Society of Pharmacy.[26]

By the end of the year Myrick had met some success with his glass bottles and decided to continue this form of packaging.

> We have prepared some samples in bottles which have excited some attention & hope to make some sale in the coming year.[27]

Once New Lebanon seriously committed itself to growing herbs for sale, the business expanded rapidly. By 1826 the demand had outstripped their supply, and the New Lebanon members began to purchase some of the products, including red roses (for rose water), sweet marjoram, and saffron, from the World.[28] Fowler summarized this productivity:

> As we find a variety of soils are necessary to the perfect production of the different plants, we have taken advantage of our farms and distributed our gardens accordingly. Hyoscyamus, belladonna, tarazacum, aconite, poppies, lettuce, sage, summer savory, marjoram, dock, burdock, valerian, and horehound, occupy a large portion of the ground; and about fifty minor varieties are cultivated in addition, as rue, borage, carduus (Benedictus), hyssop, marshmallow, feverfew, pennyroyal, etc. Of indigenous plants we collect about two hundred varieties, and purchase from the South, and West, and from Europe, some thirty or forty others, many of which are not recognized in the Pharmacopoeia, or the dispensatories, but which are called for in domestic practice and abundantly used.[29]

"Alonzo Hollister, the famous Shaker chemist, concentrating the Shaker Extract of Roots, or Seigel's Syrup, in Vacuum Pan." (Collection of New Hampshire Historical Society, Concord, New Hampshire)

By 1831 the New Lebanon Shakers were shipping boxes of herbs around the world.[30]In the next three years they were harvesting four thousand pounds of roots and herbs annually. At the same time, they published their first catalog offering 137 herbs for sale. In 1849 they had sold 16,500 pounds of herbs and 587 pounds of extracts. The following year they had fifty acres devoted to herb gardening and had sold twenty-one thousand pounds of herbs and seven thousand pounds of extracts.[31]

Other Shaker villages also established physic gardens. Taking the lead in the herb sales were the communities of New Lebanon and Watervliet, New York; Canterbury and Enfield, New Hampshire; Harvard, Massachusetts; and Union Village, Ohio. Of the seven western villages, Union Village was the only one with an herb business large and profitable enough to issue catalogs. The remaining western communities grew herbs for their own use and sold their surplus to the World but fared better with the sale of seeds. As did the New Lebanon community, Union Village apparently grew herbs long before its members officially recorded the founding of a physic garden. The community was growing sage and sassafras by 1819 but did not establish its herb garden, under the care of physicians Abiathar Babbitt and Andrew Houston, until 1833. By the 1830s the South Union, Kentucky, Shakers had a profitable seed business (established in 1821) and a distillery, herb press, and buildings in which they processed herbs primarily for their own use. Traveling by boat on the Red, Ohio, and Mississippi rivers to New Orleans, they sold seeds, herbs, and brooms made from broom corn. An herb catalog from this community has not

"Shakeresses filling the bottles with the Shaker Extract of Roots, or Seigel's Syrup." (Collection of New Hampshire Historical Society, Concord, New Hampshire)

been found, but whatever herb business they did have was greatly accelerated during the Civil War because of the increased demand for medicines.[32]

> A large business is done in the seed line ... and also in pressed and prepared herbs and roots, besides many tons in bulk ... considerably many tons of powdered herbs and roots ... and many tons of extracts, both solids and fluids. The War makes great demand for all these articles. They sell in large quantities. We cannot prepare enough to meet the demand.[33]

The Shakers of Pleasant Hill, Kentucky, produced and sold several short-lived medicines. They gathered and pressed herbs and sold them on trips down the Kentucky River. Judging from the lack of any written promotional materials other than a few broadsides, however, one may assume that their herb business was not as important as those at other villages.

In many of the eastern communities, the leaders apparently made a conscious choice not to compete with one another for the same markets, but, rather, to diversify their product line. In many bishoprics, particularly where there were villages that were located close together and had the same clients, one community would raise herbs and another, seeds. If a community raised both, one would be for trade with the World and the other would be for home use.

Watervliet, and later Groveland, both part of the central bishopric with New Lebanon, raised seeds as a major industry until 1840.[34] From the first seed sales in the 1790s at Watervliet, the seed business grew in importance; and from 1811 to 1840 seed raising was the village's chief industry. By 1827 Watervliet was selling 129 varieties of herbs and extracts, including black henbane, garden nightshade, belladonna, and red clover; and three years later the community issued its first medicinal herb catalog.[35]

In the Maine Bishopric, the Sabbathday Lake Shakers maintained an herb business while the Alfred Shakers carried on a seed trade. Although Alfred's land was not well suited for agricultural pursuits, the seed business thrived. The Alfred Shakers also grew herbs but just enough for their own use and to sell to the Harvard Shakers. By 1840 the Sabbathday Lake Shakers were selling at least eighty-three herbs.[36] Twenty-four years later, their production had almost doubled.[37]

This mutual support between communities is also seen in the bishopric shared by the Shirley and Harvard communities. Shirley depended on income from the sale of its vegetable and herb seeds. In 1805 the village was selling caraway, lavender, parsley, sage, saffron, and summer savory seeds. Ten years later it was also selling balm, burnet, and fennel seeds. While the actual date of the establishment of Harvard's gardens has not been recorded, it is known that this community had prepared herbs for the Boston market by 1820.[38] The business grew slowly, but eventually the community issued eleven bound catalogs, the first in 1845. Shirley helped out its sister community by gathering green herbs and planing the wood for Harvard's herb boxes.

The bishopric comprising the Hancock and Tyringham, Massachusetts, and Enfield, Connecticut, communities maintained successful seed industries with only minor herb businesses. The emphasis on seeds was probably because the villages were located near Watervliet and New Lebanon, each having a thriving herb trade. While Hancock had a profitable seed enterprise, the Society was also growing large amounts of sage, which were sent to New Lebanon for processing. Early records indicate that Hancock was also raising blue cohosh, foxglove, gayfeather (*liatris*) angelica, green tea *(Thea viridis),* sweet marjoram, and Virginia snakeroot[39]

The Enfield, Connecticut, Shakers, who were selling seeds by 1825, claimed to have created the first major seed enterprise in the United States. The members also pressed and sold herbs. Their trade routes, as did New Lebanon's, extended into the South until the Civil War ended their large southern market.[40]

Because the villages of the New Hampshire Bishopric were located on opposite sides of the state and thus had different markets, Canterbury and Enfield could more readily support similar enterprises. The Enfield Society sold its products to Canada and Vermont; Canterbury members ventured into the White Mountains of New Hampshire and parts of Massachusetts. Canterbury was the major herb raiser, while Enfield concentrated on seeds. Enfield's herb business did not have any substance until 1832 but eventually was extensive enough to issue a catalog. According to Caleb Dyer, the roots that were the "most extensively cultivated and which [had] found the most ready sales [were] Valerian, Dandelion, Dock, and Lovage."[41] By far, however, onion seeds were the Enfield Shakers' most important crop. An acre of their garden was devoted to onions for seed, and one half of an acre was for sage, a portion of which was forced early in hotbeds.[42]

Canterbury's botanic garden, which covered an acre and a half, was said to have "a greater variety of the useful medicinal plants than any other establishment in New England."[43] Although the contents of the garden are unknown, the catalog listed two hundred herbs.

When physician Thomas Corbett began to expand his market, he established an orderly system of harvesting, drying, and packing herbs for sale in the World. At Canterbury, the leafy herbs were dried in attics. The roots and barks, which made up a large portion of their sales, were pulverized. This activity was done at the Factory Pond, one of several artificial ponds the Canterbury Shakers created to conduct much of their heavy labor by water-power. Isaac Hill observed:

> ... where no natural stream ever ran, [the Canterbury Shakers] have created a more permanent and durable water power than can be found within a distance of ten miles ... no less than eight artificial ponds covering from five to thirty acres each have been created, one rising above the other, and each furnished a stream large enough to carry different mills and factories.[44]

To crush the herbs, the Believers devised a simple mortar and pestle apparatus.

> The fourth building above on the stream erected before the mills below is forty by thirty feet, used as a factory for various purposes. In this building ... was a cannon ball in a mortar turned for the purpose of pulverizing ... medicinal roots, a machine for polishing metals, and machines for turning and boring.[45]

In later years the Shakers ground their herbs at the Carding Mill on the lowest pond of the system. In 1847 this building was thirty-five by fifty feet and two stories high. While herb pulverizing did occur in this building, the predominate activity was carding wool.[46]

The Canterbury herb business grew rapidly after the physic garden was established in 1816. Long before the first catalog was published in 1835, the business was thriving. By 1835 the Shakers were distilling medicines and manufacturing and selling trusses to the World as well as to the Shaker communities at Sabbathday Lake, Harvard, and Enfield, New Hampshire. In 1822 the Canterbury Shakers were taking "167 lbs. medicinal herbs to Haverhill and Salem, Massachusetts" with an income of $77.07.[47] By 1826 they supplied New Lebanon with the following:

30 lb. Balm	8 lb. Pleurisy Root
2 1/2 lb. Sassafras Bark	2 3/4 lb. poppy capsules
10 lb. Sweet Marjoram	1 lb. red roses [48]

Five years later their herb business was earning more than $1,400 a year. By 1840 the volume was so high that they were purchasing many of their herbs to supply the heavy demand.

> The medical establishment at the Shakers is not confined to articles raised by themselves--they purchase all the varieties of

"Shakeresses labeling and wrapping the bottles containing the Shaker Extract of Roots, or Seigel's Syrup." (Collection of New Hampshire Historical Society, Concord, New Hampshire)

> vegetable articles of extensive use in the *Materia Medica*. As a single item of purchase at one time was mentioned six tons of the Ulmus fulva or bark of slippery elm, which was procured from the northern part of Vermont and Canada.[49]

Not every Shaker was convinced of the value of the medicinal trade, however. Nathaniel Sleeper, an old farmer who tended the botanical garden, believed that "medicine killed more than it cured." Working in the garden was no doubt a trial for him because "it sometimes pained him to think his labor was producing what was killing so many of the human race."[50]

The medicinal gardens required constant work, and at times the gardeners tired of their chores. Canterbury Shaker Nicholas Briggs at one point looked longingly at the water lilies which required no care at all.

> This month we have a beautiful flower garden which brings no burden and demands no care. Hundreds and hundreds of white water lilies are spread on the surface of the water garden every morning.[51]

Despite these views, the herb business at Canterbury prospered, and in 1848 the community bought an additional eight-and-a-half acres of land along the flood plain of the Merrimack River in Concord. This investment cost them $1,150, which included a stable and the land, where they intended to raise additional medicinal herbs and roots. Since it was difficult for the Shakers to travel

Shakers packing and shipping Shaker Extract of Roots, or Seigel's Syrup, Mt. Lebanon, N.Y. (Collection of New Hampshire Historical Society, Concord, New Hampshire)

thirteen miles to the site every day, they converted the stable into a house and hired a family to live there and help with the business.[52]

From community to community, the physicians communicated freely with one another, often writing and visiting their sister Societies and ordering herbs from them. By negotiating, the doctors could guarantee high-quality herbs at a lower cost. They bargained for the best prices, offered discounts, and gave one another preference in filling orders when it was economically feasible in order to keep their fees competitive with the World's.

These inter-village orders were sent by the Shakers themselves or by public transportation. In January 1829, when Corbett tried to place an order with Eliab Harlow at New Lebanon, he wrote that he had sent the herbs via Harvard:

> Bro. Thomas Corbett wishes to have Brother Eliab informed that he has sent some herbs and roots to Harvard hoping there might be a chance of conveyance this winter.[53]

The fact that the Shakers could regularly depend on one another for high-quality herbs, even during times of crop failures and unexpected new markets, contributed to their reputation in the World as reliable dealers. Their communal lifestyle made it possible for them to sell in large volume to the burgeoning pharmaceutical market. They had enough members so that growing, harvesting, processing, and advertising their herbs and medicines could be done efficiently at a lower cost, and they could sell their products at competitive prices.

"If You Want a Splendid Garden, Buy the Shakers' Garden Seeds"[1]

When the Shakers began to settle in America, the cultivation of seeds was an important occupation. The Believers raised seeds mainly for vegetables but occasionally for herbs and flowers as well. In the early years they kept seeds for their own use and sold what they did not need to their neighbors. As their markets expanded, the business developed into a large, profitable concern and became an important source of income through the mid- to late-nineteenth century.

Practically all the Shaker Societies developed a seed business before 1800. While claims have been made that the trade originated at Enfield, Connecticut, Union Village, or New Lebanon, the Society at Watervliet may actually have been the first to take the initial steps with this endeavor.

> In the year 1790, Believers in this place had a little Family garden occupying about two acres of land. Joseph Turner worked it and began to raise a few kinds of seeds to sell. Previous to this it was not customary in this part of the country for people to raise garden seeds for sale. When any neighbor lacked seeds, another would give him what he wanted and did not think of asking pay, more than they would for a bucket of water.[2]

Although the New Lebanon Shakers were selling seeds in 1789, they did not systematically organize acreage for that purpose until six years later. Hence, the first seeds that they sold may not have been cultivated in their own gardens. By 1807, however, the New Lebanon business had picked up to the point that the community was locally selling twenty-two different varieties. From 1790 to 1800 the Hancock members were also beginning to grow and market seeds, and by 1794 the New Hampshire Bishopric followed suit.[3]

By the first quarter of the nineteenth century, other Shaker villages had also started their seed businesses: the Maine Bishopric, in 1801; Enfield, Connecticut, in 1802; and Shirley, Massachusetts, in 1805. The western communities established their trade slightly later. Union Village began selling seeds in 1816; South Union, Kentucky first sold seeds in 1821; and the business in North Union, Ohio began slowly in 1835 when the members fenced off six acres for this purpose.[4]

In setting up a competitive business, the Believers grew their seed vegetables in separate gardens and were careful to ensure the maximum harvest. As the vegetables ripened, the members staked their plants to make the harvest easier. They hand-picked the seeds, often several times in a season for one variety, depending on the uniformity of ripening. They brought the seeds into specialized buildings to winnow out the unusable pieces. For vegetables such as squash, cucumbers, and melons, the Shakers cut the pulp out of the skins and put the meat into barrels to ferment. They stirred the mixture for about five days. When the seeds sank to the bottom of the barrels, they rinsed them in sieves.[5] After the seeds dried, the Shakers packaged them for sale.

Although much credit is given to the Shakers for developing a seed industry in this country, they were not the first American seedsmen. David Landreth of Pennsylvania, who began raising and selling seeds in 1784, is thought to have that distinction.[6] The Shakers, though, made significant improvements in the trade. At a time when seeds were customarily sold in bulk in barrels or cloth bags, the Believers were probably the first people in the United States to sell seeds in individual packages.[7]

The packaging of the seeds was a labor-intensive process, but it helped initial sales. The early envelopes were plain, generally made of brown paper, and cut and glued by hand. There were eight different sizes of envelopes, tailored to the proportions of the seeds.[8] Each package was stamped to indicate the seed's variety, the community's name, the Deacon's initials, and, in some cases, brief instructions. At Canterbury, the early seed bags contained no directions but noted the variety, community, and initials of Deacon

Shaker seed envelope, South Family, New Lebanon, New York. Sage was a major crop at many Shaker villages, used for both medicinal and culinary purposes. (Private collection)

Francis Winkley. At New Lebanon's Second Family, the early packages were stamped with "D. H." for Daniel Hawkins and "S. F." for the Second Family.[9] In the beginning, printing the seed bags was done by hand, a slow and tedious process.

The Shakers worked on this trade year-round. At harvest time all hands helped gather and sort the ripened seeds. The Sisters and the elderly cut, folded, and glued the paper bags. The printers produced advertising broadsides and catalogs and stamped thousands of seed bags. The Deacons handled the correspondence and took lengthy sales trips, dropping off wooden boxes of packages to stores throughout their territory. The following season the old seeds that hadn't sold were brought home and sorted, and the boxes were washed and refilled. In the fall biennials such as carrots, onions, cabbages, and turnips that required two years to grow seeds were dug and wintered over in the cellars, to be replanted the following spring.

As with all their industries, the Shakers were concerned about the quality of their produce. Early in their growing business, they bought seeds from the World to supplement their supplies, but they stopped the practice when they learned that their high standards were not met. By 1819 the first of many inter-village agreements was recorded, restricting the Shakers' purchase of seeds to those grown in their own gardens.[10] As they did in the herb business, the villages bought and sold seeds from one another when necessary and even grew varieties for each other, thus guaranteeing uniform quality and a constant supply.[11]

As the demand for their goods expanded, the Shakers marketed their seeds and other less perishable goods more widely. Longer sales trips by horse-drawn wagon or sleigh developed. During these travels the wagons were piled high with seeds, herbs, preserves, brooms, bonnets, ox goads, whips, pipes, dried corn and apples, cloth, dippers, chairs, clothespins, and other articles. The seed boxes were left at stores along the way, with the owners keeping track of what was sold. For selling the seeds year-round, the store owners received a 33^1/3 percent commission; this was later raised to 50 percent.

As the Shakers expanded their territories, other means of transportation were also used. With the increasing demand for their products, it became necessary to send additional supplies by railroad. The western Shakers often used the rivers for transportation; the Pleasant Hill Believers had their own boat landing on the Kentucky River and traveled to St. Louis and west along the Arkansas River. In 1816 the South Union, Kentucky Believers took their first flatboat trip down the river to scout New Orleans for new markets.[12] By the early 1820s the Brethren were peddling their wares down the Mississippi River to New Orleans.

These seed journeys were long and tiring, and the Brothers had to contend with unpredictable weather conditions, loneliness, discouragement, and sickness. When they could, the Shakers found local, reliable agents on their routes to help them.

> Br. P. F. Artes [of North Union] yesterday started on the Garden Seed trip—not to distribute—he is to collect the amt. of last year's sales, ship home the old boxes, and establish Agencies where he may deem it proper to do so—This will supercede the necessity of again travelling this lengthy, tedious, and dreary road—and we think it will be much less expensive.[13]

Despite the inconveniences, the trade was productive. By 1810 the Shirley, Massachusetts Shakers were selling at least twenty-eight varieties of garden seeds, including the following herb seeds: caraway, lavender, parsley, sage, and summer savory. Five years later the Brethren added balm, fennel, and burnet seeds to their list. Production was not so high at Hancock, where only about four types of herb seeds were being sold by 1813. By 1814 the New Lebanon Shakers' annual production exceeded two thousand pounds. In 1823 Enfield, New Hampshire, reported selling 90 pounds of onion seed, 40 ^{3}/4 pounds of turnip seeds, and 11 ^{3}/4 pounds of sage seed in a year. By 1850 the Alfred, Maine community was selling ten different types of herb seeds: English sorrel, hyssop, lemon balm, marigold, parsley, rue, saffron, sage, summer

Shaker seed box, Enfield, New Hampshire. This box is one of those left by Shaker peddlers in stores in the World. (Collection of the Museum at Lower Shaker Village, Enfield, New Hampshire)

savory, and sweet balm. The Enfield, Connecticut Society offered an even wider variety in the 1850s: caraway, coriander, dandelion, dill, fennel, lavender, lemon balm, rosemary, saffron, sage, clary sage, summer savory, sweet basil, sweet marjoram, sweet thyme, pot marigold, and rue. Many of the seeds sold at Canterbury were from flowers, including: ageratum, asters, balsam, calendula, campanula, candytuft, cockscomb, columbine, gypsophilia, hollyhocks, larkspur, lathyrus, French marigold, migonnette, climbing nasturtium, dwarf nasturtium, portulacca, pansy, petunia, phlox, india pinks, double poppy, sage, scabiosa, sweet alyssum, sweet pea, sweet william, verbena, and zinnia.[14]

The seed sales made a healthy contribution to the villages' economies. From 1811 to 1840 the Watervliet members noted that annual income increased from $300 to $5,000. By the late 1830s the Alfred Shakers were selling more than $1,000 worth of seeds a year. In an 1816 Canterbury Church Family inventory, Deacon Francis Winkley reported having $1,378 worth of garden seeds on hand.[15]

Perhaps the most impressive figures were seen at New Lebanon. By 1804 the community was selling $1,240 worth of seeds. From 1839 to 1854 sales from the garden seeds at the Church Family at New Lebanon brought in more money than the booming herb sales. In 1853 $10,000 worth of seeds were sold as compared to $3,830 worth of herbs.[16]

As demand for their seeds swelled, the Shaker peddlers extended their routes into neighboring states. When this happened, permission had to be granted from the Shakers residing in the area. In a typical case, the Harvard community sent two Brothers to Canterbury to secure permission to sell their garden seeds in southern New Hampshire, an area the latter village had not yet reached.[17]

In spite of the attempt not to duplicate territories, some routes did overlap. Customers were asked to choose among communities, and trustees began to compete against one another. To avoid this situation, the Brothers tried to define their territories "to arrest the ruinous competition."[18] In 1828 the Maine and New Hampshire Shakers began a series of letters that lasted a decade on that subject. The communication indicated that there was informal understanding between the villages that the state line was the territorial boundary. However, the Alfred Brethren had encroached on New Hampshire soil, causing the Canterbury Brothers to complain in 1828:

> Beloved Deacons,
> We received your letter of the 3rd, Inst. concerning the distribution of Garden Seeds. We should be sorry to have any strife between us on that subject or any other for **We are Brethren.** We think that you have three or four times the scope that we have for Seeds. Ours is so small it is hardly worth attention.... Suffice it to say that the Society at Harvard supply the best part of our State viz. almost all of the Counties of Cheshire and Hillsboro.

The letter goes on to name the New Hampshire towns that the Maine Shakers were allowed to trade in and those they could not.

> But since the factories have started at Dover and Great Falls in connection, and so many people have gone there who used to sell our seeds and yet **claim** them and **will** have them, and as we trade largely there in other things and they are also in our State, we should be thankful to have your union for us to supply them. And we wish that the line between the States from Norraway Plains to the sea shore would divide the district as we think it would be the most proper and not unreasonable.

Ten years later the two communities were still discussing territories. In another letter, requesting more "elbow room," Canterbury cited competition with the Harvard and Shirley members, who sold their seeds within thirty-three miles of their village on the south and east; with Enfield, who sold seeds in the northern and western parts of New Hampshire; and, finally, with Alfred, who were encroaching on their territory in the towns of Conway, Chatham, Eaton, Effingham, Wakefield, and Milton.

> Now Beloved Deacons do you not think that we stand in rather a squeezed situation? Without any means of enlarging our routes, hedged on all sides by bounds which we consider sacred and inviolable until removed by mutual agreement. We are unlike our Brethren at Alfred who have a great unbounded territory North and East of which no one holds a right or privilege and a means of extending the same especially since the grant from Gloucester [an agreement between Maine Shakers]. Just compare the extent of your district with ours and upon mature deliberation, we think you will readily concede that we are asking no more of you than you would ask of us were you placed in our circumstances.[19]

In the same year the New Hampshire Believers were bargaining with New Lebanon about the same subject.

> ... we earnestly hope that you will in your arrangements not forget our entreats and think what a *pen* we are in and lend your aid to extricate us from this enclosure. This you know we would not ask of those who are not able to extricate. It would not be understood to ask for any privilege to trade in any of these towns except in Garden Seeds nor to you from all the trade you wish, for I believe it is generally conceded that any of these towns in any others are free for you to buy or sell as occasion may require.[20]

In addition to having to worry about competition with other Shaker villages, the Believers had to wrestle the same problem with their own Families. By 1819 Canterbury found it necessary to have a written agreement between its First and Second Families to establish towns with which each might trade.

> This is to certify that the First Family is not to put out or vend garden seeds in the following towns which belong to the Second Family vis. New Salisbury, Andover, New Chester, Danbury, Alexandria, Bridgewater, Begron, Orange, Groton, Coventry, Landaff, Rumney, Dorchester, Wentworth, Warren, Plymouth, Holderness, New Hampton, Sanbornton, Northfield, Gilford, except Bridge & Gilmanton & old Iron Works.[21]

In an effort to reduce labor, increase production, and offer a competitive product, the Shakers continually made improvements to their businesses throughout the nineteenth century. As other companies began attracting customers with offers of premiums, gifts, and free seeds, the New Lebanon Shakers produced a gardener's manual. Stating that a garden is "an index of an owner's mind," Garden Deacon Charles F. Crosman generously gave advice on successful vegetable raising. The purpose of the little booklet, however, was strictly commercial.

> The design of this little Manual is to enable our trading customers, while furnishing their assortment of Garden Seeds, to afford instructions, at a trifling expense, [to their] customers [who] may wish to obtain some practical information relative to the raising and management of those valuable kitchen vegetables which are considered the most useful and important in a family.[22]

The manuals accompanied each seed box and had a modest retail value of six cents. Sixteen thousand of these booklets were sold by the Shakers of Enfield, Connecticut; Watervliet; Hancock; and New Lebanon.[23] In 1843 Crosman issued a more detailed manual in which he stated that while poor gardens might be the result of inferior seeds, they were more likely ". . . owing to the want of proper management in the gardeners." The booklet contained cultural instructions as well as advice on insect control, building a hot bed, and making pickles.

Printing also became an important aspect of the business. As the market expanded, the Shakers mechanized their printing facilities, buying small home presses. Ebenezer Alden, who ran Watervliet's seed business, invented a "printing box" for handprinting the seed bags. By 1810 the Hancock community had a printing press. By 1836 New Lebanon was printing 150,000 seed bags annually; and four years later, 930,400 bags.[24]

By the 1830s and 1840s, however, the Shakers were losing ground in competing with the World. While other seed companies were enticing customers with colorful advertisements and packaging, the Deacons' early promotional efforts were limited to black-and-white testimonials in their own publications and catalogs and the local papers. Companies such as Comstock, Ferre & Company, the first to use color on their seed packets, eclipsed the Shakers' plain, brown seed envelopes and recycled boxes.

To offset the rising competition, the Brethren initially stressed quality over eye-catching devices.

> We can bear the sway in Market, if we are truly punctual to keep the *quality* of our seed good. Others may get them up in *more* nicer style, and with finer colors etc., than we deem it proper to do; but we can compete with them in the goodness and purity of the Seed, and also in convenience of package, and in *style* sufficiently neat and grand to agree with our profession and practice in other things manufactured by us.[25]

By the 1830s, however, some villages began printing their packages in the World. Whether it was because the volume was too much for their village presses or the World's printers offered an enticing variety of type styles and colors, the result was that the Believers' advertising became more sophisticated and ornate. The first catalog illustrated with colored plates was published for New Lebanon in 1853 in Springfield, Massachusetts, by B. K. Bliss & Sons. Soon the Shakers instituted a mail-order seed business as well.[26]

Despite these efforts, the Shakers' seeds were generally more expensive than the World's; and, as competition increased, many villages were forced to close their seed businesses. The Canterbury Shakers discontinued their seed business by 1829, bowing out with $1,566 worth of seeds still on hand in the Church Family and $1,047 worth of seeds left in the Second Family.[27] In the next few years they tried in vain to sell the seeds, finally handing them over to their gardeners to use. Elder Henry Blinn summarized the reasons for closing the trade:

> The business was very prosperous till many other parties entered the field. Those by ornamental printing on the seed bags, by extended advertising and the offering of premiums, soon captivated the dealers & consumers and left the Believers with their simple unattractive show bills & seed bags quite a long distance in the rear, and finally obliged them to withdraw from the market.[28]

The Civil War also had a negative impact on the Shaker seed industry. The Society at Enfield, Connecticut suffered great losses; and in 1873 the Whitewater, Ohio and Pleasant Hill, Kentucky communities both ended their seed businesses. The New Lebanon concern, however, which was still experiencing lucrative sales as high as $9,000 in 1854, managed to survive. The only village that continued its southern seed routes during the war, New Lebanon weathered considerable competition and enjoyed sizable profits. In 1868 the village reported raising $7,196.10 worth of seeds. Thirty years later the community was still having catalogs printed in the World and offering advice on cultivation and cooking and storing vegetables. Those catalogs that were issued between 1881 and 1888 listed an impressive number and variety of herb seeds: anise, balm, sweet basil, caraway, castor oil plant, catnip, coriander, dill, fennel, hop, horehound, hyssop, lavender, sweet marjoram, opium poppy, rosemary rue, saffron, sage, summer savory, winter savory, broadleaf sorrel, broad-leaved English thyme, tansy, wormwood, white mustard.[29]

The trade continued at other villages as well. In 1861 Caleb Dyer

Nineteenth-century view of onion field at the Church Family, Enfield, New Hampshire community. Onions were a major seed crop for the Enfield Believers. The Shakers often staged photographs to document their activities. In this image the men are wearing top hats, and the women are equally overdressed. (Private collection)

estimated seed sales at $3,000 at Enfield, New Hampshire. This community's business reached a peak with sales at $4,700 in 1869. Although income declined to $500 by 1882, Enfield continued the trade until 1919, with seed records reported at $940.49.[30]

The Canterbury Shakers also sold seeds in a limited fashion for many years after Blinn announced the closing of the trade; in 1872 they sold $1,505.30 worth of seeds. Although the business diminished, the Shakers continued to save seeds for their own use and sold the excess on a small scale.[31]

With only minor sales after the 1880s, the Shaker seed business was for all purposes ended. The Shakers' herb industry fared better because it depended less on expensive, colorful graphics. The advertising campaign for their herbs also targeted members of the medical community who were less inclined to be dazzled by creative packaging than they were by the purity of the products. While the Shakers did publish some ornate medicinal herb catalogs, they never developed the extensive colorful advertising used for their seeds.

Shaker Gardens Today

*M*ost of the present-day herb gardens on Shaker sites evolved when these communities made the transition from an operating Shaker village to a museum. By 1890 virtually all of the remaining Societies that ran herbal businesses had stopped the trade. They still retained large tracts of land, however; and when these villages were incorporated into museums, their large acreage enabled horticultural demonstrations to become an important part of the interpretation of Shaker life. These museums have not tried to duplicate the original Shaker herb industries but rather attempted in various ways to represent the different types of herbs that were raised and sold by the communities.

Seven re-created Shaker herb gardens are described here—those of Canterbury and Enfield, New Hampshire; Hancock, Massachusetts; Mount Lebanon, New York; Pleasant Hill and South Union, Kentucky; and Sabbathday Lake, Maine.

This chapter opens with Galen Beale's account of her work with Mildred Wells in expanding and maintaining the herb garden at Canterbury.

Shaker Village, Inc., Canterbury, New Hampshire

The Canterbury community is still active today with one Sister, Ethel Hudson. The Lead Minister of all the Societies, Eldress Bertha Lindsay, died in October 1990. Since 1969 the site has served as both a home for the remaining Shakers and a museum for the public.

The placement of the museum's first public garden, situated near the North Shop on the foundation of the old Sheep Barn, was determined by practical concerns. While the spot was not the site of a former herb garden, the location worked well for the museum; for it was on the path of the tours and was easily accessible to the visitors who might want to return to visit it.

The first plants were obtained through the help of Jack Auchmoody, Canterbury Shaker Village's first museum-trained director. Auchmoody had a strong agricultural background, having been involved with the establishment of the Heritage Orchard at Old Sturbridge Village in Massachusetts. With his help, Caroline Smith, the museum's first herbalist, obtained plants from Old Sturbridge Village. When Caroline returned to college in the fall of 1979, I took over the garden and served as herbalist from 1979 to 1986.

After doing some research the first year, I came across Canterbury's catalogs and realized the scope of the Shakers' herb business and the importance of a garden to represent this activity. From these publications, I selected plants that would grow successfully in full sunlight in the village's herb garden. Since there were more than two hundred varieties from which to choose, it was soon necessary to enlarge the original plot. Many of the plants, such as boneset, joe-pye weed, and blue flag, are native to the area; and I was able to dig them up in the fields and move them into the garden as the Canterbury Shakers once did. I raised others from seed and received many plants as gifts from other gardeners.

As the plants grew, new challenges arose. Some of the plants that I moved from the wild when they were young, such as lovage and elecampane, grew so tall when raised in the garden's improved soil that I had to dig them up and move them to the back of the garden. The many mint varieties were a continual problem, spreading throughout the beds. The garden eventually expanded to include ninety-five herb varieties growing in six plots, each eighteen feet square, separated by grass paths.

As the garden grew and the work increased, it became necessary to mulch. David Lamb, who was working as a cabinetmaker in the North Shop, saved the sawdust and wood chips from his shop, and

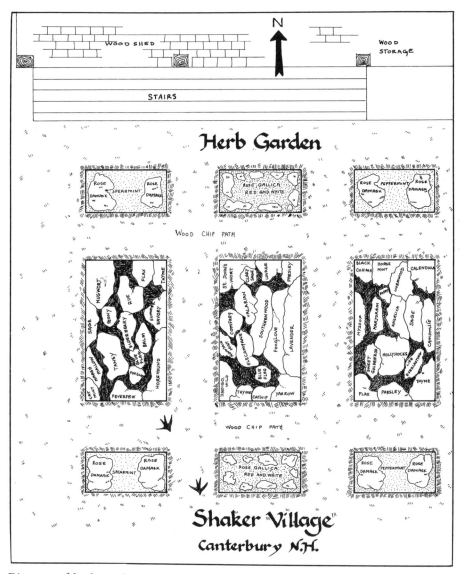

Diagram of herb garden designed from a plant list in Canterbury's 1848 catalog. Drawing by Ann Saunderson. (Private collection)

I used these for a mulch. The colors of these chips varied according to his project, but the colors were graduated from bed to bed so the variations were not immediately noticeable.

I began giving workshops on planting, harvesting, drying herbs, and putting a garden to bed as part of the museum's summer offerings. There seemed to be endless possibilities, including workshops on making various herbal products such as potpourris, cosmetics, and candies.

Garden tours were a part of the program; but in trying to incorporate as many of the catalog plants into the garden as possible, I realized that many had to be excluded because they were either aquatic or needed lots of shade. To interpret these plants, I began to lead walks into the fields and woods and around the ponds where they were growing. These walks were instructive to all of us; for while I identified plants and talked about the history of the Canterbury Shakers' industrial endeavors along their artificial ponds, many people also shared their knowledge of birds, insects, and modern-day uses of herbs.

As the large herb garden grew, it incorporated many herbs that were not listed in the Canterbury catalogs. Materials needed for workshops, plants donated by the Shakers, and other herbs grown as experiments were also in there. While these plants were necessary, it seemed also that a pure Shaker garden was needed.

With the help of Julia Fifield, an experienced gardener and past president of Shaker Village, Inc., we planned a second garden that was based solely on Canterbury's 1848 medicinal herb catalog. A raised bed garden was placed in front of the wood shed, which provided a weathered brown backdrop. The intersecting paths of this garden were of pine bark mulch, delivered by a local tree-trimming company then working on the road.

The new garden presented an opportunity to have roses for the first time, and Mrs. Fifield generously donated a selection of damask and gallica roses. These were kept in separate beds because of their size and rapid growth habit and were underplanted with pennyroyal and foxglove. In the remaining rectangular beds, tall plants were placed in the center and surrounded by others of graduated sizes. Thirty of the catalog's two hundred varieties were displayed. After the initial addition of rabbit manure, nothing was added to the soil, and the plants thrived.

Mildred Wells, who moved to the Canterbury community in 1921 from Alfred, Maine, maintained her own gardens at the village. She would frequently come over to see what I was doing and often invited me to see her garden where she pointed out her favorite varieties. I noticed that Mildred would frequently go on long walks through the fields and woods and that she was well acquainted with the property. I once asked her why she took these walks, and she replied, "The woods are my Church." After a while, she invited me to accompany her. Mildred knew that I was looking for plants for the garden and told me that she used to lead the Shaker children around the property looking for plants to fill their botanical scrapbooks. On our walks together, she always led the way. Rarely would we leave Shaker land, but we never returned to the same place twice.

Her recollections of sixty-six years at this village were mainly about the places where things happened. Certain sites, trees, and rocks would trigger memories that she would recount. There was so much she wanted me to see: Union Hill (where we came upon the remains of an old orchard), the spot where the Indians worshipped, the rock that tipped over the wagonful of Sisters who were on their way to the Holy Ground, the stump of a once-magnificent chestnut tree, the swamp where the best sphagnum moss grew, the best fishing spots, the rocks where the turtles sat, and the places where cranberries grew. We traced the watercourse of the Shaker ponds, examining the many hand-dug ditches and stonework that made these ponds possible. Often I could not determine how she knew where she was going because there were no roads. When I asked her, she said she could tell by the spacing of the trees. She knew the Shakers' names of all the fields and orchards and always referred to them that way. Mildred knew what was happening in all her territory: where the birds lived, where the beavers were working, and what plants were in bloom.

Over the years Mildred had grown fond of a number of places around the property. Some of these spots had her favorite plants growing in abundance, and others she thought were naturally beautiful. At the appropriate season she would take me on visits to these places: glades where literally thousands of bloodroot were in bloom, a site where there was a carpet of lavender blue hepatica, and a stone cliff that was covered with ferns. Sometimes our walk was to an enormous stone pile made by earlier Shakers or to the spot where they once had manufactured bricks.

I often noticed that she had a much more accepting philosophy on the natural course of things than I. I was often saddened by the realization that some of the major works of these Shakers were falling into disrepair and would disappear. When we would come across a dam that had broken or some eroding stonework, she would remind me that these were works of man, and the land was simply returning to its original form.

These trips were often long, rambling walks undertaken to find a particular plant. Long after I thought she had forgotten my request, she would stop and point out the very plant I had been seeking. When she was too busy with her own garden to accompany me, she would give exact directions to a particular plant far away. These directions were not always easy to follow. I quickly realized she was much more observant than I, and her directions were given by the description of the various stone shapes, the ditches, or the peculiarity of some tree.

Mildred always took time to note the passage of the seasons. Every year we would observe the changing of the maple leaves on the Meeting House Lane and speculate on the reasons the trees changed at different times. She watched for and reported on the migration of the birds; she always knew when the geese were resting on the Shaker ponds and when they left to begin their flight anew. If I were not at the village, she called me at home, hoping that I would go outside and see the Canada geese as they flew over my house. When the snow geese came to the North Barn Field, she would call regardless of the time of day.

Mildred helped the village in many ways. She provided bouquets at several of the public spaces—spectacular arrangements of flowers from her garden that had the touch of both an artist and a gardener. She sold herb products in the gift shop, continuing a long Shaker tradition. She collected rose petals from around the village and added them to her lavender, making a potpourri to sell in the store. (Mildred maintained two large lavender beds on the south side of her house, having started them from a single plant, and she tended these beds with love, giving away much of the lavender as gifts. If there were extra, she would give it to me.)

She would rarely accept help in her garden although she was always gracious about the offer. It was only in retrospect that I realized I never once helped her harvest the lavender. The harvesting was a much-anticipated event. Mildred would watch the flowers and the weather until she felt the time was right. For days beforehand, we would examine the beds and discuss the upcoming moment. As Mildred did not like to work outdoors when the public was about, she did the major work in her garden in the early morning and late afternoon. For many years I would arrive early, hoping that this was the day to harvest the lavender, only to see that the bushes were bare and the sea of blue had vanished. She would dry the lavender in built-in drawers located in several of the buildings on the property.

In addition to the lavender, Mildred raised large amounts of lemon balm and catnip, which she grew under the maples of the Meeting House Lane. She also cultivated a patch of four-leaf clovers in the Meeting House Field that she would never show me, but she would often present one to me on top of a potpourri mix or with some other gift.

Mildred maintained the largest garden area in the village. She took care of plants and trees throughout the village so one was not immediately aware of the scope of her cultivation: a catnip/catmint patch, a rose garden, a peony bed, a production herb garden, a bed of spring bulbs (she called tulips the "rich man's flower" since they lasted only a few years), a vegetable patch, and an orchard. She also maintained the Shaker cemetery. Her gardens were full of experiments: new, unusual seeds she had ordered (cotton, coffee, amaranth); new vegetable varieties; outrageous plants from Gurney's Seed Catalog; plants she had moved from the woods to watch grow; and volunteer plants that were allowed to remain.

Her main garden was located south of the Enfield House, where she lived. It was a historic garden maintained by Sister Miriam Wall before her. This garden was formally laid out, but it was the kind that required a guided tour in order to understand what was going on. By no means, however, was this part of a public tour! Although it was visible from many parts of the village, one had to have Mildred's permission in order to walk through it.

Her garden was edged in several varieties of parsley, with an interior path lined with peonies. The parsley was seeded each spring, then covered with a long metal pipe from part of a former building. Hotbeds, built of enormous timbers probably taken from the cow barn when it burned in 1973, were covered with window sashes and occupied the center of the garden for most of the season. Concentric iron rings from bygone wooden wagon wheels were found in the garden, and there were little paths made of roof shingles that led to important places. California poppies rioted throughout, bunches of corn streaked skyward, grapevines rambled, and young trees stood like sentinels. It seemed as if Mildred had one of every kind of plant somewhere in there. Additionally, there were many birdbaths spotted about that were ringed in leopard's bane and were carefully refreshed every day.

Mildred worked on her projects year-round. I remember seeing her pour boiling water on the ground in November to soften the soil so that she could plant her bulbs. When she was not cultivating, she was observing; and often she would call me to come look at something with her: a plant unfurling, a new color variation in the poppies, the bees drinking at the birdbath.

When not gardening, we would often spend time together gathering ingredients. We would take trips in the truck to gather pine needles in the woods, manure from a farm, or plants for terrariums she was making for Christmas. Mildred did the weekly shopping for the Sisters, and on those outings she noted many things that required a second trip. We returned for the seeds of a fruit tree that was growing at the bank, for pine cones that she had seen lying by the road, and for piles of lime or leaves that she had asked permission to take.

Mildred read extensively and had a large garden library she frequently shared. For herself she would accept very little help, but she assisted me endlessly. She grew herbs, dug up plants, dried flowers, and vigilantly watched the garden for infestations. To control insects, she usually hand-picked them off the plants and dropped them into boiling water. She occasionally sprinkled the plants with a variety of dusts made from such things as garlic ground in her blender. She often worked the soil with a pickax, not because the soil was hard but because she thought the ax an efficient tool.

Mildred was in her mid-seventies when I knew her, but her lifetime of work had made her very strong; and she continued to enlarge her garden until she died in 1987. In the traditional sense, Mildred removed herself from the World; very few people had the opportunity to know her. In the years that I spent with her, she embodied the Shaker characteristics of creativity, resourcefulness, keen observation, dedication, and generosity. Her gardens were testimony to her special skills.

The Museum at Lower Shaker Village, Enfield, New Hampshire

In 1927 the Enfield Shakers sold their remaining land and buildings to the LaSalette Order of Roman Catholic brothers and priests, who in 1985, sold much of the property to a group of private investors. In 1986 the present herb garden at Lower Shaker Village was established—the same year the museum opened. As the museum's programming developed, Happy Griffith, a gardener and teacher of herb culture for six years, was invited to give a workshop. The following spring she became the village's herbalist.

The investment group had envisioned an herb garden, but the garden's original placement was not feasible so Griffith looked for another spot. Given all the variables and restrictions, such as rock piles, shade, and development plans, she eventually chose a flat, full-sun location near Route 4A, south of the Church Family cemetery.

The beds of this new garden are forty feet long, six feet wide, and are divided by four-foot-wide paths made of bark mulch over a layer of newspaper. Due to the garden's proximity to the road, Griffith found it necessary, visually, to have its shape follow the road's contour, resulting in a parallelogram 100 feet by 110 feet. It was also necessary to plant the herbs diagonally in the beds, but because the garden is well planned and fits well into its location, its unusual shape is not immediately noticeable.

The original soil for the herb garden was poor and was initially supplemented with bonemeal, horse manure, peat, lime, and compost. Today Griffith occasionally uses liquid seaweed or fish emulsion. Three compost piles, made in Lincoln-log fashion, are near the site; and the garden refuse as well as food wastes from the restaurant in the Shaker Dwelling House are added to these piles. Every two weeks the log sides are broken down, the piles turned, and the sides re-built.

More than one hundred herbs are grown in this garden. Each bed represents a theme, with herbs for cooking, medicine, fragrance, and for dried material for workshops. Along the north end of the garden are two eight-foot-wide beds containing old shrub roses, most of which were donated by Helen Ford, a rose expert from the town of Enfield. Among the roses donated by Mrs. Ford are the *duc du guiche*, cabbage, moss, damask, *rosa mundi*, and Jacobite varieties.

At the opposite length of the garden is a border featuring a variety of shrubs that would have been grown at the time the Shakers were living at the village. This border includes privet, honeysuckle, spirea, and high mountain cranberry bushes. While both of the end gardens are mulched with buckwheat hulls, the main garden is left without a mulch to encourage propagation of new plants. The plants are sold in the museum's gift shop along

Diagram of herb garden at the Museum at Lower Shaker Village, Enfield, New Hampshire. (Collection of the Museum at Lower Shaker Village, Enfield, New Hampshire)

with seasonal products such as lavender wands, tarragon vinegar, and calendula oil.

The herb garden is thriving, and generally pests are not a problem. The museum staff uses organic pest controls or removes the unwanted bugs by hand and drops them into soapy water.

To ensure the garden's continued maintenance, Griffith launched a highly successful "Village Gardener Program." To participate in this program, volunteers commit themselves to three hours of work a week preparing the beds in the spring, planting, weeding, harvesting, and putting the garden to bed in the fall. The volunteers choose their own hours and receive village aprons to wear. Griffith and her assistant Kitty Scherer review the tasks daily with the gardeners and lend assistance if needed. With a donation of $25, these volunteers are treated to an herb-related program by Griffith every other week. At these times the Village Gardeners gather in the West Brethren's Shop for a pot-luck supper and to hear a lecture by Griffith on an aspect of herb culture that may include gardening, cooking, or herbal crafts, such as making lavender wands, tussie mussies, potpourris, fragrances, or wreaths. These get-togethers also make scheduling easier and provide an opportunity for members to discuss the progress of the garden. The Village Gardener Program includes fourteen volunteers a season, and this year there is a waiting list of ten people, a testament to its success.

In addition to the Village Gardener Program, Griffith gives workshops throughout the year on herbal crafts, such as living and dried wreaths, advent wreaths, edible petals, potpourris, and dyeing as well as many hands-on workshops, such as composting. Other herbalists give lectures and herb walks as part of the village's herb program. Each spring the museum hosts an Herb and Craft Day, a time when a variety of plants and herbal products are sold by local vendors.

With the herb garden now established and the work organized, Griffith hopes to expand her programs into the community, working with local public schools. She plans to invite fourth-grade students to the garden to plant, weed, and harvest the herbs. This program would give young people an opportunity to feel, smell, and taste many plants, and strengthen their connection with nature.

Enfield has about an acre of land on which to conduct the garden programs. For several years, the village maintained a vegetable farm stand on the property, but in 1990 a production organic herb garden was begun on the land directly behind the main herb garden. Fresh herbs from this garden will be sold to local stores and restaurants between mid-July and the frost date.

Like the soil in the herb garden, the production garden's soil is poor. In an effort to improve the heavy clay soil, each year half of this plot is planted with buckwheat, which is plowed under in the fall, and every year the plot is rotated. The production garden is managed by a full-time staff member who plants and maintains the garden and stocks outlet stores. Markets for these organically grown fresh herbs have already been established locally and will be supplied daily. Depending on their availability, basil, borage, cilantro (coriander leaf), lovage, mint, nasturtium, parsley, summer savory, and tarragon will be sold, and each bunch of herbs will be accompanied by a recipe card.[1]

Hancock Shaker Village, Inc., Pittsfield, Massachusetts

Probably the best known of all the herb gardens on public view at Shaker villages today is the one created by Amy Bess Miller, past president of Hancock Shaker Village, Inc. Miller, who studied at the Sorbonne at the University of Paris and holds four honorary degrees, modestly does not refer to herself as a professional horticulturalist, although she gave the museum the impetus to start the garden and has since written many books on the subject of Shaker herbs.

When the Hancock community opened in 1961, a centrally located herb garden that was accessible to museum visitors was one of the goals. The existing garden interprets how a Shaker herb garden might have looked on a small scale. It has ten beds, each 108 feet long and three feet wide, separated by grass paths. Eleven beds, twenty-five feet long and four feet wide, are located at each end of the garden.

The choice of having grass, instead of dirt, paths was a difficult one. Miller had consulted the library at Sabbathday Lake and found a text that said grass paths were used, but she also came across a photograph that showed a Shaker standing in a dirt path. Her conclusion was that each village probably tried something different, depending on the terrain and the preference of the current gardener.

In the initial planning stages of the garden, there were two schools of thought as to how to plant the beds. One was to make a production garden; the other was to have a specimen garden. Over the years both interpretations have been tried. At first many of the beds contained a single type of herb in order to simulate a production garden, but because of the limited space and few staff members, a specimen garden was decided to be the most practical.

The selection of plants was also difficult. While the Hancock Shakers grew a large amount of sage for the New Lebanon community, the village never produced an herb catalog. Research began several years ago and continues as the staff members try to learn more about what the Hancock Shakers would have raised. The garden currently has 110 herbs representing varieties that were sold by the New Lebanon community; the shrub rose, *Rosa Gallica officinalis,* grows on the fence next to the garden.

The museum has several public programs that relate to the gardens, including two half-hour tours. The morning tour emphasizes the Shakers' medicinal herb business, and the afternoon tour, which includes a visit to the production vegetable garden across the street, covers the village's once prosperous seed industry. Each spring interpreters give lectures in local schools about life at a Shaker village. These programs are followed by an on-site visit to the museum where students view the herb and vegetable gardens as well as the working farm with its animals, barns, and machinery. Younger children, three to five years old, are given special tours of the herb garden where they can taste, feel, and smell the plants. To supplement the educational programs, the gift shop sells culinary herbs in cannisters that are reproductions of original Shaker herb containers. Sometimes lucky visitors are given excess herb plants when transplanting is being done in the garden.

Tom Weldon, who is in charge of both the herb and vegetable gardens, hopes to expand the educational programs. His goal is to interpret Hancock's important nineteenth-century seed industry. He plans to construct another garden in order to raise heirloom or antique vegetables and seeds. The varieties chosen would be taken from one of the village's original seed lists. The proposed site would be near the herb garden so that the two gardens could be interpreted together. Subjects such as nineteenth- and twentieth-century horticultural practices would be covered.[2]

Mount Lebanon Shaker Village, Mount Lebanon, New York

New Lebanon, the community that had the largest acreage of herbs under cultivation, has an herb garden once again. With a grant from the J. M. Kaplan Fund, Inc., the staff installed an herb garden in 1990 next to the Wash House at the North Family.

The new garden was inspired by a handwritten herb list found in the museum's collection. The garden is situated on a hillside, and the rows of plants are contoured to the slope to prevent erosion. Each bed is five feet wide.

Staff members are planning to host workshops and educational programs based on the garden. Already underway, the garden is to

Seed and Herb List (A to Y) circa 1850-1860s. Center Family, Mt. Lebanon. (Collection of Mt. Lebanon Shaker Village)

be incorporated into the "Hands on History" program at Darrow School, a private school located on the New Lebanon site. The students will help plant, maintain, and harvest the herbs, at the same time deepening their understanding of their surroundings.[3]

Shakertown at Pleasant Hill, Kentucky, Inc. Harrodsburg, Kentucky

The museum at Pleasant Hill has re-created an herb garden on a historic cultivated site west of the Center Family Dwelling House. The development of this garden was initially funded by the Glenview Garden Club of Louisville, Kentucky in 1968. In 1977 Debbie Larkin Pope became the village's herbalist and installed the herb garden.

The museum's first garden had raised beds, five feet wide and of varying lengths, arranged in a square with paths on all sides and planted in two mirrored halves. In 1979 the garden was redesigned based on information found in Benjamin Dunlavy's 1843 journal. The manuscript revealed the dimensions of the garden of the Society's physician John Shane, but the garden's location remains unclear. The plot now consists of three beds eleven feet by twenty-eight feet each, with a fence row of apothecary and damask roses.

To enrich the soil and control pests, Pope uses organic methods. The garden is supplemented with compost and sheep manure; the beds are mulched with straw, and insects are removed by hand.

Interpretation at Pleasant Hill focuses on the period from 1830 to 1840, and the garden interprets the Shakers' use of herbs during that time. The plot has more than fifty varieties of herbs, all documented as having been used by Shakers, although not necessarily at Pleasant Hill. Herbal demonstrations abound during the museum's September Harvest Festival with the making of wild cherry cough syrup, calendula salve, elder flower cream, rose water and glycerine hand cream, tinctures, and fragrant waters.

The lower floor of the Farm Deacon's Shop, the earliest Center Family house, has been set up as an apothecary shop where many demonstrations take place year-round. This building contains original Shaker medicinal artifacts: a large herb press of cherry wood, a medical cabinet made at Pleasant Hill, pill boards, and documented herb baskets. The apothecary shop also has a still that produces peppermint and other fragrant oils. The copper, pot-bellied base of the still is filled with herb leaves and heated over coals in the fireplace. The oil condenses in the top ball of the still and drips out of the long copper snout, perfuming the air.

Demonstrations also include the manufacture of soup bags, closet bags, and potpourris, which are, in turn, sold in the gift shop. Fresh herbs from the sauce or kitchen garden are used in the dining room.

Researchers are reviewing Shaker manuscripts in the hope of finding references to dye plants that then could be grown in a dye garden.[4]

Shakertown at South Union, Kentucky

The South Union, Kentucky, herb garden was designed and planted by the Kentucky Garden Clubs in 1988 as a demonstration garden to display the varieties of herbs that were readily grown in the locality. The museum's garden has forty-eight herbs that are known to have been raised at many of the Shaker villages. While there is currently insufficient documentation to substantiate the types of herbs the Kentucky Shakers actually grew, research has indicated that during sales trips to Clarkesville, Tennessee, and New Orleans, Louisiana, the South Union Shakers sold herbs such as thyme, pennyroyal, and sage. In addition the members sold herbs to other villages.

In establishing this garden, volunteers consulted a village map dated 1836 that showed one herb garden in the North Family and one in the Church Family. The present site of the demonstration garden is located near the 1824 Center House, chosen for its proximity to the museum with consideration given to visitor traffic and available sunlight. Since the spot had been the site of former sheds and garages, raised beds were made to avoid disturbing the soil, in case an archeological excavation were ever to take place. Railroad ties contain the soil in the beds.

After the garden was established, Dory Hudspeth became the village's herbalist. She formerly owned a business selling plants and fresh herbs to restaurants. While the land available at South Union is too limited to conduct similar ventures for the museum, Hudspeth has been able to interpret the Shakers' herb business by using plants in the garden as examples. Herb programs at South Union include the Shaker Festival, which takes place annually during three weekends in June and features Shaker music, food, and crafts as well as guided tours of the garden.[5]

United Society of Shakers, Sabbathday Lake, Inc., Poland Spring, Maine

The Sabbathday Lake community is still active today and has a successful commercial herb business that the members revived about 1971. After the earlier pharmaceutical side of their herb business died out in the beginning of the twentieth century, the Sabbathday Lake Sisters continued to sell a variety of herbs, such as sage, savory, and calamus root, in the gift shop. When the 1960s brought a renewed interest in natural foods and herbs, Brother Ted Johnson began to research the possibility of reviving the herb business on a commercial scale. A site near the barn was chosen, and plants were selected from the village's 1863 catalog. Stephen Foster, a sixteen-year-old student at the time, undertook to plant and manage the organic herb garden.

The site, although historically a garden spot, had lain fallow for forty years since Brother Delmar Wilson had run the dairy farm, and it was well suited for an organic garden. The first plants were collected in the wild as there were still many old varieties that had naturalized over the community's 1,900 acres. Sister Francis Carr,

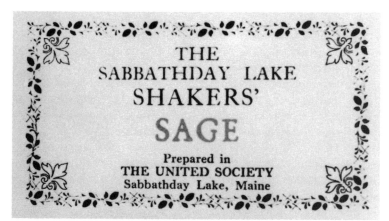

Herb label from the Sabbathday Lake Shaker community. This label, printed in the twentieth century, is an adaptation of an earlier version made at the village. (Private collection)

Kitchen Deaconess, transplanted some spearmint that she found growing down by the lake, and pipsissewa was found in the granite quarry one and a half miles away.

Eventually, the garden grew to one acre, was maintained by six people, and contained fifty of the seventy varieties of herbs that the Sabbathday Lake Shakers marketed to the World. This garden was recently moved to a site across the street next to the Meetinghouse and the vegetable garden. This new space, which was also historically a garden spot, has two advantages over the old location: its proximity to the vegetable plot makes the garden's management much easier, and it is more accessible to visitors. The new garden is managed by one full-time employee; another person is in charge of processing and packaging the herbs; and members of the village's loyal volunteer corps frequently lend a hand in the garden.

The Sabbathday Lake Shakers have been pragmatic in their selection of herbs. The original plant list has been narrowed to eliminate some of the less popular herbs such as hyssop and goldenrod. Many herbs continue to be gathered in the wild, particularly those for tea, such as wintergreen, raspberry, clover, and dandelion. Most of the plants are grown from seed, but because of Maine's short growing season and hard winters, the community sometimes finds it necessary to purchase organically grown seedlings elsewhere.

The community uses several methods to enrich the soil. Each spring the village tractor plows sheep manure into the garden. At one time, according to Sister Frances, the community tried chicken manure but found it too offensive. Compost, wood ashes, and leaf mulch have also been added, and several on-going compost piles border the garden. Other than some specific side dressing for heavy feeders, such as tarragon, no other fertilizer is used.

One disadvantage of the new garden site is that it is bordered on one side by an apple orchard that attracts deer who often wander into the garden. Over the years, the Shakers have tried many methods to discourage these animals; some have worked temporarily but, eventually, the deer grow accustomed to the measures and ignore them. Sister Frances recalls stopping at barber shops to collect human hair to lay around the garden in an attempt to ward off the deer. After that became ineffective, she tried dried blood, which also worked for a while. To control insects, the Sabbathday Lake community members hand-pick them and use organic sprays.

The Sabbathday Lake community harvests the herbs continually over the season, many being gathered from the same plant several times. Herbs such as comfrey are picked five or six times; basil, lovage, and parsley are harvested twice. Straw is spread beneath the plants to keep them clean before harvesting and to eliminate washing.

Once the herbs are gathered, they are air dried in several different attics on the property. The Sisters' Shop is used to dry and process herbs. The attic of this building was initially designed to dry clothes and is equipped with revolving racks and a woodstove. The members tie the herbs in bundles and hang them on racks. Other herbs are placed on "flakes," the original wooden-slatted drying screens used by the Shakers. These have proved to be so effective that the community is in the process of making new ones. The members are following the original design of the screens but are increasing the air spaces slightly. To dry the herbs, the members stack the screens and separate them at the four corners by four-inch clay flower pots. On damp days, to hasten the process, the wood stove is used, and a fan keeps the air circulating. With limited space, it is necessary to dry the herbs quickly and put them into containers in order to process all the herbs in the garden. The herbs are stored on the second floor of the building and are packaged for sale in a separate room.

The attic of the 1824 Herb House is also used as a drying space. This two-and-a-half-story building was once totally devoted to the processing of herbs. The roots were boiled in the basement, and the first floor was used for storage and shipping. The second floor was designed for sorting and packaging the herbs that were dried in the attic. Today, much of the building serves as a woodworking shop, but the attic is strung from post to post with wire in groups of three strands which support a fine screening on which to dry herbs.

Sabbathday Lake is licensed to sell herbs; the operation is inspected once a year by the FDA and the state. The licensing process requires that the old crocks in which the Shakers originally stored their herbs be replaced with heavy cardboard containers with covers that lock. Rows of these bins, each filled with specific herbs, are carefully labeled and are stored in the ironing room of the 1821 Sisters' Shop.

Herbs are shipped throughout the United States and to England. They have been sold in such places as the Smithsonian Institution, the Museum of Fine Arts in Boston, Bloomingdale's in New York, and L.L. Bean in Maine. The community has used various means to package the herbs. At one time the herbs were put in glass jars. Later the members duplicated an 1860s tin canister from the collection, a type of container they still use today. The label on these tins is an adaptation of one from the nineteenth century. Minor changes in the text were made as required by law. These new labels are still printed at Sabbathday Lake.

This community publishes an herb catalog that includes six kinds of vinegars: basil, chive, garlic, lemon verbena, mint, and tarragon; rose water; and four potpourri mixtures: Shaker Woods Mixture Potpourri, Shaker Garden Potpourri, Eldress Hester Ann Adams 1858 Receipt, and Shaker Lavender Potpourri. The catalog also lists their Shaker Insect Repellent Mixture, which is designed to ward off moths and household insects. Their fir balsam pillows, first sold nearly a century ago by Sister Aurelia Mace, are also offered for sale. In the winter the community makes fir balsam wreaths decorated with dried herbs.

The village also sells culinary herbs, with the most popular products being the culinary herb mixes such as Salad Seasoning, Fine Herbs, Bouquet Garni, Herbal Bouquet, Dill Dip, and Poultry Seasoning. Sabbathday Lake also offers a wide variety of herbal teas.

The Sabbathday Lake Shakers' herb business is an ambitious effort. Each year the community works on new products for the herb line and succeeds in reaping the benefits of its long herb history.[6]

"Persevering Faithfulness": Creating Your Shaker Herb Garden

Weeding should be early performed and continued with Persevering Faithfulness, as often as necessary, through the season . . . .[1]

*T*he land on which the Shaker villages were situated provided the communities with nearly all their needs. The Shakers raised their own food and animals and harvested timber for their buildings and furniture. They raised plants for medicines and clothing. The Brothers and Sisters lived and worked on the same sites for more than a century and grew to know the land's resources and limitations.

The Believers became excellent horticulturists as they used the land to its fullest potential and raised superior plants from which they made many products. Their herb businesses would not have been successful had they not been so skilled, for the reliability and potency of their products were regulated by the health and vigor of their herbs. New techniques, gleaned from their own experiences and from their contact with the World, were continually incorporated into their established practices. These horticultural skills were passed on from gardener to gardener and shared among the communities.

With their seed businesses, one of their many profitable agricultural industries, the Shakers found it necessary to teach the World their gardening techniques. Some of the villages published pamphlets that described their methods. Most of their advice is as applicable today as it was a hundred years ago.

A widely distributed Shaker publication of cultural instructions was the *Gardener's Manual*. This inexpensive guide was left with the Shakers' seed boxes in stores throughout their peddling territories. The first booklet was published by Charles F. Crosman of the New Lebanon Society in 1835; a second edition followed the next year. The early version sold sixteen thousand copies and was issued two more times between 1843 and 1860. New Lebanon also reprinted copies for the Enfield, Connecticut Shakers to sell, and at the end of the century they published seed catalogs that contained the same information. The Sabbathday Lake Shakers did their part to share gardening hints. From 1849 to 1856 Deacon James Holmes published three small books that contained what the members considered to be the most useful, up-to-date agricultural techniques.

All of these publications were intended to furnish a convenient set of practical instructions for those who had "little experience in cultivating a kitchen garden." The Shakers wanted to give their customers the best chance of producing fine vegetables.[2] By educating future gardeners, they knew they would build up their market base and increase their sales.

The Believers were not the first to publish cultural directions. By 1843 many books had already been written on the subject. The Shakers, however, felt that those publications were aimed at an elite few, and they wanted to target "the common classes, those to whom a garden [was] of most value."

> The manners of cultivation recommended by some, are expensive in a corresponding degree, well calculated for lords and nobles, who can afford a tenant to every square acre, but quite impracticable by those who have to tend their own gardens and conduct a farm, or some mechanical profession besides, which is the case with the majority of garden holders in this country . . .[3]

While the Believers published their *Gardener's Manual* as a tool to promote their seed businesses, they also took a wider view of their responsibilities to humankind. They claimed that the condition of one's garden reflected the state of one's mind, and they were concerned about the disorder they saw in the World.

> The present condition of the majority of gardens in this country, is susceptible of much improvement, which the spirit of the age, and the progressive improvements in agriculture, loudly demand. Many are unfavorably situated, and not large enough; many are of ill shape, and not well laid out internally. Very many are deficient in a variety of vegetables cultivated; and a majority not properly prepared before stocking with

seeds and plants, and but poorly cultivated when stocked. These things should not be; the garden is said to be an index of the owner's mind. If this be true, many who otherwise might be acquitted, must be judged to possess minds susceptible of much improvement in order, usefulness, and beauty. But a claim, as strong perhaps, as any that may be urged for the improvement of the kitchen garden, is its usefulness, and the superiority of a well cultivated garden, over the poor neglected patch.[4]

The *Gardener's Manual* began with basic instructions on choosing a garden spot, improving the soil, and planting and raising vegetables and herbs. The Shakers felt that if close attention were given to these concerns, the farmer would improve his plot, his vegetable yield, and his mind. The first consideration was the choice of the garden site. The Brethren recommended that it be located on

a spot of even land, slightly inclined to the south, or east, and having the full benefit of the sun … It should be situated near the dwelling, and neatly enclosed with a high wall, or a tight board fence.[5]

Its size depended on the number of people it supplied and the kinds of vegetables intended to be raised from it.

For a family of six persons, one quarter of an acre is sufficient for most of the kinds raised from seeds commonly retailed at the country stores. But if desirable to have fruit trees, shrubs, strawberry beds, early potatoes, &c, enclosed within the same fence that encloses the garden, it must be made larger, in proportion to the quantity wanted.[6]

The Shakers stressed quality over quantity.

If farmers will cultivate less land, and do it more thoroughly and perfectly, there can be but little doubt that greater crops will be obtained and the profit on the labor be comparably greater.[7]

The Believers' approach to design was practical. The shape of the plot was to be either "square or oblong, both for convenience and looks."[8]

. . . it will generally be found most convenient to have the rows of vegetables run lengthwise of the garden, so that the plough or cultivator may run through freely without interruption, allowing an alley at each end for the horse and plough to turn round upon.[9]

They felt that the initial conditioning of the soil was fundamental. The soil is the link between the rock core of the earth and all the living things on the surface. It consists of minerals, organic matter, water and air, in varying proportions. The best earth is deep, dry, light, and rich, but most soils do not naturally occur this way. When the proportions are out of balance, it is necessary to make corrections to ensure good plant growth. The Brethren called this work to improve the tilth of the soil an art.

The *Gardener's Manual* offered advice on how to improve a variety of poor soils.

> If wet, draining should be resorted to; if too shallow, deep ploughing; if poor, manuring; if stony, they should be got off; and thus should every impediment and obstruction to a good sweet soil, be reversed or removed, by industry and art.[10]

If the plot were sandy, then "the clay marl, [a soft, impure form of limestone] neutralized with lime" was recommended.[11]

Church Family, Enfield, New Hampshire, nineteenth century. A Shaker is preparing a seed bed with a horse-drawn plow. The distillery is on the left. (Private collection)

In the early nineteenth century, American farmers looked to Western Europe for leadership in scientific agricultural practices. Because their soil was similar to Europe's, New England gardeners were successful in applying European counsel.[12] The Shakers also corresponded with agriculturalists abroad. As early as the 1820s, Garrett K. Lawrence was seeking advice from an apothecary in Rouen, France, who was experimenting with muriate of lime.[13]

Lime was an important soil supplement that New England farmers used to correct the natural acidity of their newly cleared soils. To detect the level of acidity, these early gardeners tried to determine the amount of sulfuric acid in the ground.

> This may be done in several ways; first by the water that filtrates through the soil; if the water is what women call hard it contains sulfuric acid. Second, land that contains sulfuric acid is slow to sod over. When such land is sown with grass seed, it frequently fails of a catch as it is called or it catches but poorly.[14]

They also identified the kinds of grasses present, examined the roots of these grasses, and looked for the appearance of oxide of iron. Once the acidity was determined, the Shakers added lime as well as other nutrients such as compost, wood ashes, manure, and salt to improve the soil's fertility.

> It is not a matter of very great importance how lime may be applied to land which may need it, the great object is to get it on the land and distribute it evenly over the surface and then to harrow it in, so as to ultimately mix it with the surface soil. This presupposes the previous preparation of land by plowing and harrowing.[15]

> If the lime . . . has been previously slacked, [i.e., hydrated, or heat and water treated, to make it more readily available to the plants], then . . . [the farmer] should, in addition to the lime, broadcast two bushels of salt per acre over the land, and . . . add five bushels of ashes per acre . . . to place his land in the best possible condition to be benefited by whatever putrescent matter he may have to apply, whether that be stable and barnyard manure, or compost formed of two loads of that to every one of wood's mould, marsh, river or creek mud, or any kind of substance.[16]

The practice of adding salt is an indication of the depth of the Shakers' agricultural knowledge, for the members evidently observed that salt, in proper amounts, would make the micronutrients more readily available to plants. This method, however, is not recommended currently, for modern soils are quite different from those a century ago, and salinity is now a major problem. It is known today that excessive salt reduces the entry of water into plants and restricts their growth without producing specific symptoms of deficiency.[17]

The Shakers had large, readily available supplies of cow, horse, sheep, and poultry manures which they believed were essential for soil improvement.

> Lime in some form, must be the basis of every system of improvement; but it is futile to attempt to build up the constitution of any worn out land, without the aid of nutritive manures—what we mean by nutritive manures are such as by putrefication and decomposition will afford as one of its resultants ammoniacal elements. Stable manure, barn-yard manure, fish or any other animal substance, marsh mud, river mud, and leaves will do this.[18]

> ... even if the land be quite fertile, if it has been used much, a slight manuring will be beneficial. Poor land should be manured at the rate of 40 ox cart loads per acre; on good land, less will suffice.[19]

In addition to applying manures directly to the soil, the Shakers also recommended composting manures with other soil amendments.

> The best manure for a garden is a compost, of one part mineral substances, as ashes, lime and or clay (as the soil may require), salt &c; five parts vegetable matter, as weeds, straw, leaves, roots and stalks of plants and tan bark or sawdust to make the soil light, if necessary; and six parts of animal excrement. These should be collected in the course of the season, and mixed well together, to cause them to ferment. In the fall, this compost should be spread evenly upon the garden, and ploughed in, that it may be ready for action as soon as the state of the ground will allow, in the Spring, without having to wait for an operation that may much better be performed in the Fall.[20]

Peat was also a useful ingredient in a compost.

> Peat ... may be converted into an excellent manure by means of a mixture of lime and a little barn yard manure or any animal matter; thus, three or four cords of the peat, mixed with one cord of animal manure, and treated with a cask or two of slacked lime, will make a compost superior in value to five cords of the best stable manure alone. They ought to be placed in alternate layers thus: Peat, Lime, Animal manure, &c. The whole forming a regular compost heap.[21]

Isaac Hill, Governor of New Hampshire at the time, was so

impressed with the Canterbury Brothers' method of composting that he cited their methods in his annual message to the Merrimack County Agriculture Society in 1837:

> One of the Shakers recently told me they had been in the habit of buying the best of Thomaston lime, which with transportation cost them at least three dollars a cask; of breaking and slacking it and mixing it with mud collected from bog-holes or turfs from the sides of the highways, in proportion of four or five casks to an hundred common ox-loads; and after due fermentation and mixture, they have found this composition not less valuable than an equal quantity of the best [stable manure].[22]

After the Shakers spread the lime, manure, and compost in the spring, they plowed, harrowed, and cultivated their plots until they had achieved the ideal tilth.

> The ground was plowed early in spring to a depth of eight inches; instead of receiving a single harrowing, was worked with harrow and cultivator until ... it was as mellow as an ash heap, and a man in walking over it would settle in to his ankles in the fine earth. Here was the whole secret of the great crop. The land was finely and thoroughly pulverized, a mellow tilth was obtained, the soil retained its moisture uniformly, the roots found no obstruction to their movements in search of food, the nutritive matter in the soil was so reduced and evenly distributed as to be readily and easily taken in by the mouths of plants.[23]

In the nineteenth and early twentieth centuries, horses were used to plow. Although modern techniques are mechanized, the Believers' directions are still useful.

> [Plowing] ... should not be done till quite dry; for ploughing it when wet in the Spring, will cause it to be much more lumpy, and harder through the whole season, than it would be if suffered to get thoroughly dry before ploughing. Deep ploughing is the only kind wanted in preparing a garden, the deeper the better in most soils. Next comes the harrow; this should do the work faithfully, when a second and last ploughing, dividing the garden into beds, should be resorted to.[24]

> The essential advantage of deep ploughing is not only best calculated to give room for the roots to expand freely, but the crops on a deep ploughed soil will be much less liable to injury from the extremes of wet and dry weather.[25]

The last step before seeding was to hand rake the plot until smooth to eliminate any stones that would impede the growth of young plants. Recognizing this was a large job, the Shakers conceded that the plots reserved for larger seeds, such as squash and melons, could be raked less finely than the others.

Garden Design

Much of this Shaker advice about how to lay out and prepare a garden remains relevant. Location is very important, but most people do not own as much land as the Shakers did; and a modern site is often limited by such things as houses, driveways, and shade. Nevertheless, an herb garden is possible in a variety of situations because of the adaptability of herbs. In determining the size of a plot, consider how much time is really available to work in it; start with a small area that can be expanded. Although it is no longer necessary to reserve space for a horse to turn around at either end of the plot, this area may be left for a rototiller or future expansion.

There are many types of herb gardens, ranging from a collection of favorite plants to gardens made entirely of plants used as dyes, teas, or fragrances, and there are many design books that are excellent sources. With a group of plants in mind, begin to study them individually for their size, shape, and habit of growth to determine their placement in the garden.

Designing a garden on graph paper first will save time and avoid costly mistakes later. While there are many possibilities, too elaborate a plan may be discouraging to make as well as to maintain. The Shakers' basic geometric shapes were chosen for their simplicity as well as for the economy of time and motion. A garden may be made with raised beds or inside a low fence which, while no longer a practical necessity, may be used as an attractive landscaping technique.

There are three classes of plants: annuals, biennials, and perennials. An annual is a plant that can be sown from seed and will mature to harvest stage within one growing season. Annuals are killed by frost and need to be planted again the following season. Basil, chervil, coriander, dill, and summer savory are some examples.

A biennial is a plant that takes two years to mature. Its root structure survives the first winter, but the second year the plant will flower, set seed, and die. Parsley, hollyhocks, and foxgloves are biennials.

A perennial returns every spring. While the top vegetation dies back with the frost, the roots will live through the winter and send up new growth in the spring. Mints, tarragon, and sage are a few examples. In colder northern climates, some perennials, such as bay, lemon verbena, rosemary, and scented geraniums, need to be brought inside in the winter or treated as annuals.

Since most perennials are permanent inhabitants, they need more room than annuals, for they expand every year. It is useful to know how they increase, whether by underground runners, such as mints, or from the base of the plant, such as echinacea (coneflower). Herbs that have underground runners may spread rapidly but can be managed by growing in pots that are sunk into the ground.

The following five designs for herb gardens use the same varieties of plants the Shakers offered for sale in their catalogs. These modern designs are meant for relatively small plots and use a basic rectangular shape the Shakers might have preferred, but the herbs are not placed in long straight rows. Instead, the plants have been arranged with consideration given to their hue, texture, and size.

The border plans are intended to be placed in a garden location with seven to eight hours of sun each day. The plans for three-sided gardens need a backdrop of some kind, such as a wall, hedge, or a large planting. The beds drawn here should be fifteen feet long and eight feet wide, a size that will provide easy access to the plants if a narrow path between the backdrop and the rear of the garden is provided.

There is no limit to the number of forms a garden can take or to the plants arranged in them. The rectangular shape will give a more formal appearance, but the beds can be pulled and curved into interesting variations that are compatible with the naturally occurring features on your own property.

The plants depicted here were grown by the Shakers for their medicinal herb business. However, in choosing plants for these modern designs, consideration was also given to appearance, color harmonies, and length of bloom. Each plant grouping is intended to have three plants in it; however, the entire garden may be enlarged by either adding more plants in each section or by repeating these groupings at either end of the beds.

In the early spring lay out the design on the ground with a string and prepare the soil for planting. Place marker sticks with the plant's names in the center of each group or mark the location of each plant with a handful of sand so when planting time comes, it will be a simple matter to place the varieties.

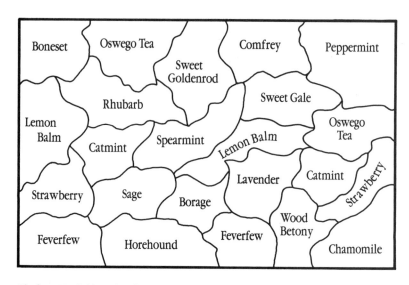

Shaker Herb Tea Garden

Shaker Herb Tea Garden

Boneset, *Eupatorium perfoliatum*
Borage, *Borago officinalis*
Catmint, *Nepeta cateria*
Chamomile, *Anthemis noblis*
Comfrey, *Symphytum officinale*
Feverfew, *Chrysanthemum parthenium*
Goldenrod, Sweet, *Solidago odora*
Horehound, *Marrubium vulgare*
Lavender, *Lavandula vera*
Lemon Balm, *Melissa officinalis*
Oswego Tea, Bee Balm, *Monarda didyma*
Peppermint, *Mentha piperita*
Rhubarb, *Rheum palmatum*
Sage, *Salvia officinalis*
Spearmint, *Mentha viridis*
Strawberry, *Fragaria virginiana*
Sweet Gale, Sweet Fern, *Myrica gale*
Wood Betony, *Betonica officinalis*

This primarily perennial garden will provide a family with a large sampling of teas throughout the year. Three each of the perennial plants are recommended for each space while the annuals, borage and chamomile, are easily started from seed and thinned to fit the space. In order to avoid the ravages of local cats, it is best to plant the catmint from seed. One plant each of sweet gale, bayberry, or rhubarb, which will grow quite large, is all that is necessary.

There are many plants from the mint family in this garden, and they will spread rapidly. Try to keep the peppermint and spearmint separated, and transplant extra plants to another area where they can grow freely and provide enough leaves to dry for winter use. Establishing plants to grow in the wild creates a lot less work for the gardener!

The leaves of almost all of these plants can be steeped in boiling water, and the brew sweetened when necessary to provide many flavorful teas. A mixture of herbs may be tried for interesting variations. The leaves of rhubarb should not be used, but the stems may be stewed in water and then sweetened and diluted with more water to make an excellent summer drink. Borage was an essential ingredient in Eldress Bertha Lindsay's summer drink; its flowers add a special touch to any beverage. When steeped, wood betony resembles the taste of oriental black tea. Oswego tea, which was used by the American Indians, has its own distinctive taste. Peppermint is a familiar and popular drink. Spearmint tea is milder and more fragrant than peppermint and is a favorite with children. Horehound is another mild tea that benefits from sweetening with honey. Sweet goldenrod leaves have a licorice flavor, and lavender tea has its own special fragrance. Chamomile is a good tea, hot or cold, at the end of a meal and is said to ward off nightmares. For variation, add ginger or fennel to chamomile tea. Lemon balm tea is good plain or mixed with lavender or spearmint and may be flavored with cloves or rosemary. Sage has a strong flavor, but a weak tea made from the leaves is very good. Sweeten it with maple syrup or brown sugar; for variation, add cinnamon, lemon, or orange.

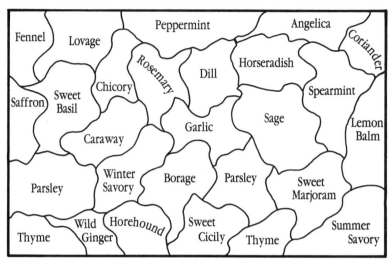

Shaker Culinary Herb Garden

Shaker Culinary Herb Garden

Angelica, *Angelica atropurpurea*
Borage, *Borago officinalis*
Caraway, *Carum carvi*
Chicory, *Cichorium intybus*
Coriander, *Coriandrum sativum*
Dill, *Anethum graveolens*
Fennel, *Foeniculum vulgare*
Garlic, *Allium sativum*
Horehound, *Marrubium vulgare*
Horseradish, *Cochlearia armoracia*
Lemon Balm, *Melissa officinalis*
Lovage, *Levisticum officinale*
Peppermint, *Mentha piperitas*
Rosemary, *Rosmarinus officinalis*
Saffron, *Crocus sativus*
Sage, *Salvia officinalis*
Savory, Summer, *Satureia hortensis*
Savory, Winter, *Satureia montana*
Spearmint, *Mentha viridis*
Sweet Basil, *Ocymum basilcum*
Sweet Marjoram, *Oreganum marjorana*
Thyme, English or Common, *Thymus vulgaris*
Wild Ginger, *Asarum canadense*

Each plant in this garden has a culinary use today, although the Shakers grew these herbs mainly for medicinal purposes until the mid-twentieth century.

While there is some color in this garden, the plant shapes are the most interesting feature. Lovage and angelica are large background plants; sweet cicily, coriander, and caraway are delicate plants that contrast with the rough foliage of the borage and horseradish plants. This garden contains many annuals that may be grown easily from seed: coriander, summer savory, sweet marjoram, caraway, parsley, basil, dill, fennel, and garlic. The rosemary plants will have to be wintered inside in most cooler climates.

Herbs do not improve with prolonged heating, so in cases of roasts and similar long-cooking dishes, add the herbs during the last hour of cooking. The seeds of fennel are used in black breads, rolls, and soups. Coriander seeds, a source of vitamin A, iron, and calcium, are also added to breads, pastries, and pickles. While the leaves of sweet cicily have a licorice flavor, the seeds are spicy and may be used in soups, salads, and stews. The stems and root of angelica may be eaten like asparagus. Historically, angelica has been used for perfumes and to flavor liqueurs. The leaves make a good substitute for China tea. Angelica can grow to eight feet; it dies after it flowers, which may not occur for two years. Peppermint and spearmint are good in cold drinks, vinegars, and sauces. Horehound makes an excellent candy. Saffron, which comes from the three scarlet-orange stigmas of the flower, is the most expensive spice in the world. It is a rich source of vitamin B-2 and is used in breads, cakes, and rice dishes. Wild ginger is not so strong as the commonly known Jamaican ginger and, consequently, the root may be used more freely. The root of chicory was used as a coffee substitute by the Shakers. Today, it may be roasted and added to coffee for a rich, smooth flavor as well as for decreasing the amount of caffeine. Lemon balm provides a light lemon flavor to drinks, fish, and salads. Rosemary is used in lamb and pork dishes. Summer savory is a wonderful addition to vegetables and bean dishes with its slightly peppery flavor. Winter savory is a shrub-like perennial.

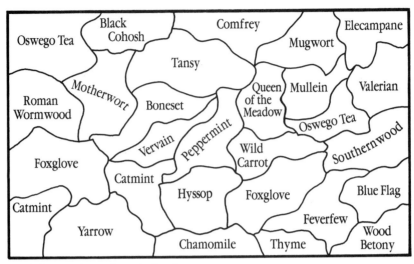

Shaker Medicinal Herb Garden

Shaker Medicinal Herb Garden

Blue Flag, *Iris versicolor*
Boneset, *Eupatorium perfoliatum*
Catmint, *Nepeta cateria*
Chamomile, *Anthemis noblis*
Cohosh, Black, *Cimicifuga racemosa*
Comfrey, *Symphytum officinale*
Elecampane, *Inula helenium*
Feverfew, *Chrysanthemum partienium*
Foxglove, *Digatalis purpurea*
Hyssop, *Hyssopus officinalis*
Motherwort, *Leonurus cardiaca*
Mugwort, *Artemesia vulgaris*
Mullein, *Verbascum thapsus*
Oswego Tea, Bee Balm, *Monarda didyma*
Peppermint, *Mentha piperita*
Queen of the Meadow, Joe-pye, *Eupatorium purpureum*
Roman Wormwood, *Artemesia pontica*
Southernwood, *Artemisia abrotanum*
Tansy, *Tanacetum vulgare*
Thyme, Common, *Thymus vulgaris*
Valerian, *Valerian officinalis*
Vervain, *Verbena hastata*
Wild Carrot, Queen Anne's Lace, *Daucus carota*
Wood Betony, *Betonica officinalis*
Yarrow, *Achilea millefolium*

Many herbs prized for their medicinal qualities are not so refined looking as other garden plants; therefore, this collection has a "wild" look about it. Nonetheless, these plants are beautiful in their own right. Elecampane, comfrey, queen of the meadow, and mullein are large and rangy plants. Other medicinal herbs, such as foxglove, blue flag, thyme, valerian, and Oswego tea, are also appreciated for their flowers. Their addition makes this a colorful as well as useful garden. Yellows in the garden are provided by tansy, yarrow, feverfew, chamomile, mullein, and elecampane; pinks are furnished by thyme, comfrey, foxglove, motherwort, and betony; Oswego tea supplies scarlet red; and whites are found in the flowers of boneset, cohosh, valerian, and wild carrot. Wormwood, southernwood, and mugwort add a silvery appearance; and blue shades are provided by blue flag, hyssop, vervain, and catmint.

Although the Shakers relied on these plants for their curative powers, the medicinal use of these herbs is not recommended as many of them are very powerful and often dangerous to those unskilled in their application. The root is the most valuable, curative part of comfrey, wild carrot (its seeds are also valuable), valerian, blue flag, elecampane, queen of the meadow, and black cohosh. The Shakers saved the leaves and flowers of boneset, peppermint, hyssop, mullein, catmint, yarrow, feverfew, thyme, motherwort, vervain, Oswego tea, southernwood, mugwort, and Roman wormwood for their medicines. They also used the flowers of chamomile and the leaves of wood betony and foxglove in their medicinal preparations.

Practically all the plants in this garden are vigorous, making them an even match for one another. Only the catmint, chamomile, and wood betony need to be protected from the other plants' invasive habits by ensuring they have a space to grow.

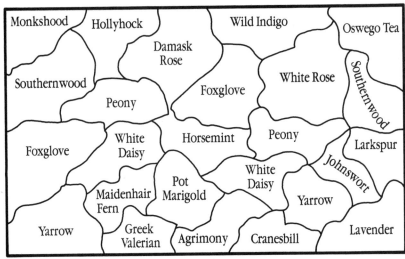

Shaker Flowering Herb Garden

Shaker Flowering Herb Garden

Agrimony, *Agrimonia eupatoria*
Cranesbill, *Geranium maculatum*
Foxglove, *Digatalis purpurea*
Greek Valerian, *Polemonium reptans*
Hollyhock, *Althea rosea*
Horsemint, *Monarda punctata*
Johnswort, St. Johnswort, *Hypericum perforatum*
Larkspur, *Delphinium consolida*
Lavender, *Lavandula vera*
Maidenhair Fern, *Adiantum pedatum*
Monkshood, *Aconitum napellus*
Oswego Tea, Bee Balm, *Monarda didyma*
Peony, *Paeonia officinalis*
Pot Marigold, *Calendula officinalis*
Rose, White, *Rosa alba*
Rose, Damask, *Rosa damascena*
Southernwood, *Artemisia abrotanum*
White Daisy, Ox-Eye Daisy, *Leucanthemum vulgare*
Wild Indigo, *Baptista tinctoria*
Yarrow, *Achillea millefolium*

This predominately perennial garden is planned for a colorful flowering display from June to frost. Larkspur and calendula are annuals and will need to be replanted each year; hollyhocks will also require replanting unless they reseed themselves.

Blues are found in monkshood, lavender, Greek valerian, and larkspur, and whites are found in daisies and roses. Wild indigo, St.

Johnswort, yarrow, calendula, and agrimony have flowers in strong yellows. Pinks are represented in cranesbill, foxglove, peony, damask rose, and larkspur. Southernwood provides a silver background, and the maidenhair fern adds a soft green.

While the varieties used by the Shakers are suggested in the plant list, substitutions may be made for more color. The white medicinal yarrow can be replaced by yellow or other pastel varieties of the plant. The simple white daisies may be replaced by larger Shasta daisies. Foxglove comes in a wide color range other than the medicinal purple.

Three plants of each variety are recommended; however, only one of each shrub rose is necessary. Several of these herbs will spread rapidly once established, such as southernwood, Oswego tea, and wild indigo, but can be restrained by pulling out the invasive plants each spring.

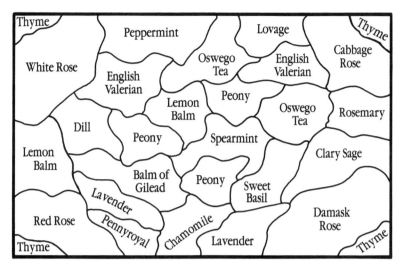

Shaker Fragrant Herb Garden

Shaker Fragrant Herb Garden

Balm of Gilead, *Dracocephalum canariense*
Chamomile, *Anthemis noblis*
Clary Sage, *Salvia sclarea*
Dill, *Anethum graveolens*
Lavender, *Lavandula vera*
Lemon Balm, *Melissa officinalis*
Lovage, *Levisticum officinale*
Oswego Tea, Bee Balm, *Monarda didyma*
Peony, *Paeonia officinalis*
Pennyroyal, *Mentha pulegioides*
Peppermint, *Mentha piperita*
Rose, White, *Rosa alba*
Rose, Red, *Rosa gallica*
Rose, Cabbage, *Rosa centifolia*
Rose, Damask, *Rosa damascena*
Rosemary, *Rosmarinus officinalis*
Spearmint, *Mentha viridis*
Sweet Basil, *Ocymum basilcum*
Thyme, Creeping, *Thymus serpyllum*
Thyme, Common, *Thymus vulgaris*
Valerian, English, *Valerian officinalis*

This is a garden that should be planted where there is foot traffic, or under a window, or near an outdoor porch in order to enjoy its fragrances. These plants are meant to be touched and rubbed to release their scents and should be placed in a spot where this will be possible.

Shrub roses anchor this aromatic perennial garden. One each of the Shaker varieties will be enough as they will grow quite large and increase by underground runners. When they bloom in June, pick some of the petals to dry for potpourris and pick the leaves of the Damask rose as well for fragrance. The flowers of the other herbs may also be dried for potpourris. In addition to potpourri ingredients, the flowers in this garden may be used for such projects as clothes sachets, bath sachets, herbal rubbing lotions using alcohol, and rose beads. Daffodils and violets may be interplanted for fragrance and early spring bloom.

Once established, the mints will need to be kept under control. Plant them in the garden in containers or dig many of them out in the spring. The new rose plants, which will pop up once the garden is established, may be cut from the parent plant and moved elsewhere. The rosemary plant should be dug up in the fall and wintered indoors. Dill and sweet basil should be reseeded every spring.

Preparing the Soil

Once the spot is selected and the garden's size and contents planned, the next step is to turn over the new ground. Depending on the amount of land, this can be done mechanically or by hand. After the ground has been worked, it can be either leveled or mounded for growing beds. The 1843 *Gardener's Manual* described a technique for throwing the earth with the plow to create ditches between the rows and ridges on which to plant the seeds. This method is excellent for herbs that like a well-drained soil, and it is a variation of the modern raised bed.

> Have your ground well prepared, as directed for the garden, throw two furrows together with a large plough for one ridge, level, and pulverize with a rake, and it is prepared for sowing or planting.[26]

In smaller gardens raised beds may be permanently made by raking up the earth in a pile and then surrounding it with a barrier of untreated railroad ties, stones, or concrete. These materials create interesting landscaping effects and lend themselves to a variety of designs. Raised beds have the advantage of eliminating a lot of bending over; if the beds are less than three feet wide, it is possible to sit on the edge and cultivate the plants. Hand cultivation also has the benefit of reducing the earth's compaction, an unfortunate result of machine cultivation. In a large garden a few stones may be strategically placed where it is necessary to walk in the garden.

After the soil has initially been turned over, it is important to

Seed onion field, Enfield, New Hampshire Shaker community. This post card was another way the Shakers documented and promoted their products. This view shows the Shakers' raised beds and meticulous cultivation. (Collection of Dartmouth College Library, Hanover, New Hampshire)

have it tested to determine what supplements are needed. In many states the County Cooperative Extension Service will provide written recommendations for either chemical or organic additives, whichever are requested. While there are several good soil testing kits for home use on the market today, the most difficult part of testing is the interpretation of the results. The County Extension Service not only knows how to read the information but is also familiar with the area and can make recommendations for specific crops.

The addition of organic matter and necessary minerals is all that is needed to sustain a healthy soil. Compost is added when preparing the ground initially and throughout the season. The addition of this organic matter loosens heavy soils and holds sandy soils together. Compost piles are easy to make, are a form of recycling, and produce a free source of plant nourishment. Most of the nineteenth-century additives, such as peat and manure, are available in packaged form. Composts may be made out of a variety of materials even without the use of animal manures since any organic matter is important for soil improvement, and any ingredients, once composted, are equally effective.

Compost piles need only five elements to be successful: carbon, or dry fibrous materials such as leaves or straw; nitrogen, which is obtained from green vegetation such as pea vines, grass clippings, or weeds; oxygen, which will occur naturally if the pile is not compacted; water, enough to dampen the pile; and bacteria, which comes from the addition of soil, compost, or a commercially available bacterial activator.[27] Maintaining a ratio of thirty parts carbon to one part nitrogen in the pile is important, and the addition of lime is not recommended. A compost pile is made by piling a series of four- to six-inch repeating layers of garden refuse (nitrogen) covered with soil or compost (bacteria) and covered again with leaves, straw, or other similar materials (carbon). The pile is periodically turned when the internal temperature has peaked. When the matter is thoroughly decomposed, the pile is ready for use and should be covered to prevent the nutrients from leaching.

As a result of the soil test, the addition of various minerals may be necessary. Sulphur will increase acidity. A neutral to slightly alkaline soil is best and is preferred by beneficial organisms, which work to improve the soil's tilth. Limestone will reduce acidity, increase the supply of calcium and magnesium, and help produce high-yielding crops. Today, ground limestone is easier to handle and costs less than the burnt or hydrated lime the Shakers used. Rock phosphate or colloidal phosphate may be added to supply needed phosphorus, and greensand will provide potassium and a broad range of micronutrients.

Some soil improvement is often necessary; but if radical changes in the soil type are recommended to achieve a particular garden, it is perhaps better to work with existing conditions and to rethink the choice of plants. If the plot is surrounded by dense pine trees, select shade-loving plants that grow in acidic soils and do not attempt to grow sun-loving plants. There are between 200,000 and 800,000 members of the plant family from which to choose, and working with the local environment will result in a more natural-looking garden.

The goal should be to improve the quality of the soil which, in turn, will produce superior plants. Feeding individual plants is merely a stopgap and does not solve the underlying problem. If the initial quality of the soil is good, the herbs will need no more than some compost dug in around them during the season. Too much fertilizer creates excessive leafy growth and will diminish the manufacture of essential oils from which most herbs get their distinctive aroma and flavor. However, salad herbs, such as corn salad, cress, mustard, roquette, and sorrel, which are cut primarily for their leaves, will benefit from fertilization throughout the growing season.

The first plants for a garden may be acquired in a variety of ways. The quickest way to have a full herb garden the first year is to purchase them. Large plants may also be made from cuttings or by dividing established plants, and often other herb gardeners are willing to share their plants. Finally, most herbs can be easily grown from seed. While this method is slower, the process is very educational, less expensive, and usually results in healthier plants.

Dividing Plants

Once a garden is established, its plants increase in size. After a few years it is beneficial to divide and move them, creating new plants. In the spring (before June) water the plant intended for division, dig it up, shake the dirt off the roots, and separate it into smaller units. Each clump should have part of the root system and an above-ground shoot. Always protect the exposed roots from the sun and air by shading and watering them. Replant and water the new clumps. Chives, comfrey, St. Johnswort, and tarragon are easily propagated by this method.

Some woody herbs, such as lavender, sage, and santolina, may be increased by the simple technique of soil layering. This is done with established plants in the spring or early summer. Choose a nonflowering lower branch of this season's growth that will easily reach the ground about ten inches from the tip. Loosen the earth under the place where the branch will touch the earth. On a small section of the part that will come in contact with the ground, remove the leaves and scrape off the outer bark on the underside of the branch. Press this scraped section of the branch into the earth, cover the section with dirt, and weigh it down with a stone. Keep the plant watered. Next spring roots will have formed from the scraped portion, and the new plant may be severed from the branch of the mother plant. Several branches may be layered at once in this manner.

Another quick way to obtain new herbs is to take stem cuttings of established plants in the spring. This method works well for herbs that are more difficult to start from seed, such as anthemis, hops, horseradish, hyssop, lavender, rosemary, and winter savory. To take cuttings, prepare a potting mixture. Combine one-part sand and one-part perlite, moisten, and pack into a container. Materials such as soil and peat moss tend to retain too much moisture and are not recommended for cuttings, which are very susceptible to fungus growth. With a sharp knife, cut off the top three inches of the tip of a soft, green, nonflowering lateral shoot of a plant. Make the cut on an angle and be sure there are at least three leaves on the stem above the cut. Strip away the lowest leaves and trim the stem to just below the lowest leaf node or joint. Make a pencil-size hole in the earth and insert the stem one half to one inch deep into the potting mix, making sure that the soil covers the leaf node. Press the earth around the cutting and water the plant. A rooting hormone, available at garden centers, may be applied to the cutting before inserting it into the pot. Either mist the cuttings several times a day or form a plastic tent over the container of the plant and put the container in a warm place out of direct sunlight. If cuttings are taken in cool weather, bottom heat is recommended.

In two or three weeks, the cuttings will be ready to transplant into their own individual containers. A gentle tug will tell if the roots have formed. Once well rooted, carefully remove the cuttings, gently shake off the excess perlite and sand, and transplant them into regular potting soil and thoroughly soak them. After a few days of adjustment, the cuttings may be placed in bright sunlight. In about a month, or when the plants are three to four inches high, pinch out the center of each plant to encourage side growth. As warm weather approaches, slowly acclimatize the cuttings to the outdoors by first putting them outside in a protected, shaded place and then gradually moving them into direct sunlight, finally planting them where they are to grow.

Many herbs resow themselves around the base of the original plant during the growing season. Keep this in mind when harvesting the herbs and let some branches go to seed. Some plants that readily reseed are dill, cosmos, hollyhocks, and sweet william.

Starting Seeds Indoors

The Shakers undoubtedly used many ways to increase their plant supply, but most of their herbs were grown from seed. Because they were conscious of the low cost of this method, their 1843 *Gardener's Manual* gave thorough directions on the subject:

> Stretch a line from end to end, over your bed, for a guide in drilling, then with the corner of your hoe, a pointed stick, or an instrument made for the purpose, drill shallow furrows across the bed from north to south, in depth and distance a part, accommodated to the kinds of seeds you wish to sow...[28]

"Sowing" referred to planting seeds while "planting" meant putting certain seeds in hills, such as melons and squash.

> Stretch the line as directed for sowing, but instead of drilling, make hills, or slight elevations of the soil, a foot in diameter and three inches high, with a southern inclination. In a dry season, the earth should always be pressed upon the top of the seeds. On level beds, it may be done with a roller; on seeds planted in hills, with the back of the hoe.[29]

These directions were meant to be followed in the spring, but the Shakers also planted in the fall.

> Some seeds may be sown in the Fall, with success; and the plants will be up considerable earlier next Spring, in consequence. But as Fall sowing is attended with considerable risk and extra labor, it should be generally avoided, except for such needs as vegetate very slowly, and will be greatly forwarded by the action of the frost, without the risk of losing the seed by premature vegetation. Perhaps Asparagus and Sea Kale are the only kinds of this description. For Fall sowing, the ground should be prepared as directed for Spring sowing, and the various seeds put in just so late as they will not sprout before winter sets in, for sprouting will spoil them. As soon as the frost has fairly closed the ground, the beds should be covered a foot deep with litter, straw, or boughs of ever-green, to prevent the frost from penetrating too deeply; these should be removed early in the Spring, and you will have the plants quickly up.[30]

Today, many gardeners still rely as heavily on growing plants from seed. All annuals may be started from seed sown directly into the ground or started earlier indoors. Perennials may also be grown from seed, but the process takes much longer. Winter is the time to plan for next year's garden and to order seeds.

In northern climates annuals are often started indoors in March, and the seedlings are transplanted outside when the ground is warm. Traditionally, indoor seed planting begins on Town Meeting Day or three months before the last frost date. Raising seedlings indoors takes very little special equipment, and it is an easy and enjoyable thing to do in the late winter months. Young seedlings should be placed in a window area that receives seven to eight hours of sun a day; if necessary, supplement with fluorescent lighting.

Indoor seeding may be done with regular soil that was brought inside in the fall. If using garden soil, lighten it with equal amounts of sand and peat moss and some perlite. There are also many commercially available potting mixtures, which have the advantage of being sterile, more convenient, and free of stones.

Prepare containers by filling with the potting mix, leveling the soil, watering thoroughly, and allowing them to drain. Plant the seeds according to the package directions, sowing a single variety in each container. Plant the seeds in rows in order to check their germination when they sprout. If seeds are to be covered, sprinkle fine, clean sand or soil over them to hold them in place. Sand is preferred because it gives them excellent surface drainage. Label each container cover it with either plastic or newspaper, and place it in a warm spot—about seventy degrees. The plastic covering will create an artificially higher temperature for the seeds and will retain the moisture so misting is not necessary, but remove the cover promptly when the first seeds sprout. If using newspaper, remove each morning and mist the surface until the seeds sprout; thereafter, water the plants at their base. When they emerge, place the seedlings in good light and water them when the surface of the soil is dry. Thin the young plants to allow air circulation and proper growth. If damping off begins, promptly remove the affected plants and water very sparingly with a weak solution of chamomile.

When the plants are two to three inches high, use an organic fertilizer, such as fish emulsion. Most herbs will need no further feeding except basil, dill, and parsley, which should continue to be fertilized every two or three weeks.

When seedlings become crowded in their containers, transplant them to larger pots containing a regular potting mixture, set them slightly deeper than grown originally, and protect them from direct sunlight for a few days. When the weather grows warmer, move them to a place outside with indirect sunlight and gradually accustom them to the full sun.

Starting seeds indoors is a method of expanding the growing season, a matter of great interest to the New England Shakers. While they started some seeds indoors, they needed such a large volume that they found it more practical to use hotbeds to start plants for early greens or plants that required a long season of growth. When the weather grew warmer, they transplanted these seedlings outside.

Hotbeds

Today, there are many products available that the practical Shakers would surely have used to increase their growing season: plastic mulches, floating row covers, slitted row covers, and greenhouses. Yet in spite of these improvements, hotbeds are still common today. Following are the Believers' instructions for making a hotbed:

> To form a cheap and convenient hot bed for a family Garden, select a warm dry place, near the south side of a building or high wall; make a boarded box or frame from three to five feet wide, and extend it east and west to any convenient length, but so constructed as to descend towards the south about fifteen degrees from a level. This frame is to be covered with glazed sashes, fitted in tight on all sides, to prevent rats and mice from entering the enclosure. Within this frame put a quantity of unfermented horse manure, with about one-third part of short straw or leaves, mix the whole well together by

pitching it over, spread it even all over the bed, keeping it inclined to the south as above directed; the depth of manure should be from 12 to 36 inches, according to the season, heat required &c. Then put on a layer of well rotted manure three inches thick, let the whole now be covered with sashes or boards. If the weather be cold, put on a coat of straw or mats, keep it covered, until the heat begins to rise, then cover the surface of the manure with rich garden mould, about eight inches deep, and lay on your [s]ashes. As soon as the earth gets warm and of the proper temperature, stir the top of the bed thoroughly over and rake it fine, reserving enough of the fine mould to cover the seeds; mark your drills across the bed about four inches apart, and half an inch deep, then sow your seeds, and sift the mould equally over the whole covering them about half an inch deep. Press the surface with a board or back of the shovel equally all over; put on the sashes and cover with straw or mats when exposed to frost. The bed will now require very close attention to keep the temperature right; if too hot, raise the covering, to admit a circulation of air; or make holes in the bed with a sharpened stake; if more heat is required, add some fresh manure to the outside of the bed. When the plants are up, give them water frequently, and air when the weather is mild. After the plants have attained sufficient size, and the weather is favorable, they may be transplanted into the open ground. In this climate, we commence making our hot-beds from the 20th to the end of March; if plants are wanted earlier, we sow the seed in boxes of fine rich earth, about the first of March, and keep them in a warm place exposed to the rays of the sun as much as possible, and remove the plants into the hot bed when they have attained sufficient size, and the bed is prepared for vegetation.[31]

Transplanting

Growing plants indoors or in artificially created climates and transplanting them outdoors means the gardener does not have to rely on the unpredictable early spring weather, thereby ensuring a more dependable yield. Transplanting is also quick, easy, and highly productive. The Shakers preferred this method and felt it was an area of horticulture about which many people were ill informed.

A prevalent, but erroneous opinion concerning transplanting is that it should be done just before a shower, in order to succeed well; but experience has shown that a day or two after, when the ground has become dry enough to work again, in the evening is a preferable time, and perhaps, with the exception of cloudy weather, is the best that can be selected. The ground should be prepared as directed for sowing, the plants should be taken up with as much dirt as possible ad-

hering to them, which will be promoted by watering plenti-
fully, before taking them up. A hole deep enough for the roots
to enter at full length, should be made, the plants set upright,
and the fresh earth gently pressed against the roots on all sides.
Tender plants will sometimes need watering and shading a
day or two after transplanting.[32]

The Shakers recommended that transplanting be done "immediately after the ground has been newly ploughed or dug." They
advised using a "trowel or a flat pointed stick." When returning the
plants to the ground, the farmer should raise the earth around the
stems to support the plants.[33]

They also recommended a dip that promotes root growth:

> . . . dip the roots into a mixture of rich mould or rotten manure
> and water, with the addition of a little lime or ashes, and
> reduced to the consistency of thick white-wash.[34]

The high phosphorous content of this mixture, which is similar to
modern starter fertilizers, is beneficial for strong root development.
Today, there are many commercially available solutions that can
be used for the same purpose. Another method to encourage
strong root growth is to move the plants into progressively richer
soils which will encourage the roots to move toward the nutrients.

Starting Seeds Outdoors

Sowing seeds directly outside where they are to grow is the
simplest method of raising new plants. If the ground was particularly dry, the 1835 *Gardener's Manual* recommended:

> . . . let the seed be soaked a few hours in water strongly
> impregnated with sulphur or soot, and keep the ground moist
> by frequent watering. This will have a great tendency to
> forward the vegetation and prevent the ravages of insects.[35]

When the seeds sprout, the young plants are often crowded, and
thinning is necessary in order to give them space to fully develop.
Seedlings may be thinned by uprooting the extra plants until the
correct spacing is achieved or by transplanting some of them to
bare spots in the garden.

> Thinning may be performed twice, the first time as soon as
> the plants are fairly in sight, the second after they are large
> enough to show which will make thrifty plants. As the
> quality of the crop, as well as the quantity, frequently
> depends very much upon this branch of cultivation, it is

important that it be seasonally and faithfully performed. Leaving plants too thick is a prevalent error, and one to which gardeners are very liable.[36]

Cultivation

Once the plants are properly spaced and begin to grow, the rest of the season is spent hoeing, watering, and protecting the plants against insects. The Shakers stated that the benefits of clean cultivation were "beyond the calculation of most farmers" and should be "early performed, and continued with persevering faithfulness, as often as necessary, through the season . . . ."[37] They considered the hoe to be the best tool for the job.

> There are three manners of hoeing necessary to be made use of in the garden, which may be distinguished by the names of 1st., flat hoeing; 2nd., digging and 3d., hilling. The first is made use of merely to kill the weeds; the second to promote the growth of the plants by mellowing the soil, and the third to support and nourish some plants in their more advanced stages by drawing the earth up around their stems, or stalks.[38]

Today there are a variety of specialized tools available, but the hoe remains as useful as ever.

While they felt that cultivating the plants would encourage the moisture deep in the soil to rise to the surface, the Shakers also recommended watering during dry spells. The 1843 *Gardener's Manual* outlined the proper method of watering.

> Some gardeners spend much useless labor in sprinkling water over and around their plants. When the ground is very dry, at the time you wish to transplant, watering the ground where you intend to set the plants, a day or two beforehand, may be beneficial; watering hot beds is also necessary and indispensible. But to plants in open ground, that have good roots, watering in the customary way, with a hand watering pot, is of but little use. If you have a stream of running water at your command, which can be turned upon your garden, something more effectual may be performed. But in default of this, digging and stirring the soil should be resorted to, which will cause the moisture below the surface (the life and dependance of plants in a dry time), to rise freely.[39]

Mulches

Herbs generally tolerate drier conditions than many other plants but may require watering during the season. In order to eliminate the need for supplemental watering, mulching is a common practice today. There are a variety of materials that can be used for this purpose: a "living" mulch of clover, which will also benefit the soil, and dry mulches, such as salt hay, pine bark, and buckwheat hulls. A mulch has several other advantages—it saves time by controlling weed growth, and it protects the leaves from mud splashed up in the rain. The disadvantages are that mulches tend to keep the earth too moist, attracting slugs and promoting fungus; and their decomposition alters the character of the soil.

The Shakers did not recommend mulching until probably the twentieth century. Mildred Wells, who lived at Canterbury from 1921 to 1987, recalled that the members went to the woods to collect sphagnum moss to use as a mulch because of its water-retention properties. Several years ago when the mid-nineteenth-century Ministry Shop at Canterbury was being repaired, sphagnum moss was found in the walls as insulation. As it was being removed, Wells collected it for her garden.

Pest Control

As the growing season progressed, the Shakers took precautions against harmful insects with a variety of dusts, powders, and sprays.

> Every garden should have a good supply of well rotted manure or old compost, ready for use when wanted; also a portion of soot, tobacco, dust, ashes and lime, for the purpose of scattering over seed beds and hills of plants in dry weather, to destroy insects which often cut off the young plants as fast as they come up.[40]

Their methods were organic; their emphasis was on raising healthy plants that had a natural resistance to insects.

> But as plants are subject to material injury from these insects only while in an infant state, the chief aim should be to have the land so prepared, seeded and cultivated as to give the plants a vigorous, thrifty growth, which will soon place them out of danger.[41]

The Believers advised that farmers begin their pest control early before the problem grew to be unmanageable. In the 1843 *Gardener's Manual* their pest control recommendations reflect their keen observation skills, experience, and organic bias.

> Cutworms, root-worms, slugs or snails, cabbage-lice, turnip-flies and yellow bugs, are the insects that most trouble the kitchen

gardener...Cut-worm...commits its depredations in the night; and immediately, upon the appearance of daylight, secretes itself under the dirt, near the plant which it last attacked; consequently, there it may be found and easily destroyed which perhaps is the most effectual and only sure method of killing them.[42]

They also used another method of dealing with cutworms as described in an 1839 issue of *The Farmers Monthly Visitor*.

[The Shaker]...gathered the skunk weed or cabbage, that being the earliest and most easily obtained. He dropped the leaves from six to seven feet apart between the rows, and found it to succeed to admiration; as on an examination a few days afterward, he found the corn untouched, but under each leaf or weed he had dropped he found from twenty-three to forty-seven worms. The ground under the leaves and the leaves themselves were completely perforated. The worms being thus collected were easily destroyed.[43]

The 1843 *Gardener's Manual* also gave instructions on destroying other insects; slugs could be discouraged by "strewing ashes or quick lime over them."[44] A remedy for cabbage lice was to rub "plaster, ashes or quick lime" into them with a cloth or brush. The plaster was gypsum, a fine powder that would also act as a fungicide. Alternative measures were "a decoction of tobacco, administered with a sponge" and "fermented urine." Turnip flies or garden fleas could be controlled by "covering the plants with chaff, fine shavings, or sawdust till they are out of danger." When this was impractical, the manual recommended "snuff, soot or sulphur finely pulverized, and sprinkled over and under the plants while wet with dew."

The great enemy, the yellow or striped bug, was treated either with "water saturated with cow dung" or by "sprinkling the plants when wet, with a composition of Rye-flour, Ashes and Plaster having equal quantities of each, thoroughly mixed."

Tent caterpillar infestations were common wherever there were orchards. The Believers often included in their publications directions for controlling these and other fruit pests. This remedy found in *The Farmer's Second Book* is an example:

To destroy caterpillars on fruit trees, various plans have been resorted to, and recommended; such as shooting a charge of powder into the nest—burning the silky nests and their inmates, by using a flaming torch—swabbing the nests with suds made from whale oil soap, or common brown soap, seeking out the nest while the caterpillars are young and crushing them with the finger and thumb: faugh! none, but confirmed snufftakers ever ought to be allowed to perform this delicate operation. The best thing we have used... was in the use of a Pickering brush, fixed to the end of a light, straight pole. By thrusting this into the nests in the morning, before the caterpillars have left them. (and they are usually at home till about nine o'clock in the morning), they can be very readily wound around the brush, from which they are easily cleared and crushed by the foot. A few times passing through an orchard during one week, soon after the broods are hatched, and a careful application of the brush will pretty effectually use them up and leave none for seed.

... but if any one is too poor to buy one of these spiral brushes, to rid his orchard of these useless intruders, we will just say to him, that the head of a last year mullein stalk tied to a pole answers a tolerable substitute for the wire bristles.[45]

In 1878 the Shakers found a recipe to control the plum curculio:

We tested the plan of strewing tomato vines under plum trees, as a preventative of the curculio; and on a tree that we have invariably lost all, or nearly every plum, we had a nice quantity of most beautiful fruit. We shall practive the simple provision[46]

Insects on houseplants were a concern for late nineteenth-century Believers; in earlier times ornamental plants were not allowed. By 1878, however, the members were publishing such directions as setting "a little smoking tobacco on fire under the plants, and let[ting] the fumes be directed thence to all parts of the plants" as a means of arresting household pests.[47]

Fortunately, herbs have a natural resistance to insects. The safest way to control these pests is simply to follow the Shakers' advice by preparing a healthy soil, practicing clean cultivation, and harvesting at the proper time. Well-grown plants are the best protection since bugs attack unhealthy specimens, and the number of destructive insects grows in proportion to the number of poor plants. Pesticides are a short-term solution; the basic problem to be addressed is the health of the plant, which is a reflection of the health of the soil.

Pests often do need to be controlled, however, particularly as soil-building techniques sometimes require many years. It is necessary to use nonpoisonous preventative measures since herbs are generally grown for culinary or cosmetic purposes. With organic pest controls, birds and beneficial insects, such as ladybugs, lace wing, and praying mantis, will come into the garden and become the guardians of the plants. Even biological pesticides, particularly nicotine, rotonone, and pyrethrum powders, need to be handled carefully. Diatomaceous earth, which is very abrasive, will injure the lungs. Dusting with a harmless powder often works, particularly in dry weather, for it will destroy the insect's protective wax coating causing it to dry out. Hand-picking the larger bugs and dropping them into a can of hot water is an effective method if done frequently. A propane torch may be used against such large insects as the Japanese beetle, but this must be done early in the morning when the dew is still on the plant. Insects may also be sucked up in a vacuum cleaner.

Organic repellent sprays may be concocted in the home blender and are an effective alternative to chemical sprays. Spraying should begin as soon as the insects appear and should be continued once a week. Both sides of the leaves should be sprayed. A concoction of santolina and hyssop will work against white flies. Another recipe is made by blending a garlic bulb, a small onion, and a tablespoon of cayenne pepper with one quart of water. Add a tablespoon of liquid soap to this mix, which will help it adhere to the leaves, and refrigerate for use. Spray infested plants once a week.[48]

To ensure against bad weather or rampant bugs, the 1843 *Gardener's Manual* suggested overplanting. This is still good advice; if extra plants result, they can be given away or traded for others.

> . . . as all means of preventing the ravages of insects may at times fail, it is well to put in plenty of the seed of such plants as are attacked by them, which with the precautions heretofore given, to take means for having thrifty plants. . . . [49]

Harvesting and Storing

Harvesting herbs may be done lightly throughout the season and can begin a few weeks after the plants have begun to grow as this cutting stimulates new growth. Later in the season, just before the herb begins to flower, is the time when the plant's oil content is the highest. Then the full new growth may be harvested. Late morning on a sunny day after the dew is off is the best time to cut the plants, and harvesting should always be done before the first frost. Twice a season annuals receive heavy cuttings. The top two or three inches of the branches can be removed without cutting into the plant's woody growth. Established perennials are harvested in their second year and may also be cut a couple of times a season. A sharp knife or pruning shears are the only tools needed. If the herbs are dirty, hose them off and let them dry before gathering.

Once gathered, the herbs may be saved by drying, freezing, or storing in vinegar. If the herbs are to be dried, choose a well-ventilated spot, free from light, such as a closet or an attic. The darkness will preserve the herb's color, and the ventilation will help prevent molding. Hang the plants in small bunches or lay them in thin layers on clean paper or screening. To dry seeds from herbs such as dill, put the seed heads in a paper bag, which will catch them as they fall. The best drying temperature is below ninety degrees Fahrenheit; higher temperatures will cause more rapid evaporation of the essential oils and changes in the plant's chemical elements. If possible, keep the air temperature in the mid-eighties at first, increasing the temperature at the end of the drying cycle. Depending on the weather, this process takes from two days to two weeks; plants are dry when they feel crisp to the touch. They may also be dried in the oven at a very low heat (below 150 degrees) but should be watched carefully. Many ovens do not function below 200 degrees, but there are commercially available food dehydrators. It is also possible to dry the plants in a microwave oven. Place a few herbs between paper towels, heat on high one to one-and-a-half minutes until dry and crumbly. Check frequently.

Once dried, herbs should be stored in a dark place away from excessive heat. Check the containers for several days to see if any moisture appears inside the jar. If this happens, the herbs need to be removed and re-dried. Dried herbs are three to four times more powerful than those in their fresh form. One year is about the maximum length of time they may be stored before their flavor deteriorates.

Herbs may also be frozen. Basil, chives, dill, lovage, mint, oregano, parsley, and sorrel are some that freeze well. To prepare the herbs, clean and chop the plants and put them in plastic bags. Covering herbs with water and storing them in ice cube trays in the freezer is another way to have small amounts readily available. The ice cubes may be removed and stored in plastic bags in the freezer. Frozen herbs should be used in the same proportions as when fresh.

Vinegar is also a convenient and foolproof way to preserve herbs such as purple basil, chives, dill, and tarragon. Choose glass bottles with nonmetal caps. For a fast method heat, but do not boil, the vinegar, using either red or white depending on the herb. Stuff a bottle full of herbs, pour the hot vinegar over them, and seal. They may also be covered in cold vinegar and set away in a cool place for a month or so. A jar of white vinegar may be left in the garden and gradually filled with fresh chive blossoms. The resulting chive blossom vinegar, which will be a lovely shade of pink, is ready for use after a few weeks in the sun.

Broadside from the Harvard Shaker community. While the typefaces on this advertisement alone would attract attention, the Shakers also used green-flocked paper to catch the eye. (Collection of Fruitlands Museums, Harvard, Massachusetts)

Preparing the Garden for Winter

Each fall the garden must be put to bed for the winter. A few simple tasks will ensure that insects do not remain over the winter and will reduce the work in the spring. Remove the annuals and put them in the compost pile. Cut the perennials down to three inches from the ground and add the cuttings to the pile as well. In colder climates, cover the garden with a mulch after the ground freezes. Winter mulching protects the perennials from the deep frosts of an open winter and will keep them from growing prematurely during a mid-season warm spell. Mulching is especially important if there has been a series of consecutive mild winters. In that case, the herbs have been acclimatized to those conditions and are even more vulnerable when a hard winter comes. The time to mulch is when the ground is frozen solid to a depth of one inch. Use a six-inch layer of salt hay or leaves or some small branches. The following spring, remove the mulch as soon as all danger of snow is past. Leaving the mulch on too long may heat up the ground prematurely and allow young plants to emerge before the weather has settled.

Growing Four Culinary Herbs

The Shakers gave specific directions in the 1843 *Gardener's Manual* for growing some of their seeds. The recommendations for their four major culinary herbs are given below.

> Sage—*F. Sauge. S. Salvia*—This useful herb requires a good rich soil, and may be sown in drills, about two feet apart, when of sufficient size for culinary purposes, it may be thinned out as it is wanted. The plants intended to be kept over the winter may finally be left at the distance of two feet each way. They may stand through the winter covered with straw or litter or they may be taken up and put in the cellar. After the first year they will grow and bear seed a number of years in succession, but new seed should be sown once in three or four years as young roots produce the most thrifty shoots. The leaves that are to be preserved … may be collected and dried and packed away for future use. Our botanists press them into hard packages and put them up in papers for market—we also grind and sift it and put it up in that state for the sausage makers.
>
> The Clary Sage is much used for medicine as well as for tea, and bids for to equal its rival the common sage of which we sell great quantities pressed.[50]

There are at least five hundred varieties of sage, many of which are not hardy in colder climates. Garden sage, *Salvia officinalis L.,* is hardy and has a good flavor. It may be grown from seed or from cuttings taken from established plants. Seeds sown to a depth of one-half inch will germinate in three weeks. While it can grow in almost any soil, this herb needs good drainage and full sun and should be mulched in the winter. The leaves are used as a flavoring for poultry stuffings, sausage, lamb, and pork. Sister Ethel Hudson, of Canterbury, remembers using it to flavor cheese.

Clary Sage, *Salvia sclarea*, or common sage, is a biennial. Its lavender-like scent is used in potpourris and perfumes. Clary has quite a different appearance from the culinary sage, having large, downy, oval leaves on three-foot stems bearing white or blue flowers. It has been used in making wines and beers as well as a flavoring in egg dishes and soups. Clary was also known as "clear eye" because of the medicinal use of its mucilaginous seeds.

> Savory, Summer—*F. Sariette de fete*—This plant will grow in almost any soil. It may be sown in drills about twelve or fourteen inches apart so as to pass a hoe freely between the rows. Let it be kept clean from weeds—and if it comes up too thick, let it be gradually thinned out as it is want for use, and it will not require any further trouble. To dry it for winter use, it should be cut when in blossom and spread on the floor of an upper room or garret, where it can have air, and not be exposed to the sun. When it is sufficiently dry, tie it up in bunches, and wrap it in paper, or put it away in clean bags for future use.[51]

There is both a summer savory, *Satureja hortensis,* and a winter savory, *Satureja montana L.,* Summer savory, the preferred of the two for culinary purposes, is a delicate annual; winter savory is a woody, low, shrub-like perennial. Summer savory may be sown directly outdoors after the last frost date and will germinate in about a week and grow quickly enough to give a good crop by the end of summer. If a few plants are left uncut, it sows itself freely.

Summer savory has been used in America since the seventeenth century and was probably very popular in the nineteenth century; it is not commonly used today. It has a strong, biting taste (best known as a flavoring for fresh beans) and is also good with cabbage, peas, potato salad, sausage, soup, stuffings, and salads.

> Sweet marjoram—*O marjorana*—Is a hardy biennial, a native of Portugal. Sow about 1st of May broadcast on a bed prepared—have the ground made very fine, and sow the seed on the same without any drilling. The seed will not want any covering, lay a board on the bed and walk on it, which will be all that is necessary to ensure it to vegetate. When the plant becomes large enough to transplant, set them at a distance of six inches. Water the plants if the weather is dry. When in

blossom the herb is cut over, and dried for winter use, so that a sowing requires to be made every year. The herb is much used in soups, broth, stuffings &c.[52]

Marjoram, a member of the oregano family, is a popular, strongly scented culinary herb. It is a tender perennial and is usually treated as an annual. Marjoram can be easily propagated by seeds sown in the spring and can be dug in the fall, kept indoors, and again replanted outside in the spring. It is harvested as soon as blooming starts. *Majorana hortensis* is the best variety for culinary use and is especially good with tomato dishes and meats.

The Shakers cultivated sweet thyme in the same way as they did marjoram.[53] While there are more than sixty varieties of thyme, each distinctive in flavor and growth habit, *Thymus vulgaris*, common or English, is the standard choice for cooking. Thymes are creeping, woody, evergreen perennials. They may be propagated by almost any method, but root division is the easiest. A mulch in the winter will prevent the herb from heaving during a spring thaw, and it should be divided every three or four years. Harvest thyme just before it blooms. The Believers recommended it specifically to flavor meat dishes, but today it is used primarily to season fish chowder, poultry, eggs, and cheese.

"A Good Garden"

The Shakers' agrarian lifestyle supported their large communities and fitted well with their belief in "hands to work, and hearts to God." Throughout the Shaker's history, these lands continued to support a variety of profitable enterprises. Today, the benefits of creating a well-kept, healthy garden are still as numerous as they were a hundred years ago.

> A good garden, well supplied with useful vegetables, in a healthy, thriving state, kept neat and clean from weeds affords a striking evidence that the cultivator possesses a good portion of wisdom and economy and is attentive to his business; but ...a garden containing a small quantity of such as are evidently from good seed, promiscuously planted, without order or regularity, faintly struggling among the weeds for a feeble existence, . . . [indicates] the proprietor's mind needs cultivation, and that some noxious weeds of domestic or foreign growth have taken deep root there, which will require the strong hand of an industrious and persevering cultivator to eradicate.... The numerous benefits afforded to a family from a well-cultivated garden are too little considered by many of our country farmers, for their own interest and the health and prosperity of their families. The cheap and healthy varieties which may be furnished (much less expensive, and far more

healthy than the same quantity of meat without vegetables) the pleasing and healthy exercise and enjoyment attending their cultivation, is beyond description; indeed, the cultivation and produce of a good garden are the life and health of a family, upon every principle of rational enjoyment and temporal economy.[54]

"The Power to Heal": The Shakers' Medical Practices

The promise of the power to heal diseases and to live free from sickness is held by the Church of Mother Ann's founding[1]

*A*lthough the sale of herbal medicines eventually became a lucrative business for the Shakers, the early Believers preferred the practice of spiritual healing to a dependence on medicines, and they avoided doctors whenever possible. New Lebanon Shaker Isaac N. Youngs recalled that a "learned" physician of the World was "needless" in those early communities:

> It was recommended to rely more on the power of god, and zeal energy of spirit, than on the skill of a doctor. Now especially it was enjoined not to apply to world doctors, if it could be avoided in reason. The principle was adhered to in a good degree and much in Family was surmonted without medical aid; and indeed there were many real gifts of healing, in consequence of refusing medical means.[2]

Spiritual healing was considered to be a "gift" from God. Beginning in the eighteenth century, many Believers received such spiritual "gifts." These were thought to be received by individuals who were particularly suited to accept them and were meant to be shared with the rest of the community. Mother Ann, for example, was said to have possessed many gifts, including the power of healing.

101

Instances of Mother Ann and some of her followers curing diseases by the laying on of hands have been recorded by several Shakers. Benjamin Youngs recorded a testimony of 1808 by Mary Southwick:

> That about the beginning of August 1783 (being then in the twenty-first year of her age) she was healed of a cancer in her mouth, which had been growing two years . . and which occasioned great weakness and loss of appetite. That she went one afternoon to see Calvin Harlowe to get some assistance. That Mother being at the house, Calvin asked her to look at it. That she accordingly came to her, and put her finger into her mouth upon the canker; at which instant the pain left her, and she was restored to health, and was never afflicted with it afterwards.[3]

These stories were passed down for several generations. Many years later two North Family Sisters from the New Lebanon community, Anna White and Leila S. Taylor, recorded another instance of Mother Ann's healing abilities:

> Zaccheus Stevens . . . was at one time taken very sick at Watervliet and was not expected to recover. He told Mother Ann that important matters at home demanded his attention. She said to him: "Take faith and you will recover. You may set out tomorrow morning, return home and settle your business." This command amazed everyone. But Zaccheus obeyed and started promptly on his journey of one hundred and fifty miles, going thirty miles the first day, increasing in strength daily, until he reached home in good health.[4]

According to Elder Henry Blinn, Joseph Meacham, who led the Church after Mother Ann's death, continued this reliance on spiritual healing:

> At the gathering of the Church at New Lebanon, a man professing to be a Believer came to Father Joseph for liberty to consult a physician not of the Believers' Order. Father walked the room, considering the matter, and laboring to gather a gift. He then said, "They who have my spirit, have no occasion to go to a physician not of our Order, for there is power sufficient to heal soul and body," whereupon Ezekiel was Healed.[5]

Throughout their history, however, the Shakers acknowledged that not everyone had this "gift" and that other means to cure the sick were necessary. Isaac Youngs admitted as much in his journal:

> . . . but the gift of healing by supernatural power was too precious to be granted as a common favor; and as the body is

> subject to disease, it was indispensable that there should be
> some means for the relief of the afflicted. Therefore, an order
> of physicians, two males, and two females, was set apart . . .
> to officiate in the medical line, & to these the Brethren and
> Sisters were to apply, each in their own order, males to the
> males & females to the females.
>
> These physicians were to obtain skill and information in their
> line, to enable them to do their duty by books and by applying
> to more experienced doctors in the World, as was found to be
> necessary & proper: and such doctors, were, & have been to
> this day employed, in cases of surgery, & many, peculiar
> instances of disease.[6]

Thus, an Order of Physicians and Nurses was established, and
buildings were set aside to house and care for the infirm.

When the first generation of Shakers was establishing their
Order of Physicians, the traditional practice of heroic medicine was
being challenged by several popular theories. The conventional
remedies of the late eighteenth and early nineteenth centuries
relied on harsh procedures such as bleeding, blistering, and the use
of leeches and mercury. Seeking gentler ways of healing, many
people began to experiment with herbal cures and other methods.

The concern the Shakers had to heal their own kind led to the
systematic growing of medicinal herbs. The folk medicine of New
England was generally adopted by the early Believers; undoubtedly, some of the Shaker converts had a knowledge of herbal
medicine when they joined the Society. Because physicians were
few and far between in the World, many families had, of necessity,
acquired a knowledge of folk medicine which had been passed
down from generation to generation. Indian herbal recipes found
throughout the Shakers' early medical books indicate that the early
Believers also relied on the local native knowledge of indigenous
plants.

Medicine was simple in the eighteenth century: relief from
symptoms was the primary concern; diagnosis was mainly given
in general descriptions such as cankers, colds, and sore throats.
Several treatments were often tried in succession. Remedies such
as "sugar added to the moss obtained from the north side of a maple
tree" were recommended for cough syrup. Elder flower tea was
considered infallible in the early stages of influenza. In the
treatment of lung disease, the patient had to be "well greased,"
preferably with skunk oil. To prevent rheumatism, a person was
advised to carry a horse chestnut in his pocket. At South Union,
Kentucky, one Shaker graphically described the treatment for a
spider bite in this way:

Andrew Barnett, while rising, was bitten by a spider and soon life despaired of. A great many things done, given black snake root, plaintain, sweet oil clusters, warm baths, drafts of raw onions, spirits of Harts Horn. Did not get about until the next 3rd day and not entirely well for over two weeks. Note: [from H. L. Eades who transcribed this 1804-1836 record] the spirits of Hart Horn perhaps was the only thing that did any good. In a precisely similar case, I gave the patient nearly a half gill of Harts Horn and brandy mixed, and though previously screaming with pain, was relieved in 5 hours and well as common next day.[7]

Spring tonics proliferated, consisting of sulfur, molasses, wormwood, and poplar bark mixed with burdock. Many of the herbal tonics were heavily laced with alcohol, and contemporary newspapers advertised the glories of these "cure-alls."[8]

In addition to folk medicine, several unorthodox schools of medicine were also popular. The American Reformed System—started by Dr. Wooster Beech—substituted vegetable remedies for chemical ones. The Water Cure, or Hydropathy, and Allopathy, which professed to cure patients by producing symptoms opposite from those created by the disease itself, were widely practiced. The Thomsonian School of Medicine was another well-known medical philosophy in the beginning of the nineteenth century.

The son of a poor Baptist farmer, Samuel Thomson of Alstead,

Samuel Thomson, a self-taught New Hampshire doctor, established a school of medicine based primarily on the healing powers of the herb lobelia (pictured here). By the 1830s the Shakers began relying on his course of treatments. (Collection of New Hampshire State Library, Concord, New Hampshire)

New Hampshire, learned medical practices largely on his own. As a boy, he befriended an elderly female herbalist who taught him the medicinal properties of several plants. Thomson believed that four elements were present in all animal bodies: earth, air, fire, and water. He concluded that cold was the primary cause of all illness. To cure disease, "the practitioner had to restore the natural heat and clean the system of obstruction."[9] He advocated using lobelia (an herb which was said to promote free perspiration), and cayenne pepper to "cleanse the stomach by giving an emetic." When necessary, he also recommended the use of a steam bath, followed by a concoction of bayberry, sumac, hemlock bark, witch hazel leaves, red raspberry leaves, and marsh rosemary.[10] The following letter from a practitioner describes the first day's treatment:

> When the sweat rolls off as thick as your finger, the body is washed with cold water and the patient is straightway put to bed with hot bricks to bring back his heat. Then a powerful vomitive is administered, composed of bay berry, of cayenne (red pepper) and lobelia, which suffer naught impure to remain in the stomach, and all these herbs are mixed in 40 proof brandy, after which warm water is drunk until there has ensued the most extraordinary vomiting. Next, the patient rises and takes a second bath, like the first. He takes again to his bed, after having been laved with cold water and surrounded with hot bricks and remains in bed for an hour. At the end of this time he takes two injections [enemas] of penny royal, cayenne pepper, and lobelia, and the treatment is over for the day.[11]

In 1804 Thomson began traveling throughout New England promoting his claims and treating anyone who answered his advertisements. In 1812 he published a set of rules and regulations for an organization he established known as the Friendly Botanic Society. He obtained a patent for his medicinal system and published the *Thomsonian Materia Medica or Botanic Family Physician,* which, for twenty dollars, entitled the reader to become a member of the society. A membership certificate, located at the end of the book, gave the reader the "right" to heal himself and his family, using the Thomsonian system. Members of the society were not necessarily licensed to practice medicine but were given the privilege to procure drugs from Thomson's company.

In 1822 Thomson issued *A New Guide to Health or Botanic Family Physician,* a book filled with information he felt was important for the public's health and safety. The first 157 pages discussed "the Life and Medical Discoveries of the Author" and were followed by sections on "the Cultivation of Bees," "the Bad Consequences of Stoves in Tight Rooms," and "the Value of Guards and Sentinels in War or Peace and the Danger of their Signals being Neglected."[12]

In 1835 another edition was published in which more emphasis was placed on herbs. Also included was a section answering some commonly asked questions, such as: "Why do old people die more in a warm and rainy winter than in a severe cold one?"[13] The book was reprinted thirteen times and sold more than 100,000 copies.[14]

Botanic practitioners such as Thomson were bitterly opposed by the regular medical fraternity. Several efforts were made in the legislature to ban them from receiving fees for their work; and, at one point, Thomson was briefly sent to jail.[15] The botanics, however, took a patriotic stance, stating that such laws were an insult to democracy. Job Haskell, defending the Thomsonian school before the New York legislature, charged:

> Intrinsic merit, sir, is the only qualification which ought to be required of any man to entitle him to practice physic or surgery; it is the only qualification necessary to carry a man from the humblest station under our republican government to the presidential chair.[16]

Such arguments were successful, and by 1844 all laws regulating the practice of medicine were repealed. Thomson died in 1843, but his influence remained. In 1901 there were still several thousand

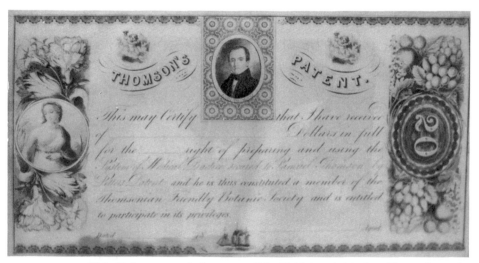

This diploma was the last page of the 1841 Materia Medica. *The student who read Samuel Thomson's book signed the diploma and was then certified to practice Thomsonian medicine on family members. (Collection of New Hampshire State Library, Concord, New Hampshire)*

"botanic, reformed, physiopathic and physio-medical" doctors in the United States treating patients pretty much along the lines he laid down eighty years earlier.[17]

By 1831 the Shakers had formed an eclectic medical system that included Thomson's "pepper puke" and other cures, simple massage, and a prudent diet.[18] Their buildings revealed an attention to proper ventilation and light, and their meals reflected a concern for nutritious and properly prepared foods. In 1893 a Sister wrote:

> We are increasing our fruit crop every year. Grapes are especially wholesome and are much cheaper and more palatable than drugs. We have not had a fever in the family for 50 years. Judicious water treatments, simple massage and the use of hot herb drinks are our methods of cure in cases of sickness.
>
> Some must always battle inherited tendencies to disease but if they live strictly moral lives, and adhere to hygienic laws, they will live more comfortable. Great good is attained in this direction by fortifying the mind against the ills of the body, and rising superior to them.[19]

In 1854 Eldress Betsy Smith commented on the rather flexible medical philosophy of New Lebanon's physician, Barnabas Hinckley:

> ... he considers water is good in some cases, but don't consider it a specific for all diseases. Uses medicine in some cases ... and says he would make use in certain cases, any human remedy to mitigate pain. But at the same time, he would be more cautious about using strong medicines of all kinds, and not use them where one more simple would answer.[20]

For the most part, the early Shaker medical system was a combination of several elements. Shaker patients were given an assortment of cures ranging from steam baths to emetics:

> [Dec. 1835] William L. began to doctor for a hammering in his head. Br. Joseph Mayo ordered him to take Hellebore snuff &c &c some times to snuff up some Pepper, Cayenne, anoint his nose & put hot stones to his head nights.
>
> [Jan. 1836] Br. Nathan had a poultice of Charcoal & yeast, applied to his legs. Sister Sarah Kendall came from the Square house to see Br. Nathan; he had a poultice of stewed pumpkins applied to this. . . .
>
> [Jan. 1836] Ziba Winchester came here in the p.m. sick enough. Mumps had settled on his lungs; he could but just speak or breathe. Dr. Joseph Mayo sent for. He ordered him to draw steam from the spout of the tea pot into his lungs.

[Jan. 1835] Daniel Myrick hurt his right wrist. He went into town saw Dr. Holman. He said the bone was not injured, he called it a contusion of the joint. He ordered a liniment for it $^1/_3$ opium $^1/_3$ Oil of Origanum, three part Volatile Liniment.

[Oct. 1837] Augustus H.'s humour troubled him very bad; he had a constant pain in his head. He went to Dr. Parker's for advice; he ordered him to take a teaspoonful of Epsom Salts every day till a cure was effected; he was to take it as follows: Put one teaspoonful of Salts into 2 tablespoonful of scalding water, let it stand a few minutes, then add 2 tablespoonful of sour cider & salrutus enough to cause it to effuse, then drink quick. His diet must be light.

[Dec. 1837] Dana White's health was very poor. The Dr. (Parker) ordered him to take $^1/_2$ oz of Castor Oil, & $^1/_2$ oz of Spirits Turpentine once in 3 hours till it operated well; he thought it might be he had worms.

[Aug. 1838] Sarah Ann Finch, one of our little girls, had six convulsion Fits in succession. We gave her about 30 drops of strong Laudanum to no effect, then we gave her some of the Compound Tinct. of the Seed. This caused her to throw up a pint or more of thick phlegm, then her fits abated.[21]

Hydropathy was another popular cure adopted by the Shakers. Eldress Betsy Smith from Kentucky recorded on a visit to New Lebanon a trip to Lebanon Springs:

> . . . spent the forenoon in company with Brothers Jonathan Wood [herbalist], and Allen Reed, John Dean. They took two carriages and escorted us to the Lebanon Springs. Spent some time looking at the surrounding scenery; the springs are beautiful, the water deep. There did not appear to be anything peculiar in the flavor of the water; only it is quite warm, as it boils up and is said to continue so through the winter . . . A short distance below where the water rises, they have made beautiful pools for bathing, one for each sex in different apartments.[22]

The Sabbathday Lake Shakers owned three springs, known as Poland, Rock, and Valley, which were said to have curative powers. Early in their history, the Sabbathday Lake Shakers exchanged part of their property, which contained Poland Spring, for a piece of land in Alfred, Maine. Philemon Stuart, who was living at Sabbathday Lake at the time, issued a broadside advertising the virtues of the two remaining springs. Desiring to "live secluded and retired," however, the Believers would allow no public resort to be built around their springs. Instead, they constructed their main stone dwelling over the powerful Rock Spring, which had been drilled to thirty feet, and bottled and sold the excess water to the World as a cure for scrofula, cholera morpus, rheumatism, liver, and kidney ailments. The Shakers also used these waters for their distillations and implied that the process improved the already powerful healing powers.

> In fine these three springs do not vary so very essentially in their curative properties, when applied in equal quantities and in the same condition of the patient. But when used for distillation, with simple roots and herbs, their curative properties seem to work quite different.[23]

The Harvard community also had their own spring, which they recognized as a valuable asset. Once they realized its potential, they took great care to preserve the water's purity.

From the early nineteenth through the twentieth century, the Shakers took trips to the ocean as part of their health care regime. In this view, Bertha Lindsay of Canterbury is seen at the Nubble Light in Maine with other Shakers and friends. In the twentieth century, the Canterbury Shakers also had a cottage at Lake Winnisquam in New Hampshire, which they used as a retreat. (Private collection)

Advertisement for spring water, Harvard Shaker Community. Both the Harvard and Sabbathday Lake Shakers promoted and sold the spring water on their properties as a cure for many diseases. (Collection of Fruitlands Museums, Harvard, Massachusetts)

During the protracted drought of 1854, the water supply of the village failed, and there was no other reliable source to obtain water but from the "never-failing Spring," situated one mile distant, at an altitude of about one hundred feet, which flowed in sufficient quantities to warrant laying an aqueduct. The first requisite was to get the best advice how to construct it and the kind of pipe that would not impair the water. This was secured in the persons of E. N. Horsford, Professor of Chemistry, of Harvard College, and E. D. Chesbro, Civil Engineer, of Boston. They came and ... advised the use of the cement-lined iron pipe, forming a perfect stone tube ... At that time little attention was given to the relative quantities of water as a remedial agent; and it was not until the general improved health of the community gave palpable evidence of the healing virtue it possessed—giving a new lease of life, effecting some remarkable cures, with the entire freedom from some diseases common elsewhere ... [The] mouth of this spring was cleared of loose earth, decayed leaves and other rubbish, and a well of stone work formed around it and roofed over with masonry save a small aperture closed by a locked iron door, while around the fountain the whole space was fitted in with stone, and covered with a thick layer of turf sloping on all sides to exclude all surface water and organic impurities.[24]

As the spring grew in popularity, particularly with the tourists and boarders who lived at the nearby Rural Home (a three-story hotel in the town of Ayer), the Shakers began to sell the water.[25] The waters were thought to cure a variety of diseases, including dyspepsia, chronic rheumatism, paralysis, and scrofula.[26] This site and resorts such as Saratoga Springs in New York attracted the World's people and Shakers alike, who gathered there to experience the fresh air, exercise regimen, and famous waters.

The Canterbury Shakers took a broad view of health care, including many different healing systems that would ensure their well-being: steam baths, herbal preparations, dietary measures such as vegetarianism, the manufacture of their own medicines, and trips to the spa or the ocean. In 1820 a small group of Shakers began the first of these trips, traveling to the New Hampshire shore for fresh air and a change of scene. On some occasions, members of other villages would join the group; at times, healthy visitors would accompany them as well.

Not everyone was convinced the trips were planned entirely for health reasons. Elder Henry Blinn indicated his doubts in his history of the village:

[1820] This is the first note that is found where special care is mentioned for the health by taking a ride and a rest, in a journey to the beach. It was, no doubt, a wise proposition to

accept the remedies which nature had so bountifully provided and which at the same time was so congenial to the
mind ... The company was John Jewett, Levi Stevens, Molly
Drake, Mercy Elkins and Ruth Stevens. They went from home
on the 25th of September and returned on the 30th which
could not have afforded them only three days at the beach.
Supposing that they were sick on their departure, their recu-
peration must have been very active to have warranted much
of a change in so short a time.[27]

Blinn's doubts extended to the physician as well:

[1821] Another company was induced to visit the seashore this
season in search of health. This time it included the Physician
of the Family, which would show that he did not rely wholly
on his own skill for the cure of his patients. They also tarry
longer at the beach—this time—not less than five days. The
company that enjoyed this privilege was Elder Brother Micajah
Tucker, Thomas Corbett, Tabetha Williams and Hanna Muffett.
In July on Independence Day another company started for the
beach. This company was absent eight days, but no word has
been recorded that they were healed of their infirmities. We
are persuaded, however, that it did some good, as others
followed the same course.[28]

These excursions to the shore continued into the twentieth
century.

Members of the Enfield, New Hampshire, community started
visiting the seashore by 1847. On one recorded journey six Enfield
Shakers stopped at Canterbury for the night and spent seventeen
days at the beach. The Enfield Shakers, as well as those from Alfred,
Maine, continued taking trips to the ocean until 1876.[29]

Canterbury's physician Thomas Corbett firmly believed in the
curative powers of hydropathy, and he not only visited the New
England shores but the waters of Saratoga Springs as well. There
is evidence that later in his life he was not a healthy man. In a letter
to the New Lebanon Ministry in 1827, the Canterbury Ministry
expressed their concern for Corbett's well-being:

Most beloved and esteemed Ministry,

We write a few lines to inform you that the two Brethren
Thomas [Corbett] and James [Daniels] have undertaken this
journey at this time on account of their health particularly
Thomas who has been recommended by the physicians at
New Lebanon and also by those of the world to try the
Saratoga waters ... The Saratoga and Ballston water appeared
to [Brothers Eliab and Garret] as holding out a rational hope
of a permanent cure. The length of time he would need to

drink the water could be better ascertained upon trial; but thought that a tarry of two weeks at the spring or at Watervliet and occasionally ride to the springs and bring the water away in bottles, and finally take a few Dozen home, would be a thorough trial. However they said they should like to see him before he commenced the use of the water, or have David Miller examine his case. We greatly desire that Thomas may get help as he is the only physician in this place, and a very useful member too.[30]

Hancock's ailing Elder Grove Wright, who frequented many seaside resorts throughout the East Coast, also visited the famous waters. Unlike many of his Brothers and Sisters, however, he had little faith in their effect.

The first week [at Saratoga Springs] appear'd rather favorable for me, but after that, rather lost ground. The Dr. thought, however, that if I could stay 6 or 8 weeks, he could cure me up. He probably thought I had money enough to last about that length of time . . . I went thro' with quite a diversity of treatment in the water cure line, and after the *forments & baths & dashes, etc.,* the attendants would give me such a rubbing that they nearly wore out the *hide* in some places where the bones were near the skin.[31]

The Believers were constantly concerned with the rampant contagious diseases of the day, such as smallpox, typhoid fever, measles, and mumps, that passed through communities. Blinn recorded that this fear was prevalent at Canterbury.

An anxious care in regard to contagious diseases passed over the Family this season. The Believers had learned that the fearful malady small pox was quite prevalent in some of the cities and villages and that some cases had proved fatal. As a hopeful safeguard they concluded to inoculate every person unless they had already passed through the ordeal. . . .[32]

Although no case of smallpox was recorded, the Canterbury community was not immune to other diseases.

The village, however, was not so fortunate with regard to measles. One of the Trustees, Benjamin Warren, who had been away on business, returned with this malady, and before it could be arrested, not less than eight additional persons were infected, and one case proved fatal.[33]

In 1814 there was an outbreak of mumps as well as typhus fever.

> During the months of April and May not less than forty persons were confined with the mumps [at Canterbury]. Last season a malignant fever raged at New Lebanon and Hancock and forty-two persons died . . .[34]

The early Shakers fought against disease with their simple herbal cures and medicines. Their communal lifestyle caused them to have a great concern for their members' health. Their desire for self-sufficiency and the very best medical attention led them to grow their own herbs, produce their own medicines, and establish an Order of Physicians and Nurses.

The First Herbalists

Drs. E. Harlow and G. K. Lawrence, of our Society, the latter an excellent botanist, gave their attention to the business, and introduced a more systematic arrangement and scientific manner of conducting it, especially as to the seasons for collection, varieties and method of preparation ...[1]

*T*he story of the Shakers' herb industry is about people as much as it is about plants. The physic gardens were overseen by physicians and those knowledgeable in the cultivation of medicinal plants. Many of the Shakers' medicines and promotional materials bore the name of the physician who was responsible for its manufacture; furthermore, the physicians worked with prominent members of the medical community in the World to produce and sometimes patent these medicines.

Before the *Millennial Laws* dictated in 1821 that an Order of Physicians and Nurses be established, Shaker Sisters were already serving as nurses and caring for the sick. These women possessed a variety of medical knowledge; in extreme cases of emergency, they hired doctors of the World to assist them.[2] Even in the twentieth century, when there were no physicians at the villages and doctors of the World began treating the Believers routinely, the Shaker nurses continued managing the infirmaries and helped the aged members live out their lives comfortably in their own villages.

The Canterbury community's first nurse was Elizabeth Avery. Born in Kingston, New Hampshire, in 1753, she visited Mother Ann

Eldress Marguerite Frost at the Infirmary, Canterbury Shaker Village. In 1965 Eldress Marguerite was appointed as Lead Minister of the United Society of Believers. By that time the Canterbury Shakers were giving tours of their village. (Life *magazine*)

and the Elders at Watervliet when she was thirty. Mother Ann is said to have told her:

> Young woman, as you have not been married and have no family of your own to care for, what have you ever done to help others or to bring about any good in the world?[3]

These words apparently inspired her to join the Canterbury Society and become a nurse. In 1792, the year the community was formally established, Avery was appointed head of the nursing department. She had an associate, Anna Carr, who was said to be "very prudent and careful."[4]

After living at Canterbury for fourteen years, Elizabeth Avery moved to the Enfield, New Hampshire community. She was replaced by Martha Wiggins, whom she had trained. Wiggins was born in Hopkinton, New Hampshire and remained as a nurse at Canterbury for forty years. Martha was described as:

> gentle, cautious, and conscientiously punctual to the regulations of the Family. While she was thoroughly devoted to her temporal duties, she was equally as interested in her spiritual devotions. She was patient, wise, and chaste in her whole course of life...and through the care of the physician [Thomas Corbett] . . . they were eminently successful in breaking up fevers and restoring their patients to health.[5]

During those early years, the nurses primarily relied on popular folk treatments to cure their patients. According to Henry Blinn,

> the medical aid...was very simple. Assistance from physicians not of the Society was seldom called. Simple doses of roots or herb tea entered into nearly every prescription.[6]

Prescriptions consisted of not much more than sugar and alcohol, as shown in a list of medical supplies bought for the Church Family in 1802:

3 gall. Brandy	2 pt. Alcohol
2 gall. Rum	3 lbs. white sugar
1 pt. Gin	29 lbs. brown sugar[7]
11 lbs. Honey	

It soon became evident that experienced physicians were needed in times of epidemics, accidents, and other serious medical problems. When the New Lebanon Ministry decreed that an Order of Physicians and Nurses be established, many communities set about to train some of their members in the medical field.

The Canterbury Shakers' first physician was Thomas Corbett, who moved with his family to the Enfield, New Hampshire village as a young boy. Many members of Corbett's family were Shakers, including his grandmother and his parents. His grandmother, Mary Fowler, was born in Hopkinton, Massachusetts in 1730 and moved with her parents to Hopkinton, New Hampshire when she was twelve years old. In 1746 she, her family, and three others were captured by Indians who took them to Canada. During the three years she was imprisoned, she was separated from her family, and her mother died of yellow fever. Her father managed to escape and hired a doctor to give her medicine to feign sickness. As she was no longer able to work, she was sold by the Indians to a French gentleman and was taken back to Hopkinton.[8] Mary Fowler later married Jesse Corbett and had two children, Jesse and Josiah. Years later, she moved to the Second

Family at Canterbury, where she died at age one hundred.

Josiah Corbett was born in 1758 in Hopkinton, where he lived until age seventeen when he left to fight in the Revolutionary War. Four years later he married Elizabeth Lankester, and the couple settled in Hopkinton, where they had two sons, Jesse and Thomas. During the next ten years a religious revival developed in the area, and the Corbetts converted to Shakerism. In 1790 they and four other Hopkinton families moved to Enfield, New Hampshire, where the Shakers were gathering to form a community.[9]

Thomas Corbett spent several years at Enfield, but in 1794, at age fourteen, he left his mother and brother and followed his father to Canterbury to live in the Church Family. Corbett quickly revealed himself to be intelligent and inventive.

About 1809 Corbett developed a device called the rocking truss to alleviate hernias. These were manufactured for sale by the Canterbury Shakers, and, over the years, Corbett improved and reimproved his design. By 1820 the Shakers had produced 192 trusses for sale. Five years later, 552 were made. Trusses continued to be a popular item, and in 1852 Corbett sold $376.50 worth of them.[10] Isaac Hill, editor of *The Farmers Monthly Visitor,* described the item in 1840 as "one of the very best articles of the kind that were ever invented to alleviate the pains of humanity."[11]

In 1810—at age sixteen—Corbett built a static electricity machine.

> It consists of a glass cylinder, revolving against a chamois pad, producing frictional electricity. This charge was drawn off into a Leyden jar.[12]

The electricity produced by this machine was applied for curative purposes to afflicted parts of the body.

In 1813 the New Hampshire Ministry appointed the young Brother "to qualify himself for a physician in this Society."[13] In compliance with the Ministry's wishes, Corbett began an intense study that lasted throughout his life.

His education, which included what he learned from the village's extensive library, involved an apprenticeship to Dr. William Tenney of Loudon. Although not a Shaker, Tenney was a familiar sight at Canterbury, for he was the physician the Shakers called upon in case of emergency. Tenney was one of the first doctors to discard the practice of heroic medicine, preferring the milder Thomsonian system. The Canterbury Shakers' adoption of the practice was probably due to Tenney's influence.

It is probable that Corbett also gained some of his medical knowledge from Jesse Wright, a physician who lived at Canterbury. Born in 1776, Wright entered the community in 1793 from Enfield, New Hampshire and lived there until 1837. According to

Blinn, he "never engaged largely in the practice of medicine" but spent his time supervising the botanical garden and the pressing of herbs for the Boston market.[14]

Although Wright oversaw the herb garden from time to time, Corbett is given full credit for starting it. By 1831 Corbett had built up such a market with the herb business that he was assigned an assistant, William Tripure, who had followed his brother to Canterbury in 1823 at the age of thirteen.[15] Once appointed, Tripure was sent to Concord to attend medical lectures.[16]

As did Corbett, William Tripure had many talents. He taught for several years and, after a stint serving as herdsman and shepherd, eventually was appointed Family Deacon, a position he held until he left the Society. Tripure lived at the village during a time of religious revival when there was much dancing and speaking in tongues at Shaker meetings. Considered a fervent Believer, he was said to be one of several Brethren who took on the spiritual manifestation of a native Indian during those times.[17] In 1843 he was given the high honor of helping print the Shakers' *Holy, Sacred and Divine Roll and Book*. Written in New Lebanon, it was thought to be the Shakers' most remarkable gift of inspiration.[18]

Another "jack of all trades," Henry Blinn took up medicine as well. Born in Providence, Rhode Island, in 1824, Blinn entered the Canterbury community when he was fourteen. As a young man, he learned several occupations including beekeeping and teaching and later dentistry. In 1852 he was appointed to the order of the Elders and was placed in the Ministry. In 1860

> a shop [was] fitted up for the purpose of working Dentistry which [had] become quite a benefit. Vulcanized rubber for plates [had] been introduced which [gave] general satisfaction.[19]

The dentist's office was placed in the Ministry Shop, no doubt at Blinn's convenience. According to Whitcher, it was well outfitted: "We have now a good set of tools for making plate work, also for plugging." By 1861 the Church Family was practicing dentistry for the entire Society as well as for other visiting Shakers. Typical work was to prepare "a set of 14 teeth on vulcanibe for the Second Family and [charging] $15.00."[20] Blinn also taught the Enfield, New Hampshire Shakers this process. Beginning in the twentieth century, however, with the death of Elder Henry Blinn, dentists from the World would visit once a year, on a Sunday, to do dental work on the Shakers.

The early nineteenth-century physicians at Enfield, New Hampshire were similar in age and experience to Thomas Corbett. Benjamin Warren, who became the Church Family's first physician

Church Family, Enfield, New Hampshire, 1870. The small white building in the center of the photograph is the village's dentist office. (Private collection)

at Enfield, was the same age as Corbett and entered the community the year that Corbett joined the Shakers. Warren was appointed as physician in 1815, two years after Corbett's appointment. Warren's father, as Corbett's had been, was also a member of the Society, and both men had been soldiers in the Revolutionary War.

The South Family at Enfield had an herbalist, Ezekiel Evans, who was the same age as Corbett and Warren. He was said to be a well-read physician who studied medicine with Warren and learned from several professionals in the World. Evans died in 1821 and was succeeded by his apprentice Samuel Brown. Born in 1797, Brown was also a contemporary of the other three New Hampshire physicians. He was an Elder in the Second Family, but his early interest in medicine led him to devote all his time to that calling. Largely self-taught, Brown studied under Evans and gained a reputation as a careful and skilled physician.

There must have been other physicians at Canterbury and Enfield, but Corbett, Warren, Evans, and Brown formed the core of the New Hampshire physicians who developed and operated the successful medicinal herb business. After they died, the

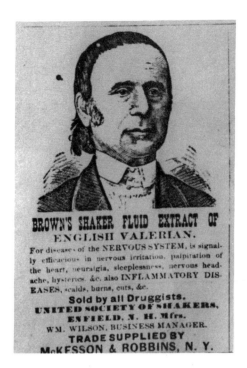

This advertisement in the Shaker Manifesto *reveals the portrait believed to be of Samuel Brown (1797-1856), who originated the Shakers' formula for the Extract of English Valerian. The medicine helped support the Enfield, New Hampshire community for many years. (Private collection)*

profits from their gardens continued to make a large contribution to the bishopric's income.

How the other Shaker physicians gained their medical education is only recorded in fragments. The doctors at New Lebanon organized early under Eliab Harlow and Isaac Couch (who was later replaced by Garret Lawrence). These physicians traveled among the villages and shared their knowledge. Harlow provided the Canterbury nurses with their first recipe book in 1793, and in 1819 he returned to the community again and helped with a difficult operation on Mother Hannah Goodrich, the Shakers' beloved leader. When Lawrence and Harlow died in the late 1830s, they were followed by their apprentice Jonathan Wood, who was succeeded by Barnabus Hinckley and later by Edward Fowler.[21]

In 1821, when he was only three years old, Barnabus Hinckley's family moved to the New Lebanon Society. By the age of nineteen he was appointed as the community's doctor and became known as a careful physician. In 1858 he received a degree from Berkshire Medical College in Pittsfield, Massachusetts. Hinckley died at the age of forty-three.

At the Watervliet community, David Miller, Senior Elder in the Church Family, functioned as physician while Corbett was in

Infirmary at New Lebanon, New York, nineteenth century. (Private collection)

practice. He was assisted by Chauncey Miller, a Trustee. Doctors in the World (as well as other villages) would frequently send their patients to David Miller for consultation.

The Order of Physicians was predominately male at New Lebanon; Union Village, Ohio; and Canterbury and Enfield, New Hampshire. At Harvard there were many doctors who were women. Their first recorded female physicians were Sarah Jewett, Tabitha Babbit, and Salome Barrett.[22]

The Shaker doctors had great responsibilities that extended well beyond their caring for the sick. In addition to maintaining the physic gardens and fields, at times they were called upon to help with the livestock.

> [Jan. 1834] One of the Colts got hurt very bad, they were frightened by some Dogs. Joseph M.M. had a bad cold, Susan K. Myrick [a physician] gave him a sweat.[23]

They also visited gardens and distributors in the World and haggled over sales. Corbett and Chauncey Miller (who served as an herbalist as well as a Trustee) dickered frequently over herb prices. Many of the Shaker doctors probably led similar lives. The journal

*Chauncey Miller (1814-1901) was a trustee and herbalist
at the Watervliet, New York, community. (Collection of the
Western Reserve Historical Society, Cleveland, Ohio)*

entries about Miller give a glimpse of how the herbalists spent their
time:

> [July, 1848] Chauncey Miller went out about the neighborhood
> somewhere, after Elecampane Root, &c, to find out where it
> grew, so as to know where to go to again.
>
> The farmers have been thrashing Oats—got them nearly all
> thrashed. C. Miller helped them today.
>
> [Oct.] C. Miller started out somewhere towards Balstown &
> Saratoga after Herbs &c.
>
> [Nov.] C. Copley, C. Miller, C. Prentiss (with Eunice and Emeline
> for cooks) went down to the Island [in Mohawk River] with
> teams &c to sow Dock seed.
>
> [3 days later] C. Miller & co. at the Island, pretty much finished
> planting &c. their Docks and returned home.
>
> Wm. Thrasher, and a young brother (Anthony Lake) with a

crippled arm, from East Family, Holy Mount, arrived here via Railroad, for advice from D. Miller, our physician.

[next day] David Miller, C. Miller, Wm. Thrasher and the lame youth or brother, started for Albany this evening. They visit Dr. Marsh for advice about the crippled arm.

C. Miller & the Physician Sisters went to Albany & Troy.

C. Miller started for N. York [via steamboat].

C. Miller returned from New York this morning took a team and went down to Albany after some things which had arrived from New York. From there he went to Troy, to secure a quantity of herbs &c. which he was about to lose by a broken agent.

[Dec.] C. Miller went to Schenecady to engage a load of manure, to replenish the farm purchased in Niskeyuna.

C. Miller went to Albany also, with a cutter, to carry down some Herbs &c to ship to England.[24]

Originally, the Shakers did not set aside specific buildings as infirmaries. When necessary, the sick were placed in rooms in the dwelling house. Canterbury's progression toward a permanent infirmary is probably typical of the other villages. From 1815 to 1849 the second floor of Canterbury's Church Family Dwelling House was used as an infirmary, and Corbett, who was then new as the Family's physician, probably organized the facility. In 1849 the doctors and nurses took over the "Lower House," built in 1811, as the infirmary. This two-story building was at first partially occupied by the Office Sisters, with remaining rooms designated for overnight guests.[25]

In 1825 the forty-one members of Canterbury's North Family saw an opportunity to provide more space for their sick.

The old dwelling of the West Family was moved to the North Family and a part of it used as a hatter's shop, and the upper story for an Infirmary. In 1884, the whole building was remodeled and taken for an Infirmary.[26]

The infirmary in Canterbury's Church Family still stands and reveals something about the Shakers' long history of health care. The building underwent many alterations over the years and by the first quarter of the twentieth century was predominantly used as a residence for elderly Shakers.

The rooms for the patients or elderly residents were located on the second floor. These spaces were airy and comfortable with large windows, white walls, and gossamer curtains. Shutters helped regulate the sunlight. Each room was equipped with a sink, closet, and dresser. Two rooms shared a connecting bathroom. Patients could ring for help to nurses downstairs. A hook and strap in the ceiling allowed patients to pull themselves up from the beds if necessary. The second floor also had a library for light reading, looms for weaving, and drawers for handiwork.

The first floor had a room that functioned as a doctor's office. Operations were performed there. Cupboards filled with medicines still line the walls, and a marble topped counter remains. Each drawer and cupboard was carefully labeled. In addition there was a sitting/sewing room, which also served as a medical library.

Today a kitchen exists on the first floor, but originally the kitchen was located in the cellar. During the twentieth century, the cellar was converted into a storage area to keep jars of canned goods for the sick.

The eaves in the attic are still lined with built-in, labeled drawers. A small area was set aside for embalming. One room is used to store crutches; a cupboard houses procelain chamber pots.

The New Lebanon infirmary became the model for other communities with its extensive library, floor plan (designed both for function and comfort), and specialized furniture, such as an adult-sized cradle. The Canterbury community also had custom-designed furnishings for their patients:

> A splendid Rocking Chair of exquisite arrangement ... you can lie down, or sit up just as you feel to; it is turned into a bed or a chair at pleasure by the aid of a little Machinery.[27]

The infirmaries were often a point of curiosity to visitors. At Canterbury, the Shakers included the building on their public tours.

With so many members in the communities, however, it was inevitable that some people would complain of bad treatment. While the Shakers gained a reputation for their excellent health care, they also acquired enemies who criticized their way of life. Court battles with the Shakers were common in the 1840s and 1850s.[28] In 1848 the Brethren were called before the New Hampshire House of Representatives to defend themselves against accusations of, among other things, mistreatment of their members.

Sixteen members from Canterbury and nine members from Enfield came to defend themselves against the slander. Among the doctors of the World who were called to support the credibility and practices of the New Hampshire Shakers were physicians Charles Chadbourne, William Prescott, Richard P. J. Tenney, John

Clough, and Josiah Crosby. The Shakers were represented by Franklin Pierce, who was elected President of the United States four years later. During these hearings, Corbett's reputation as the leading physician of the Canterbury Society was affirmed by Dr. Chadbourne:

> His medical knowledge is very respectable. He has a very good library of medical books. Although not a member of [the Hampshire Medical Society] he usually attends our meetings. He has performed some delicate operations on the eye and is considered very safe in all his prescriptions.[29]

Corbett's assistant William Tripure, however, did not receive such a favorable appraisal. While he was a physician at the village, Tripure was held accountable for the death of a young boy. David Parker, a Trustee when the incident occurred, recalled that he had wanted to have a coroner's inquest but was opposed by Tripure who said that there was no need.

> [The] child came into [Tripure's] hands before he died; [Tripure] said his death was occasioned by a concussion of the brain, by a fall on a stone.[30]

Corbett also testified about the event and said that Tripure had called on him for consultation. When he arrived, however, the boy was dead. When Tripure told Corbett he had given the boy laudanum and brandy, Corbett replied:

> I asked him how much? He said as much as he could get into him. I told him that I should not have dared to give him that medicine.[31]

Years later James Kaime, who succeeded Corbett, admitted to the boy's mother that the large doses of brandy and laudanum were probably more the cause of his death than the fall.

Tripure was removed as Family Deacon on February 7, 1844 and left the Society at age thirty-four. He had been at the Society at the time of its greatest apostasy—a time of much discontent.[32]

In 1847 Tripure was discovered in Ohio mimicking his former friends. In the Union Village, Ohio, records is the following report:

> 1847. June 11. Some turn backs [apostates] originally from Canterbury are going through the country gathering money by mocking Shakers in their singing dancing &c &c. This company of mockers are nam'd William Tripure, Jell Otis, J. Partridge, L. D. Tripure, A. Foster, and Julia Willard . . . This company of mockers were designated . . . as men without principle and shameless women—in a Cincinnati Paper.[33]

This broadside promoted a traveling musical program performed in the World. This "great moral entertainment" was conducted by several apostates, including William Tripure, a former physician at Canterbury Shaker Village. (Collection of Williams College Archives and Special Collection)

LAST NIGHT!

GREAT MORAL ENTERTAINMENT!

By the Celebrated and Far-famed

SHAKER FAMILY

From Canterbury, N. H.

Who have recently performed for seven consecutive weeks to overflowing houses

at the New York American Museum,

and have received the unqualified commendation and patronage of the people of Boston and other cities of New England, beg leave to announce most respectfully to the Ladies and Gentlemen of this vicinity, that they intend giving a Grand Levee,

At Washington Hall, Bradley-st.
Tuesday Evening, March 21.

Mr. Maloon, who, together with his coadjutors, has lived many years among the sect called Shakers, will give a full idea of the performances witnessed. Also, a

HISTORY OF ANN LEE.

The Rise and Progress of Shakerism in England, France and America, the firm belief of the Shakers in the reality of visions, and conversation with angels, and departed spirits, the manner of worship, and all the actions and ceremonies observed by them, will in this most extraordinary Concert, be depicted by the whole corps, together with illustrations of Shaker

Singing, Dancing, Shaking, Whirling, &c.

PROGRAMME.

PART 1.

SONG—O-le-er-lum-er-la—supposed by the Shakers to have been learned by inspiration.
BLANCO—Holy Order and Square Order.
SONG—In the Unknown Tongue, as learned by inspiration.
LA-BALA—Slow March and Quick March.

PART 2.

SONG—Of the French Consul, sung and played upon a Spiritual Flute.
LA-BALA—Square Hollow Company Labor.
SONG—Osceola and Pocahontas.
LA-BALA—Square Check Company Labor.

PART 3.

SONG—The Reapers, with motions to mortify pride.
SONG—Come Life, Shaker Life.
BLANCO—Mother's Love, Company Labor.

In conclusion will be introduced the remarkable Young Lady

MISS L. A. CHASE,

As the miraculous Shaker Tetotum. This young lady whose long experience as a Shaker, united with unheard of bodily powers, render her a general wonder, will execute astonishing Shaker gyrations, eclipsing in agility, grace, muscular ability and wonder, the wonderful Fanny herself. Through the force of long habit, and being peculiarly endowed, she can without dizziness or cessation,

Whirl Round 1500 Times.

Nothing in this performance can offend the taste of refinement or the eye of modesty.

☞ The Company will appear in real Shaker Costume. ☜

Tickets 25 Cents. Children half price. Doors open at 6 1-2, commence, at 7 1-2.

Hiram Clifford, a Shaker for twelve years who had lived at both New Hampshire communities, also complained about mistreatment. He testified:

> While I was there [Canterbury] I was sent by David Parker to take the measurement of water on a rock in the pond; worked in the water, and took cold and had the rheumatism; was sick three weeks. The Elders told me, and told an Elder of the North Family that I must have a bed and suitable food; went to the North Family. The North Family Elder told me that they had no sick room, but perhaps I could have a chance to be on a bed of one of the Brethren in the Garret. This bed consisted of an old surtout and a block of wood for a pillow; all the bed I had. No care was taken of me, and I had no diet; some time before I was able to work; as soon as able, went to work.[34]

In contrast to these incidents, there are many touching notations throughout the Shaker records of their devoted care for one another. At New Lebanon Barnabus Hinckley worked closely with the early doctors, Harlow and Lawrence, and eventually took over as physician when they died. In 1836 Hinckley began to record his mounting concern for Garret Lawrence, who was becoming unable to work. On some days they bottled herbs, cleaned the drying house, and worked in the garden together; but in November Lawrence retired to his room to prepare himself for a course of medical treatment. From the end of November until January 23, Hinckley faithfully waited on Lawrence while struggling to continue his own work preparing the gardens and tending other patients.

> Dec. 6 I steam Garret & help David Lidle unload 2 horse loads Dung on Sage bed and split and carry some wood into the . . . house.

> Dec 26 Garret H. Lawrence moved into the southwest room in the great house garret and I tend upon him till the 27th when I with . . . go over to Washington to cut timber.

> Jan 1st, 1837 I commence again taking care of Garret H. Lawrence and continue through his sickness with help of Daniel Wood after the 9th.

> Jan 9 Daniel Wood commenced helping take care of Garret H. Lawrence. This releases me some so I can tend some other Duties.

> Jan 23 Our beloved & useful brother Garret Lawrence this morning departed this life at 10 minutes past 5 ocl. having

passed through a serious & lengthy sickness and hard suffer-
ings, he has scarcely enjoyed any health since Jan. 1832 at
which time he had a severe attack of acute rheumatism.

Jan. 24 tend the funeral at 2 ocl p.m. .... This evening there is
the greatest light or Phenomanon that has ever been known
&c.[35]

The Shakers not only nursed the members of their own Families,
but they also took care of Believers at other villages and friends in
the World. When physician Richard Tenny grew ill at the end of
his life, many of the Sisters lovingly took their turn caring for him.[36]
Journals during this time reflect their concern for the doctor:

May 18, 1876. Martha Crooker [an Infirmary nurse] went to
Pittsfield to aid in taking care of him.

May 20, 1876: George Moore went to help take care of the Doctor,

*Lucy Hunt (1885-1927) and another Canterbury Shaker at the Infirmary
at Union Village, Ohio. Members would often travel to other communities
to care for the sick and elderly. Several of the Canterbury Sisters stayed at
the Ohio Society for seven years before they brought the remaining elderly
back to Canterbury. (Private collection)*

who had been our family physician for over forty years and a fast friend to Believers.[37]

When it was clear that Tenney did not have much longer to live, their nursing care increased:

> May 25, 1876: Dr. R. P. Tenney of Pittsfield, our family physician is sick unto death. A Brother and two Sisters go to Pittsfield to assist in taking care of him. [38]

The Shakers attended Dr. Tenney until his death three weeks later.

Nurses worked at the Canterbury infirmary well into the twentieth century. When Eldress Bertha Lindsay came to the village in 1905, Harriet Johns was head nurse and Alice McNear was her assistant. When Johns died in 1913, Elizabeth Stickney and Lucy Hunt assisted McNear as nurses. In two years, however, Lucy Hunt, with several other Sisters, went to Lebanon, Ohio to take care of the aged members of the Union Village community. The Canterbury Sisters stayed in Ohio for seven years, an extraordinarily sympathetic effort on the part of the New Hampshire Shakers to allow these last Ohio Shakers to live out their lives in their own community. In 1921 Lucy Hunt returned to Canterbury with the three remaining Shakers. She died shortly thereafter.

During Hunt's absence from the Canterbury community, the infirmary faltered.

> Sept. 5, 1916: Mr. Wilder, of the Fitch Co. of Concord, druggist, comes at our call to look over Infirmary stock of medicine & select saleable goods, also condemn the useless. He does so & Eld. Emma, Jessie & others pack same for transit to Concord or to the deposit for refuse."[39]

Jessie Evans eventually took Lucy Hunt's place in the infirmary. A schoolteacher and historian, Evans had no specific medical training. According to Eldress Bertha Lindsay, she was "compassionate and yet she didn't have too much use for sickness."[40] With fewer trained people on hand to care for the sick, Evans probably experienced much sadness and helplessness in her role as a nurse. The care recorded in her diaries no doubt reflects a long tradition of kindness bestowed on patients by such nurses.

> August 22, 1892: School opens this p.m. for fall term. Our little Emily absent, was taken sick today from eating unripe pear.
>
> August 23, 1892: . . Emily no better today.
>
> August 24, 1892: . . . Emily taken to Infirmary, a very sick child.

August 25, 1892: Emily no better, nurses and Mother in constant attendance. A sad 25th birthday for me.

August 26, 1892: Dr. Meagrath sent for to see the sick one, decides it a hopeless case; terrible inflammation of bowels.

Our darling Emily died at 11:20 tonight in convulsions.

August 28, 1892: Kind remembrance service for the sweet little spirit just departed, held this a.m.[40]

After Jessie Evans' death in 1937, the infirmary closed and with it ended Canterbury's long history of health care for their members.

The Shakers' physicians and nurses left a legacy of high standards of health care. Their buildings stand as examples of good lighting and ventilation; their recipes for food and medicine are published; their lifestyle, which emphasized order, sanitation, and exercise, is still studied and copied; their values of honesty and industry as seen throughout their herbal history are still admired. Most of their herbal medicines have been replaced by modern chemical preparations, but their bottles of tinctures, extracts, and syrups speak silently of a simpler period of herbal cures.

The Age of the Cure

8

The Shakers have long been justly celebrated for the excellence of their manufacturers and medicinal preparations. Their care, skill, and cleanliness are proverbial. Their honesty and reliability unquestionable.[1]

*T*hroughout most of their history, the Shakers cultivated a reputation for living a long and healthy life. This effort, no doubt, arose partly from the criticism they received for their unorthodox communal lifestyle. In an attempt to deflect the denouncements, the Shakers carefully compiled statistics to document their successes. In 1882 Elder Giles Avery from New Lebanon requested that all villages gather information to refute the claims that being a celibate Shaker led "to idiocy and atrophy and a short life."[2] Communities such as Alfred, Maine kept records of the ages of their members at death and determined the average life span to be "62 years, 9 months, 6 days, 2 hours."[3] Isaac Hill, a business associate of the Believers, reported that the average age of the Canterbury Shaker at death was fifty years and eight months. (In contrast, the life expectancy of men and women in Massachusetts eight years later in 1890 was 43.5 years.) In a newspaper article that glorified the attributes of the Shakers and their trades, Hill reasoned that a healthy way of life was the cause of their longevity:

> Very seldom does a death occur among these people, but from an originally delicate constitution or some organic defect, before passing the middle age . . . With limbs and nerves

> strengthened by exercise and labor, with the contentment of
> perfect independence and freedom from worldly fear and
> worldly care—the Shakers, in nine cases out of ten, live to a
> mature and ripe age . . .[4]

About forty years later Elder Frederick Evans, having examined a
record of the deaths at all the Societies, reaffirmed the benefits of
a Shaker lifestyle:

> I hold that no man who lives as we do has a right to be ill
> before he is sixty; if he suffers from disease before that, he is
> in fault.[5]

The Shakers' reputation for their good health also stemmed
from their interest in medicine. They became well versed in
current theories of health care and adapted them for their own
uses. Their medical regimen was based on many schools of thought
and became a unique, eclectic system.

As the Shaker physicians incorporated various medical systems
into their practices, they readily solicited advice from the established medical community of the World. The village doctors and
the World's physicians worked in harmony: the Shakers learned
much from these doctors who were usually better educated; the
World's physicians gained from the Shakers an established botanical business that provided them with the highest quality herbs.

In response to the demand for quality products, the Shakers
manufactured a broad range of medications, including extracts,
pills, ointments, wines, and waters. A few of the villages developed
one or two preparations which grew to be important income
sources.

The members of Union Village promoted the sale of wine. In
their manual, the Ohio Believers explained the medicinal uses of
this beverage:

> Good wines possess highly valuable and restorative medicinal
> properties for refreshing and supporting the sick, feeble and
> convalescent from long and severe fevers; and such as have
> been reduced by protracted debilitary complaints. They cheer
> and enliven the spirits of the weak and feeble and give
> strength and comfort both to the body and the mind. Good
> wines are agreeable and pleasant to the palate and do not
> intoxicate the brain and infuse the health as all kinds of
> alcoholic liquors do.[6]

Some medicines were formulated by the Shaker doctors themselves, who endorsed their own products; others were made by the
Shakers and marketed by a company or physician of the World.

A visual pun is used in a pamphlet promoting the New Lebanon Shaker's medicine, Seven Barks. In another pamphlet, sailing ships ("barks") were substituted for the dogs. (The Miller Collection)

The New Lebanon Shakers made two preparations at the request of physicians in the World: Seven Barks, produced exclusively for Dr. Lyman Brown, and Tincture of Veratrum Viride, manufactured for Dr. Wesley C. Norwood of Cokesbury, South Carolina. Seven Barks was a commonly used name for hydrangea; however, the Shaker preparation did not include this ingredient. It was made from the extracts of black cohosh, bloodroot, blue flag, butternut, golden seal, lady slipper, mandrake, sassafras, and stone root. The bottle was packaged with a picture of seven barking dogs on the label, making a visual pun on the medicine's name. Veratrum Viride was a liquid extract derived from the narcotic and potentially poisonous white helebore, or *Veratrum viride*, which grows in swampy areas. Originally produced by Dr. Norwood to treat pulmonary diseases and cardiac disorders, the medicine became so popular that he hired the Shakers to manufacture it for him. From 1858 to 1936 the New Lebanon Brethren printed eleven booklets devoted to promoting this medicine.

Several products bore the name of a Shaker who, for one reason or another, was chosen to endorse the product. Examples are: Mother Seigel's Syrup, produced at New Lebanon; Faith Whitcomb's

Nerve Bitters from Harvard; Brown's Fluid Extract of English Valerian, which was manufactured at Enfield, New Hampshire; and Corbett's Shaker Syrup of Sarsaparilla, made in Canterbury. Corbett lent his name to several medicines of his invention, including: Sarsaparilla Lozenges, Shaker Vegetable Rheumatic Pills, Bilious Pills, Shaker Dyspepsia Cure, Vegetable Family Pills, and Shaker's Compound Cherry Pectoral Syrup.[7]

In the 1830s the Shakers began manufacturing extracts as one branch of the trade. Fluid extracts were more dependable in strength than the infusions and teas made with herbs, and they were more convenient to handle and store. The extracts were sold in glass jars and were also put up in a solid form. Prior to 1841 the extract business was run by the Sisters; but "as the business grew, the Brethren took it over and greatly increased its size."[8]

The Shakers constantly updated their equipment to improve the extract business. In 1850 the New Lebanon Believers remodeled their two buildings designated for the drying, pressing, and distilling processes. They also purchased a new twelve horse-power steam engine to run the extract distillation equipment; a second, larger boiler; and other machines and fixtures. Three years later they purchased equipment for pulverizing the herbs and a hydraulic press for pressing the herbs.[9]

In the spring of 1851 members of the Watervliet community, Trustee Chauncey Miller and physician David Miller, went to New

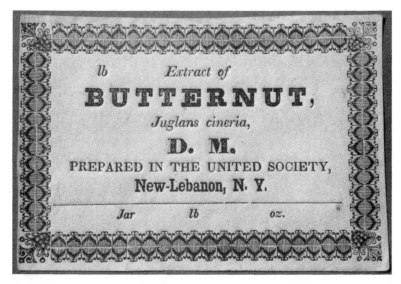

In this butternut extract label the initials "D. M." stand for Trustee David Meacham. (Private collection)

Lebanon to learn about these advancements. By summer the Watervliet members had renovated their own extract works based on what they had learned at New Lebanon. When Benjamin Lossing visited New Lebanon in 1854, he described the extract house the Watervliet Shakers had admired and copied:

> The Extract House, in which is the laboratory for the preparation of juices for medical purposes, [is] a large frame building, thirty-six by one hundred feet. It was erected in 1850. It is supplied with the most perfect apparatus, and managed by James Long, a skillful chemist and a member of the Society. In the principle room of the laboratory the chief operations of cracking, steaming and pressing the roots and herbs are carried on, together with the boiling of the juices thus extracted. In one corner is a large boiler, into which the herbs are placed and steam introduced. From this boiler the steamed herbs are conveyed to grated cylinders, and subjected to immense pressure. The juices thus expressed are then put in copper pans, inclosed in iron jackets, in such manner that steam is introduced between the jackets and the pans, and the liquid boiled down to the proper consistency for use. Some juices, in order to avoid the destruction or modification of their medical properties, are conveyed to an upper room, and there boiled in a huge copper vacuum pan, from which, as its name implies, the air has been exhausted. This allows the liquid to boil at a much lower temperature than it would in the open air . . . . These extracts are of the purest kind. The water used for the purpose is conveyed through earthen pipes from a pure mountain spring, an eighth of a mile distant, which is singularly free from all earthly matter. This is of infinite importance in the preparation of these medicinal juices. They are, consequently, very popular, and the business is annually increasing. During the year 1855 they prepared at that laboratory and sold about fourteen thousand pounds. The chief products are the extracts of dandelion and butternut. Of the former, during that year, they put up two thousand five hundred pounds; of the latter, three thousand pounds.[10]

The men working in these laboratories became skilled chemists. Unfortunately for the Shakers, the extract business took place at a time when many members left for the World, taking their skills and information with them. The Trustees battled against these departing members as well as firms which used the Shaker name for their own gains. A broadside issued in the 1860s is an example of the difficulties that the Trustees encountered during those times:

> Having dissolved my relations with the Society of Shakers at New Lebanon, I consider it due to the public that my position while there, my withdrawal, and their course towards me, should be understood. For many years I have had sole charge

of their Medical Laboratory and have prepared all their MEDICINAL EXTRACTS. The responsibility of proper preparation, putting of them up for sale with correct labeling, rested entirely with me. It being a responsible position (a mistake having occurred several years since in the putting up and selling of Belladonna for Dandelion, and the Society having had to pay a large sum to the injured party for the carelessness or officious intermeddling of members of the family with the business of the Laboratory), when I took charge of it I caused an entire change in the mode of conducting it, and adopted such a system of marks and labels, with a record of them as would not, unexplained, be intelligible to any other person, and hence would not allow of the interference of these persons, without great liability of mistake. Under such a system I conducted it for years, to the credit of the department in my charge.

After I decided to close my relations with the Society, I have them to understand its true condition, and that it would not be safe to allow the use of any article from the Laboratory, without explanation from me, which I would make when we had settled, and made an appointment with them for that purpose. At the meeting, Benjamin Gates, a legal Trustee of said Society, offered me, as a renumeration for my service, $5 a year for sixteen years, without any explanation from me, and take all responsibility of mistakes. One of the Ministry, having some recollection of the previous error, for which they had to pay, was afraid to take the risk, and offered me $8 with all necessary explanation from me—all of which I declined, believing that they should pay me at least $50 a year, which was as small a sum as any reasonable person would suggest. We parted with the understanding that we should meet again at a time to be agreed upon.

According to the writer, the Trustees sent the Sheriff after him, and he quickly went into hiding. Feeling that the Shakers were trying to frighten him, he continued his negotiations through a third person.

All efforts at an adjustment of the matter being at an end, I am advised by my attorney to notify all dealers in such preparations, that it is impossible for them to ascertain the contents of the several jars with sufficient accuracy to make it safe for them to sell them . . .[11]

In addition to extracts, the Shakers also manufactured a variety of other medicinal preparations, including sarsaparilla syrup, a popular remedy in the nineteenth century. Sarsaparilla syrup was produced by many companies in the World as well as at least five Shaker communities: Canterbury, Watervliet, Union Village, Harvard, and New Lebanon.

Most of the sarsaparilla syrups on the market, including the very first Shaker mixtures, were made from the root of the imported sarsaparilla, or *Smilax officinalis.* This herb, a trailing plant with a prickly stem, was imported in bulk from Central and South America. Canterbury physician Thomas Corbett, however, used the root of the indigenous *Aralia nudicaulis,* or wild American Sarsaparilla. The New Lebanon community made extracts from both varieties of the plant.

As the popularity of the syrup spread, the use of the term "sarsaparilla" became a popular trade name used for many products regardless of their contents.

> [It was the extensive] range of diseases to which sarsaparilla is applicable, [and] the harmless character of the remedy, that have made it a great favorite with empirics, so that there are an immense number of quack medicines sailing under its name.[12]

During this "Age of Quackery," it was generally the quality of the advertising, not the contents of the product, that made these medicines a commercial success. The medicinal value of sarsaparilla was doubtful; the U.S. Dispensatory stated that there were a great number of species belonging to this genus, but only a few possessed any useful medicinal power. The root of the *Aralia nudicaulis,* however, was thought to be as effective as the imported roots.[13]

Despite the Dispensatory's claims, the sarsaparilla syrups were heavily endorsed by physicians and satisfied customers across the country. Comments such as "it cheered while it cured" indicated the heavy alcohol content. Another fan expressed it this way: "... [the] therapeutic powers were indifferent to weather conditions ... a bottle of it [had never been known] to freeze."[14]

The New Lebanon physicians supplied the Canterbury nurses, and probably those at other villages as well, with their first medical recipe book.[15] This manual contained the formulas for several medications, including the sarsaparilla syrup. New Lebanon used the same formula concocted by their physician, Garrett L. Lawrence, for many years. This version was said to cure "diseases of the blood arising from the use of Mercury, and various other causes."[16] The New Lebanon Shakers also claimed that it cost only one third of the other preparations.

For sixty years the Union Village, Ohio, Shakers sold a syrup endorsed by Elder Peter Boyd, whose name was embossed on every bottle. Boyd believed that the manufacture and sale of this medicine was one of the "most prominent and profitable industries."

Elder Peter Boyd was head of the medicine business for more than fifty years at Union Village, Ohio. Boyd's name was embossed on Union Village's sarsaparilla syrup bottles to prevent counterfeits. At least five Shaker communities produced a sarsaparilla syrup for sale. (The Western Reserve Historical Society, Cleveland, Ohio)

So successful has the Shakers' Extract of Sarsaparilla been that the Lebanon Medical Society, the only chartered Medical Society in Warren County, although opposed to the use or sale of patent medicines, passed a unanimous resolution [in 1849] recommending the Shakers' Extract of Sarsaparilla to the profession at large.[17]

Their syrup, however, competed with one made in the World. Ironically, this version bore the name of Dr. S. D. Howe's Shaker Compound Extract of Sarsaparilla Syrup. The medicine was endorsed by D. M. Bennett, an apostate from New Lebanon who claimed that the formula was used by the New Lebanon and Watervliet Shakers. Since Bennett had been a physician at New Lebanon, he probably gave Howe the recipe. Dr. Howe's company was located in New York, but he also advertised his "Shaker" Sarsaparilla in Cincinnati, Ohio, where the medicine was frequently mistaken for that manufactured by Union Village.

Of all the medicines the Canterbury Shakers produced, and there were at least thirty-three, Corbett's Compound Concentrated Syrup of Sarsaparilla was perhaps the most well known. While Corbett originally created medicines for his own village's use, he also knew that there was a market for high quality herbal products; and he had no qualms about entering the very competitive sarsaparilla market. While he tried to promote his medicine, there were at least ten other brands of sarsaparilla being advertised. The Canterbury community manufactured two versions; the first formula was derived from a recipe given by New Lebanon physician, Garrett Lawrence. This syrup appears along with Liverwort and Black Cohosh syrups in Canterbury's first herb catalog. A later recipe was the creation of Dr. Thomas Corbett.

The Shakers often capitalized on the trends of the day, and it was probably David Parker, a young and innovative Trustee, who saw the possibilities of the Shakers manufacturing their own sarsaparilla syrup at Canterbury. To secure the backing of the medical community, he and Corbett went to the Dartmouth Medical School in Hanover, New Hampshire, to consult physician Dixi Crosby about their new formula.

> Dr. Dixi Crosby ... gave his counsel and advice to the Shakers Dr. Thomas Corbett and David Parker, to aid them in the preparation of a curative compound of herbs and roots, which should meet the wants of the medical fraternity. The learned doctor wanted his prescription honestly and conscientiously mixed; and reposing confidence in the fidelity of the Shaker community, he and his friend Dr. Valentine Mott gave the new medicine the benefit of their approval, and widely advertised its merits. The combination was of the roots of sarsaparilla, dandelion, yellow dock, mandrake, black cohosh, garget and indian hemp and the berries of juniper and cubeb, united with iodide of potassium. From the most euphonious of its constituent parts, it was called "sarsaparilla," and became so famed for its curative properties, that great fortunes have been made in manufacturing imitation or bogus articles of the same name. The medicine was designed for impurities of the blood, general and nervous debility, and wasting diseases; and, for the half century during which it has been prepared for the public, it has been inestimable boon to the sick and suffering ...[18]

Dixi Crosby was probably selected as a consultant because he was a celebrated physician and may have been a friend or at least a professional peer of Thomas Corbett. Crosby was one of the seventeen children of Asa Crosby, a physician who had earlier tutored R. P. J. Tenney, the Gilmanton physician who took care of the Shakers after Corbett died. While Tenney and Corbett were older than Crosby, they undoubtedly knew him since he had practiced for thirteen years in Gilmanton and Laconia, towns surrounding Canterbury.[19]

A second consultant, Professor Valentine Mott, was a surgeon from New York who had studied and practiced medicine at Columbia College and later helped establish Rutgers Medical College. When this college closed four years later, Mott returned to lecture at Columbia. The selection of these two men helped give the product credibility.

Several events date the establishment of Corbett's Sarsaparilla Syrup to around 1843. Dr. Dixi Crosby had moved from Laconia, New Hampshire in 1838 to assume the Surgery and Obstetrics Chair at Dartmouth. This date, therefore, would have been the earliest for Corbett to have gone to Hanover to seek Crosby's advice. It is known from a firsthand account in 1847, however, that Corbett took his formula before the New Hampshire Medical Society about 1843.

> I first became acquainted with the Compound Concentrated Syrup of Sarsaparilla prepared by Dr. Corbett of the Shakers Society somewhat more than four years ago; at this time he made its precise composition public to the members of the New Hampshire Medical Society.[20]

In an 1847 testimonial in the *Shakers' Manual* a physician from Hanover, New Hampshire gave another indication of the first production of Corbett's Sarsaparilla:

> The article has been but a few years before the public. During the three or four first years of its introduction it was comparatively unknown until, in the year 1847, having obtained a Diploma at the Mass. Charitable Mechanics Assoc. of Boston, it attracted the attention of the public, and from that period to the present, it has steadily advanced in general favor.[21]

The manufacture of the syrup was a technical, labor-intensive process involving several buildings. At Canterbury, the herbs were dried in the large attic of the North Shop and distilled in the nearby Syrup Shop, both located in the center of the Church Family. The east side of the north room of the first floor of the Syrup Shop had two kettles, one to hold seven barrels and five gallons of liquid, and another to hold 47 1/2 gallons. The west side of the room had a still, a tank, and more kettles. The original formula gave instructions to "put 100 lbs of Sarsparilla root and 80 lbs of Prince's Pine into a deep or steeping kettle." The roots were soaked for thirty-six hours, after which the liquid was pumped through a strainer into an evaporating pan where it continued to be heated. The remaining roots were again covered with fresh water and allowed to simmer for another thirty-six hours. The resulting liquid was strained and pumped into

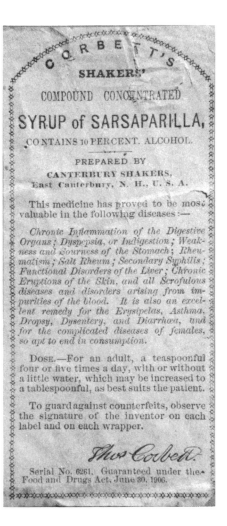

Thomas Corbett's Sarsaparilla Syrup was perhaps the most well known of the thirty-three kinds of medicine manufactured by the Canterbury community. (Private collection)

the evaporating pan. The roots were then removed by "pitching them out of the sliding door west of the kettle into a cart."

The first kettle was then filled with layers of several herbs, starting with sarsaparilla roots at the bottom and followed by prince's pine, dock, dandelion, garget, black cohosh, then mandrake, Indian hemp, and juniper berries. The larger herbs were placed on the bottom so that the smaller pieces would not burn. These herbs were steeped for thirty-six hours, and the resulting liquid was pumped off as before.

At the same time, eight pounds of cubebs (small, spicy berries of a kind of pepper) were distilled to remove their oil, and the liquid was added to the kettle filled with layers of herbs. This process was repeated three times. If the liquid did not evaporate fast enough for each successive pumping, the flat kettle on the east side of the room was also used.

Once all the liquid was pumped into the evaporating pan and the liquid measured "10 $^1/_2$ inches in the S.E. corner of evaporator," it was drawn off into a wooden tub and allowed to settle for five days. The brew was then "put into [the] round kettle in [the] arch on East side of room," heated to boiling, and mixed with four hundred pounds of brown Havana sugar. This concoction was then put back into the wooden tub. Epsom salts and sal soda were added and dissolved.

After the mixture settled for two weeks, the Shakers poured it into hogsheads in the cellar and stirred in "1 gallon of Alcohol to every 9 gals. of Syrup." After standing for three months, the syrup was ready for sale.

This formula remained unchanged until 1880 when another ingredient was added. At the suggestion of "a chemist of Boston ... under the supervision of N. A. Briggs ...," fourteen gallons of Hydriodate Potassa (potassium in a water solution) were included in the recipe.[22]

It took the Canterbury Shakers approximately four months to make one hundred gallons of sarsaparilla syrup and four days to bottle and wrap twelve hundred bottles. The syrup was put in either nine-ounce bottles or in jugs. In 1885 the cost of labor and fuel for making 120 dozen bottles was figured to be $184.43, or thirteen cents apiece. The Shakers sold the bottles for $1 each retail or $48 a gross wholesale.[23]

The Shakers heavily advertised the syrup in their publications. In Canterbury's 1848 catalog, Corbett's Sarsaparilla received an entire page describing its many uses.

> This medicine has proved to be the most valuable in the following diseases: Chronic Inflammation of the digestive organs, Dyspepsia or indigestion, jaundice, Weakness and sourness of the Stomach, Rheumatism, Salt Rheum, Secondary Syphilis, Functional Disorders of the Liver, Chronic Eruptions of the skin, and all scrofulous diseases.

This catalog indicated that the medicine already had a wide distribution.

> [Corbett's Sarsaparilla] was for sale, wholesale and retail by E. Brinley & Co., General Agents; Henshaw, Ward & Co ... and by most of the Druggists in Boston, Cambridge, Charlestown, etc. .... Salem, New York, Providence, Lowell, New Orleans, Portsmouth, Newburyport, Haverhill, Dover, Manchester,

Brother David Parker (1807-1867) oversaw many industries at the Canterbury community and helped research the formula for the sarsaparilla syrup. In his capacity as trustee, he promoted the village's medicines by sending samples to exhibitions and publishing the endorsements of physicians in the World. (Collection of the Western Reserve Historical Society, Cleveland, Ohio)

Nashua, Concord, Franklin, Meredith, Enfield, Hanover, Orford, Keene, etc. And by Druggist and Country Dealers throughout the United States.

David Parker, as a Trustee, undertook the promotion of this medicine. He gave samples to the physicians of the World and published their endorsements. He also submitted bottles to various competitions. Both Corbett's Sarsaparilla and Enfield's Valerian medicines won a diploma from the Massachusetts Charitable Mechanics Association in 1847, and the following year, according to the *Shakers' Manual,* they were awarded medals and endorsed by the association.

> It comes sustained by the names of the most distinguished physicians in the country, and from a knowledge of its component parts, the Committee cannot but express their full belief as to its efficacious qualities.

Thirty years later the Shakers exhibited Corbett's Sarsaparilla at the Philadelphia Centennial. According to John Whitcher:

> Elder Henry and Benjamin go to Concord. Benjamin is having glass made in which to place some bottles of Sarsaparilla to be exhibited in the main building of Centennial Fame at Philadelphia during the year and on.

This endeavor was rewarded by the receipt of yet another medal. The following year Trustee Nathaniel A. Briggs won a diploma for the syrup from the forty-seventh exhibition of the American Institute. In 1880 an article about Canterbury's industry was published in the *Granite Monthly*:

> But if one branch of a number of industries can be selected for particular commendation, that relation to the growth and care of medicinal herbs, roots and barks, entitle the Shakers to universal praise and gratitude. Intimately acquainted with the precious properties of herbs and plants, they have been accustomed to find in them a balm for every wound. What the Indian has been supposed to be, the Shaker has been in reality—the custodian of nature's secrets, and to him more than to the medical profession is due the knowledge and prestige attained by most of our indigenous herbs, and roots and barks. Under these peculiarly fitted to be instructors, and later under Dr. Thomas Corbett . . . the preparations of medicine for general use by the public has been carried to the highest state of perfection. In fact for 50 years Dr. Corbett's Shaker's Sarsaparilla . . . has been and is the standard remedy with physicians, druggists, and the public, for impurities of the blood, general and nervous debility, and wasting diseases.[24]

In addition to promoting sarsaparilla in their herb catalogs and other publications, the Canterbury Shakers had their wholesalers advertise their products as well. These distributors published pamphlets which marketed not only the Shakers' preparations but also their own medications. Such publications included Edward Brinley's *Every-Day Book* and *Mary Whitcher's Shaker House-keeper*. Published by Weeks and Potter of Boston in 1882, the latter bore the name of a Canterbury Eldress. It contained culinary recipes, practical household information, and discussions on Shakerism. Issued primarily as a vehicle to advertise the various medicines distributed by Weeks and Potter, the pamphlet also devoted space to such non-Shaker items as Sanford's Radical Cure for Catarrh, Collins' Voltaic Electric Plaster, and Petrocarbol.

From 1851 through 1879 the Canterbury community also published the *Shakers' Manual,* a booklet intended to sell their medicines.

> The object . . . is to make known more extensively some of the most valuable Family Medicines compounded and prepared by the United Society of Shakers, and, more particularly, Corbett's Compound Concentrated Syrup of Sarsaparilla and Brown's Shaker Fluid Extract of English Valerian, which have been thoroughly tested by Physicians, Chemists and others, some of whose testimonials we insert without comment.

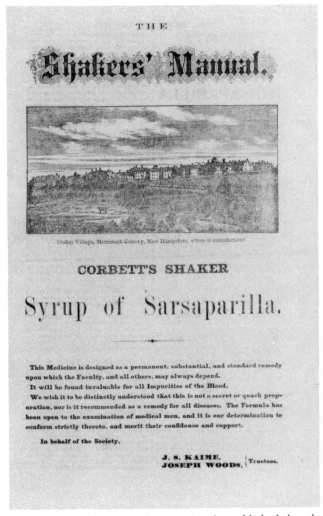

Front cover of The Shakers' Manual, *published by the Canterbury Shakers to promote their sarsaparilla and Enfield, New Hampshire's, Extract of English Valerian. (Collection of New Hampshire Historical Society, Concord, New Hampshire)*

The manual described the Shaker way of life, gave useful recipes, and was filled with endorsements from the medical community, satisfied customers, and members of other Shaker villages. Dealing with the ever-present problem of forgeries, the manual advised:

The genuine article is packed in bottles, with the words "Shaker Syrup, No. 1, Canterbury, N.H." cast thereon. To guard against counterfeits, observe the written signature of the Proprietor on the label, on the outside wrapper this signature: "Thomas Corbett."[25]

The New Hampshire Shakers aggressively marketed their medicines and became increasingly protective of them, changing distributors when they felt it necessary. In 1848 they sold the exclusive rights to sell Corbett's Sarsaparilla Syrup to E. Brinley & Co., of Boston. Later, Maynard and Noyes, also of Boston, took over the distribution; but, because of disappointing sales, Nicholas Briggs changed agencies in 1879. After consulting with the members at New Lebanon and Enfield, New Hampshire who agreed not to make a sarsaparilla syrup for the market, Briggs negotiated a five-year contract with Weeks & Potter and promised "to manufacture for them not less than 400 doz. bottles at $48 per gross." By 1885, when the contract expired, the Shakers took "the business of its sale back into their own hands and [dealt] directly with the apothecary and incidentally to the public." As the business grew and competition and fraud increased, the Shakers registered trademarks for some of their preparations, including Corbett's Sarsaparilla Lozenges (1885) and their Cherry Pectoral Syrup (1886).[26]

The records of sarsaparilla syrup sales from 1849 to 1880 show a steady increase in the business. The number of bottles recorded sold were: 551 in 1849, 400 dozen in 1854, 590 dozen and 20 gallons in jugs in 1864. In 1870 James Kaime reported that the Church Family had invested five thousand dollars in the patent medicine business. In the trade's four months of operation, the Family had paid two hundred dollars to hired hands for gathering 2,500 pounds of roots and herbs. At the time the enterprise was worth $2,250, one of the highest valued industries of the Church Family, preceded only by broommaking (valued at eight thousand dollars) and the manufacture of washing machines (valued at five thousand dollars). Other endeavors included the sale of flannel (worth one thousand dollars) and tubs (valued at six hundred dollars). In 1880 the community made nine hogsheads of syrup, and Corbett's Sarsaparilla was still listed in the *National Druggist*, indicating a wide usage. In 1880 Canterbury's Church Family reported that their income-producing ventures were washing machines, valued at $2,444; sarsaparilla, valued at two thousand dollars; socks, valued at $950; and brooms, valued at $795. The sarsaparilla business employed four men over age sixteen for ten hours a day, all year.[27] After 1880 the manufacture and sale of the medicines declined. By 1882 only five hundred gallons of sarsaparilla were made, and by 1890 only 120 gallons were produced. By 1894 there were only seven wholesale customers buying Canterbury's syrup. Although Corbett's sarsaparilla was mentioned in the 1902 *Druggist Circular and Chemical Gazette,* Canterbury's account book, which listed the last entries of sales by Maynard & Noyes, showed very little business:

1901   30 doz. [bottles] Sarsaparilla
1902   24 doz.
1905   24 doz., 2 qts.
1908   23 doz.
1910   6 doz.

In 1914 Sister Jessie Evans reported that the Elders were still trying to sell their syrup:

> [Elder Arthur Bruce] and Irving [Greenwood] go to Manchester in "Buick" in regard to setting a sale for Sarsaparilla; We are making arrangements with Walsh and Cummings of Manchester, NH to have the Sarsaparilla made and act as agents for it and pay us a certain percent of the net profits.

Five years later the two kettles were removed from the Syrup Shop, and in 1920 the still, tank, and sarsaparilla kettles on the west side of the north room were dismantled. Finally, the Syrup Shop was totally refitted for canning fruits and vegetables.[28]

Witch hazel was one of the last medicines that the Canterbury Church Family manufactured at the Syrup Shop. It first appeared in the *U.S. Pharmacopeia* in 1882, and in 1893 the Canterbury community was advertising it in their catalog. The Shakers claimed it to be

> a very useful remedy for cuts, Scalds, Headache, Sore Throat and all cases of external inflammation; also taken internally for Bowel Complaints, Bleeding of Lungs or Bowels and for all aches and pains.

It was made from fresh, young twigs of the small tree *Hamamelis virginiana,* which were "preferably gathered when the plant [was] in bloom in the late autumn." The Shakers distilled one gallon of *Hamamelis* with one pint of alcohol and sold the resulting mixture in jugs, barrels, and kegs. In 1889 Canterbury Shakers made 597 gallons of *Hamamelis* for the World and sixteen gallons for home use. Years later steam was introduced to the Syrup Shop to aid in the distilling process. Sales continued until 1917, outlasting the sarsaparilla trade.[29]

The medicine business at other villages was conducted in a similar manner to Canterbury's. For thirty years the A. J. White Company, a small, wholesale pharmaceutical business in New

This Enfield, New Hampshire, broadside advertises six Shaker medicines prepared under the supervision of Jerub Dyer. Dyer was the village's physician from 1824 until he left in 1852. (Collection of New York Historical Society, New-York, New York)

York, distributed and vigorously advertised New Lebanon's products. New Lebanon Shaker Benjamin Gates visited the company in 1875, gave White the Shaker formulas, and lent him money to expand. Gates also traveled to London to promote the Shaker products White distributed.[30] The A. J. White Company issued several booklets similar to the *Shakers' Manual*, including the *Shaker Almanac*, which was printed for nearly twenty years starting in the 1880s. Among its pages were testimonials for Shaker medicines, recipes, and practical household information. The texts in all the Shaker medicinal publications resembled one another, suggesting that frequent borrowing occurred.

Under the supervision of Jerub Dyer, the Church Family's physician, the community of Enfield, New Hampshire, also operated a successful medicinal business. As did Corbett, Dyer manufactured many products under his own name. Enfield's North Family had a profitable business with the manufacture and sale of Shaker Anodyne, made from valerian. The village's most successful preparation, however, was Brown's Shaker Pure Fluid Extract of English Valerian. This medicine was made by the Second Family from the root of the English valerian plant. Its market name was derived from the Second Family's physician, Samuel Brown, who oversaw its production.[31]

Previous to the manufacture of Brown's Extract, the medicinal properties of valerian, which were known since ancient times, were difficult to obtain in a usable form.

> We could not use [valerian] as often as we wished, because of the great bulk, both of powder and infusion, which it was necessary to throw into the stomach in order to get a full effect. Nausea and even vomiting resulted from the large doses. This compelled us to abandon its use.

Opium and morphine (a compound extracted from opium) were popular substitutes in the nineteenth century, but both had undesirable side effects. The Shakers grew poppies to obtain these drugs; Nicholas Briggs, who was raised at Canterbury, recalled his early training to maintain the kitchen garden which contained a poppy bed:

> A bed of poppies was being grown for opium and I was given the care of it. When the capsules were grown, I scarified them every morning, and in the afternoon scraped off the dried milk and gave it to the nurses.

Although Brown received little formal training as a physician, he was able to extract the essential oil of the valerian root and prepare a medicine that had the proper effect without the unpleasant secondary results.

> Several years ago Dr. Samuel Brown, a member of our Society, discovered a simple and novel process of extracting the pure and essential oil of the English Valerian Root (*Valeriana officinalis*) without destroying or injuring in the least any of the Nervine, or the medicinal properties of this invaluable Root.[32]

The Enfield Shakers claimed that Brown's medicine was

> the best remedy yet discovered for the cure of Nervousness, Lowness of Spirits, Debility, Hypochondria, Neuralgia, Hysteria, Restlessness, Tic Douloureux, Sick Headache, and every disease arising from mental affection and nervous exhaustion ... [and] an invaluable remedy for outward applications, in all cases of Cuts, Bruises, Sores, Sprains, Scalds, Burns, Lameness, Skin Diseases, and every affection requiring external treatment.[33]

The Second Family's original twenty-gallon formula required using only the fresh, green roots of the imported English valerian plant. The recipe specified dissolving eight ounces of oil of valerian in two gallons of alcohol. Two strong narcotics, four ounces of poppy extract, and one ounce of henbane extract were added to this mixture. With four gallons of burnt sugar, the rest of the concoction was water and nine gallons of alcohol. Several valerian recipes still exist; some omit the henbane extract; others include henbane and ginger but no poppy extract.

As Corbett had done, Dr. Brown sought endorsements from leading professionals in the World to help promote his new product.

> [Brown] sent a specimen of the "Extract" to some of the most distinguished Chemists, Geologists and Assayers in the Country, giving them the precise formula for its preparation. They all gave the "Extract" a thorough scientific examination and voluntarily gave their testimonials in its favor.[34]

With these endorsements, Brown set about to sell his medicine. It was advertised jointly with Canterbury's Sarsaparilla Syrup for twenty years and received several awards. Six years after the extract received its first medal, Brown died; but the medicine continued to be made and sold by the Second Family members, bringing in a substantial income of about $4,000 annually.

In the late 1870s the marketing of Brown's Valerian changed. In 1878 the preparation was no longer advertised jointly with

The distillery at the Enfield, New Hampshire Shaker community was where the Shakers made, among other things, Brown's Fluid Extract of English Valerian. (Collection of New Hampshire Historical Society, Concord, New Hampshire)

Canterbury's sarsaparilla syrup, and it was not mentioned in the *Shakers' Manual* issued the same year. By then the medicine was being promoted by Enfield's twenty-four-page booklet, "Facts Concerning Brown's Shaker Pure Fluid Extract of English Valerian." In 1879 the Church Family members took over the business as they had done years earlier with the North Family's Shaker Anodyne. The Shakers reported that the annual sale had "gradually increased from a few dozen bottles to over 50,000." In 1918, however, the Church Family sold only $445 worth of valerian and was still receiving royalties on their Shaker Anodyne.[35]

In spite of aggressive marketing techniques, the medicinal herb businesses at all of the Shaker communities were failing by the 1890s. The Shakers could not compete with the World's colorful advertising, and their declining and aging membership restricted their ability to harvest great quantities of herbs and carry on a large-scale business. Tightening governmental regulations also contributed to the problem. With the enactment of the Pure Food and Drug Act in 1906, manufacturers were forced to state on their labels the percentage of alcohol and other addictive ingredients their products contained. Many of the "miracle" cures of the day had to be adjusted or abandoned, and the Shakers' medicines were no exception. New Lebanon Shakers were forced to record that their Tincture of Veratrum Viride was seventy-five percent alcohol. They also had to attach a "Poison" label to each bottle indicating the potential danger of the primary ingredient, False Hellebore.[36]

While the Shakers' large-scale herb business declined, the members continued to grow and sell herbs in limited amounts. The Family that experienced profitable sales was ensured survival at a time when many villages were closing. In the 1880s Canterbury Trustee Nicholas Briggs approached the Church Family about having the failing North Family take over the sale of Corbett's Wild Cherry Pectoral Syrup. In spite of the fact that the trade would have helped salvage the North Family, the Church Family Elders decided to keep the medicine business to themselves. The North Family faltered and began closing in 1916, after which its remaining members moved to the Church Family. When Enfield was closing in the 1920s, the Canterbury Ministry looked seriously at forming a partnership with the A. Perley Fitch Company (which operated a drugstore in Concord) to continue selling Brown's Extract. This endeavor, however, apparently did not succeed.

As the Church Family's own medicinal business declined, the members put their herbs to other uses. Under the supervision of Deaconess Rebecca Hathaway, the members began selling herbal candies. She also maintained a large sage garden and raised catnip for making and selling toy mice.[37]

By 1971 the Sabbathday Lake Shakers revived their herb business and were offering for sale eighteen organically grown herbs, eleven herbal teas, and rose water. This new business, however, focused on the culinary, not medicinal, uses of herbs.[38]

Culinary Herbs

Beloved friends, while on our journey to this place we were comforted by some excellent cake, made at lovely Canterbury, and as we learn, expressly for us. Our comfort was not alone in the refreshment of this cake; but of that love so pure, so kind, so thoughtful, that led clean hands to prepare the cakes for us, and cleaner hearts to remember us in this our time of need. "Thank ye gude folk," for each and all, but especially for your love so pure, so refreshing, so good with which the cake was seasoned.[1]

While today the Shakers are known for their simple, wholesome cooking, it was not always the case. Over the past two hundred years, the Shakers followed dietary trends of the World, and some practices were healthier than others. Oddly enough, the issue of diet was at one time a controversial subject that caused great discord within the communities.[2]

When the Shakers first settled in America in the 1770s, the business of raising herbs could not have been farther from their minds. After establishing their village sites, they concentrated on clearing fields and building meetinghouses and dwellings. The raising of herbs for flavoring food was a luxury that neither their time nor their funds could afford. Between 1812 and 1820 the Shakers began selling herbs, but for medicinal purposes only.

At Canterbury the early industries revolved around their dairy and apple products. Elder Henry Blinn recorded that in 1801 the Shakers produced 2,222 pounds of cheese, 942 pounds of butter, and 100 barrels of cider. Ten years later they had expanded their farm products to include 5,835 pounds of beef and 5,616 pounds of pork. In 1815 they were also making applesauce.[3] The Canterbury Brethren did not start listing herbs for culinary use in their catalogs until 1847, six years after the practice began at New Lebanon.

Brother Joseph Joslin in a field at the Enfield Shaker community in New Hampshire. (Private collection)

During the first few decades of their settlement, the Shakers had no restrictions on their diet. Busy winning converts, raising buildings, and developing new trades, they had little income or time to be fussy about food. Rather, they subsisted on plain New England cooking: bean porridge, hash, minced meat, potatoes, bread, and, infrequently, milk, butter, and cheese. Food was flavored with either salt or pepper.

Following deep-rooted tradition, the Shakers also drank cider, tea, coffee, and alcohol, during and between their meals. Lightly fermented drinks were common throughout Europe and America in those times. Refrigeration methods had not yet been developed, and water sources were not always pure since many were used for mills and transportation. According to Blinn:

> It had been a universal custom for all who chose to do so, to take a glass of spirits every morning before breakfast ... and then more or less through the day as circumstances favored.[4]

"Cider wine," a mixture of aged distilled cider called "apple brandy" and fresh cider, was a popular drink at Canterbury.[5] Cider was the preferred beverage at many of the other villages as well. Working in the fields at Busro, Indiana, Benjamin Youngs reported in 1810:

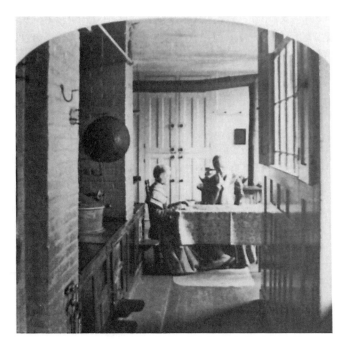

The culinary department at the Church Family, Enfield, New Hampshire. (Private collection)

We have planted a nursery—Plenty of Apples & cider by & by;
I could easily drink three egg cups full of good cider this
minute if I only had it . . . I am already so tired & sick of this
slimy water.[6]

About 1800 the Shakers began putting restrictions on their food and drink. That year the New Lebanon Ministry decided that liquor should be used for medicinal purposes only; but this recommendation was not put in writing, and it is doubtful that any other community followed it.[7] In 1821 the Shakers published their first written dietary regulations in the *Millennial Laws*—ordinances that were intended to guide all aspects of behavior. These injunctions, however, were mild; Believers were told they should not eat cucumbers unless the vegetables were seasoned with salt or pepper. Raw fruit and nuts were permitted only between breakfast and six o'clock in the evening. Intoxication was punishable by removal from the Family meeting until the guilty party had confessed and repented. No consumption of "ardent spirits" was allowed on Sunday except when there was heavy farm or kitchen work to be done. In such cases, drinking liquor was permitted only in the morning, and not before breakfast. At no time was a member allowed to drink an alcoholic beverage outside the community. An occasional glass of wine was tolerated only for medicinal purposes. If a person had a different diet, he or she was allowed to "freely go to the cooks" and have their food specially prepared.

In 1828 the New Lebanon physicians urged the "Death of Old Alcohol." At Canterbury the Shakers responded by reducing the Brothers' intake of cider to one-fourth of a pint at breakfast, one-half of a pint at dinner, and one quart throughout the day; Sisters were permitted smaller amounts at meals.[8] To discourage the manufacture of cider, the Brothers had many apple trees cut down, and they converted some orchard land into a garden.[9]

From 1820 to 1850 the Shakers became well known for their high-quality goods. As their lean and hungry years gave way to more prosperous times, their tables became groaning boards of beef, pork, lamb, gravies, heavy puddings, and pies. Red meat was served three times a day. Each meal was a bountiful event, described by Watervliet Shaker Ephraim Prentiss:

> breakfast: beef, pork, mutton, or fish, most generally fried with a plenty of grease, mostly hog's fat, with bread and potatoes— Next followed bread and butter and pies of various kinds from plain pumpkin to the high seasoned mince pie, cakes of

Apple picking at the Enfield Shaker community in New Hampshire. The Shakers grew a great variety of apples for many uses. Rose water was used as a complementary flavoring in the Shakers' apple dishes. (Collection of Dartmouth College Library, Hanover, New Hampshire)

different kinds, milk and butter, toasts and pancakes drenched
in butter—But these various articles were given at different
times for a change—Fish, clams, chicken, eggs, rich gravies,
honey, all in their turn, and according to the season.

dinner . . . the various kinds of animal food boiled, roasted,
baked or fried, with vegetables as usual with other varieties—
pickled cucumbers, peppers, rich applesauce, and various
other condiments &c.

supper . . . cold meat, bread, butter, cheese, milk and tea and
more or less of the above-mentioned articles as condiments
were brought on at every meal.[10]

This prodigious fare was common throughout America and
brought on a number of maladies including dyspepsia, the nation's
number one complaint. Temperance movements and dietary
trends swept the country. Always interested in the spiritual and
physical health of their members, some of the Shaker physicians,
such as Garret Lawrence of New Lebanon and Thomas Corbett of
Canterbury, began adopting these reforms. Harvard, New Lebanon,
and Canterbury were the first Shaker communities to adhere to the
practices of Sylvester Graham, a well-known nutritionist who
advocated eating whole-grain bread and vegetables and abstaining
from meat and stimulants. In 1835 Harvard community Believers
were trying out the new diet.[11] The next year Canterbury members
followed suit.

It was a vegetable diet and required the abstinence of condiments or stimulants. It was to be a great and radical change
for those who had been accustomed to meat and butter, more
or less, three times each day, and to tea and coffee and tobacco
to leave all these and live as simple as their formula now
stated. They were to have water to drink, were to abstain from
tobacco and were advised to take frequent or daily ablutions
in pure water.

The Ministry advocated the system especially for the young,
and believed it would be beneficial for health physically and
mentally.[12]

In 1841 the Lead Ministry issued formal recommendations
regarding the Graham diet, suggesting that Believers refrain from
eating pork, tea, and coffee. At Canterbury pork was removed from
the table, but red meat and fish were still allowed except on
Sundays. The consumption of more than one dairy product at a
meal was "uniformly avoided."[13]

Blinn reported that members were encouraged to drink herbal
and vegetable beverages. A tea made from Meadow Sweet, *Spiraea*

tomentosa, also known as Steeplebush or Hardhack, was suggested. Another recommended drink came from New Jersey Tea, or Liberty Tea, also known as Red Root, *Ceanothum americanus,* a plant that grew in dry woodlands. Blinn also recalled a beverage that consisted of "barley, peas, and roasted carrots, and the root of 'Avens,'" or Water Avens, *Geum rivale,* an herb that grew near the village ponds. When served with milk and sugar, the drink was said to taste like chocolate.[14]

A cookbook published by New Lebanon Shaker Frederick Evans, an avid Grahamite, described a very bland diet:

> Our breakfast usually consists of oatmeal or wheat mush, baked or broiled potatoes, tomatoes cooked with milk and bread crumbs, warm apple sauce and Graham [wholewheat crust] pie. Dinner [noon meal] is more varied. There are three kinds of vegetables, sometimes the addition of soup, plain fruit sauce, either pie, pudding, or other dessert. For supper we have boiled rice with sugar and cream, or mashed potato, tomato stew, apples baked, or in sauce, and preserves. We frequently have the addition of fresh creamed cottage cheese or crisp celery; the latter we think good for the nerves.[15]

It was during this period that the Shakers introduced herbs into their cooking. With such a dramatic change to their customary wide selection of foods, the Shakers probably wanted to add some flavor to what was no doubt perceived to be a tasteless and monotonous diet. They probably also wanted to cure such problems as dyspepsia. Even in the twentieth century, Eldress Bertha Lindsay, who rarely used herbs in her cooking, added summer savory to some of her recipes to make them more digestible (see her Baked Bean recipe).

As borne out in their catalogs, journals, and manuals, the nineteenth-century Shakers sold only a small number of herbs for culinary use: sweet marjoram, sage, summer savory, thyme, and, occasionally, horseradish. These were listed in their catalogs as "sweet herbs" and were sold in canisters as opposed to the medicinal herbs, which were pressed into "bricks" and wrapped in paper packages. Eight villages sold culinary herbs; the New Lebanon community took the lead in 1841; followed by Watervliet in 1843; Harvard in 1845; Canterbury and Union Village in 1847; Enfield, Connecticut, in 1854; Enfield, New Hampshire, in the 1860s; and Sabbathday Lake in 1864. From 1854 to 1873 Harvard also sold horseradish as a "sweet herb"; in later catalogs, however, it was dropped from their culinary list.

The Shakers sold a great number of other herbs that we use for cooking today, but they considered them as medicines. Believers used parsley, for example, to cure a variety of ills. They reccommended the root to treat dropsy, retention of urine, strangury, and gonorrhea; the leaves to cure insect stings and bites; and the seeds to kill lice. Sweet basil was said to stop excessive vomiting, and rosemary was made into a tea for colds, colic, and nervous condition.[16]

The Shakers were always flexible when it came to regulating what their members could eat or drink, and the Graham diet was no exception. While the younger Shakers had to follow the recommendations strictly, the older members had the choice of staying with their former ways or adhering to the new system.[17] Despite the ban on beef and pork, many Shakers continued to eat meat. Canterbury records indicate that between about 1811 and 1848 nearly six thousand pounds of pork were slaughtered each year. While some of this meat was sold, it was also consumed at the village. In 1848, however, when the Lead Ministry distributed another ban, the Canterbury Shakers totally prohibited the consumption and sale of pork. This edict permitted drinking tea and coffee only in special cases and dismissed alcoholic beverages altogether.[18]

In an effort to compromise on their diet, the Shakers failed to satisfy most of their members. The restrictions displeased the vegetarians, who felt that the regulations were not strict enough; meat eaters missed their traditional dishes; and cooks complained of having to prepare special dishes for too many people.[19]

In the second half of the nineteenth century, many of the reforms started to erode. Members began drinking cider in 1850 and tea and coffee by about 1861.[20] They also began eating beef and pork again, and cooks were flavoring food with cane and maple sugar, honey, spices, and rose water.

During this time, Shaker cooks continued to collect recipes and culinary ideas from the World and adapt them for community use. In the 1857-1886 cookbook of Canterbury Sisters Lavinia Clifford and Sarah S. Woods, some recipes originated from other communities, but the majority came from publications such as: *The Medical and Surgical Journal, The Saturday Evening Post, The New England Economical Housekeeper and Family Receipt Book* (1847), and *The Young Housekeeper's Friend* (1859). Sally Ceeley of Enfield, New Hampshire, cited publications such as *Ladies Home Journal* and *Scientific American* in her late nineteenth-century cookbook.[21]

In 1882 the Canterbury Shakers published *Mary Whitcher's Shaker House-Keeper*. The purpose of this book was to promote the medicines distributed by their agent, Weeks and Potter of Concord, who sold Corbett's Sarsaparilla Syrup. The cookbook contained not only recipes and household hints, but also advertise-

After decades of chemically-treated produce and "instant" foods adulterated with preservatives, there is today a rising interest in natural foods and sound nutrition. Health stores abound, and more cooks are showing an interest in basic cooking methods and exploring the joys of preparing healthful food from fresh, uncontaminated ingredients.

MaryWhitcher's Shaker House-Keeper

was originally published in Boston in 1882, the earliest cookbook in Shaker culinary literature, and the first

Mary Whitcher's Shaker House-Keeper was published in Boston in 1882 by the Canterbury Shakers' agent Weeks and Potter. In addition to advertisements that promoted herbal medicines, it contained culinary recipes and was the earliest Shaker cookbook. (Private collection)

ments endorsing many of the agent's products. On the cover was a picture of Mary Whitcher, an Eldress who oversaw the New Hampshire Bishopric from 1859 to 1865. Her parents donated the land that had become the site of the Canterbury Church Family. By having her name on the cover page, she was showing her approval of the products in the book in the same way that Corbett endorsed the Shakers' medicines.

The late nineteenth- and twentieth-century culinary style of the Believers can be seen in this book. Plain, simple dishes were given with a text that emphasized the nutritional value of food. A good, healthful dinner was considered to consist of soup, a red meat dish, potatoes, and pudding. Two preparations, Shaker Fish and Egg and Shaker Brown Bread, probably originated at Canterbury. Many others were contributed by married women in the World. These recipes, and ones with such titles as Saratoga Fried Potatoes, Virginia Pudding, Penobscot Stew, New York Gingerbread, Union Cake, and Cape Ann Pudding, prove that the World had a strong influence on the Shakers. A few herbs were occasionally added:

parsley, sage, mustard, and cayenne. Flavorings such as salt, pepper, sugar, molasses, cloves, nutmeg, ginger, and sometimes allspice and mace, were listed more often. Extracts of lemon, almond, and vanilla, as well as currants, raisins, citron, celery, and onion juice, were also included.

This culinary tradition continued into the twentieth century, although herbs were more frequently used in these recipes. As the medicinal herb business declined, the Shakers put their plants to other uses. The Sisters began selling herbal candies made from horehound, lovage, and sweet flag. At haying time, cool herbal drinks were brought around to the hired hands.

> One man was continuously employed with horse and wagon in carrying drink to the laborers. Three times each half day did he come with lemon, peppermint, checkerberry, raspberry and currant shrub . . .[22]

In the 1950s Kitchen Deaconess Rebecca Hathaway at Canterbury maintained a large garden of sage so that she could sell the herb to local customers. Twenty years later the Sabbathday Lake community revived their herb business; in 1971 they offered eighteen organically grown herbs for sale.[23]

In the twentieth century the sale of food products was an important source of income for the Shakers. When guests dined at the villages, it was crucial that the meals be prepared with care. Sisters were encouraged to experiment with dishes and make them look festive. As did their Sisters of the 1800s, the cooks and bakers collected favorite recipes from newspapers and magazines.

Serving beautifully prepared dishes was a source of self-esteem for many of the Sisters. As in any other apprenticeship, it took several years to become a master. Girls were taught simple tasks, such as boiling potatoes, when they first came to the village. As they proved their skills, they were given more difficult duties such as making pies or baking bread. Sometimes the Sisters were formally recognized for their successes. In her autobiography, Eldress Bertha Lindsay proudly related stories about her first casserole, her award-winning lemon meringue pie, and her role as head cook at the Trustees' Office.[24] Because the best produce and dishes were served at the Trustees' Office, where the guests dined, this responsibility was the highest honor for a Sister who prided herself on her cooking.

Up until 1988 Eldress Bertha Lindsay, trained from childhood as a cook, prepared daily meals that showed the heavy influence of Mary Whitcher's culinary style at Canterbury. Having served as head cook at the Trustees' Office for more than forty years, Eldress Bertha believed that cooking was an art to be valued as highly as

Dining Room of the Enfield, New Hampshire Stone Dwelling House. (Private collection)

furniture making and other trades. She was proud that her meals were not only delicious and nourishing, but also "eye-appealing," with foods of different colors and textures served together. Following years of tradition, she cooked from recipes that were passed down to her from older Sisters. She also referred to cookbooks from the World and adapted them for communal use.

Even in the twentieth century, the Canterbury Shakers never used many herbs in their cooking; in fact, some of the remaining Sisters confessed a dislike for herbs.[25] About 1950 the Shaker culinary style took another turn. The physician treating Eldress Bertha Lindsay advised her to reduce her intake of animal fats and salt, an idea that harks back to the Grahamite innovations from the previous century.

The study of Shaker cooking becomes even more difficult when we understand that Eldress Bertha Lindsay also saved "Shaker" recipes published in modern cookbooks of the World and adapted these for the village.

At Sabbathday Lake Sister Frances Carr, who has been Kitchen Deaconess for forty years, provides mid-day meals that follow the nineteenth-century tradition. In *Shaker Your Plate*, published in 1985, she described her cooking as "plain" and "wholesome." As the Sisters before her, she was given recipes that were handed down from older cooks. She also learned to "experiment and develop her own style of cooking."[26] Her dinners offer abundant servings of meat and potatoes, one or two kinds of bread, two or three vegetables, relishes, jellies, dessert, and hot tea. Her vegetables are grown in the garden at Sabbathday Lake; the root vegetables are stored in the cellar over the winter. Although there was "very little herb cooking" at the village when she was a child, her food today is well seasoned with herbs. Her book lists twenty-one herbs for cooking.[27]

The subject of food was an integral part of the Shakers' lives. It held much interest to all ranks, as opposed to spiritual or worldly matters, which were the responsibility of Ministers and Deacons. Food was not only a source of nourishment; it was also a main source of income for the Shakers, and it served as a form of recreation. Picnics were enjoyed by both children and adults. Fishing, and harvesting nuts, berries, and apples were pleasant seasonal activities experienced by many Believers, not only in the nineteenth century, but in the twentieth century as well. Eldress Bertha remembered large gatherings for picnics at the Ice Mill Pond, holiday dinners in the abandoned Cow Barn, popcorn parties in the Laundry, and taffy pulls in the Syrup Shop. She also recalled joyous times harvesting apples and learning how to bake with other young women.

The following recipes were selected not because they are typical of the Shakers' cooking over the past two hundred years but because they do contain herbs. Few Shaker recipes dating from the nineteenth century list herbs as ingredients. The following recipes appear in their original wording and spelling.

Condiments

The following recipe came from a handwritten book that belonged to Canterbury Sisters Lavinia Clifford and Sarah Woods. Lavinia Clifford was a member of the Church Family and died in 1857 at age twenty-nine. Sarah Woods, born in 1821, was a member of the Church Family by 1886. The front section of the book has several printed recipes from many sources pasted in it. Many of the recipes originated from the World; others came from Canterbury. This particular recipe was found in a newspaper clipping attached to the book's front pages:

To Keep Horseradish

If you want to keep horseradish, grate a quantity while the

root is in perfection, put it in bottles, fill the bottles with strong vinegar, and keep it corked tightly. You may thus have a supply at all seasons.[28]

This recipe came from Canterbury in 1879:

Tomato Catchup

Cut tomatoes in pieces, and between every layer, sprinkle a thin layer of salt; let them stand a few hours, then add a little horseradish, garlic, pepper, and mace; boil well and strain, then bottle, cork, and seal for use[29]

The next two recipes came from *Mary Whitcher's Shaker House-Keeper:*

Piccalilli

A peck of tomatoes should be sliced and sprinkled with a handful of salt. They should stand over night and in the morning, all the liquor should be turned off. Then chop them together with a cabbage-head, 7 onions, and 4 green peppers. Mix with this mass half a pint of whole mustard, half a teacupful of fine sugar, half a teacupful of horseradish, and vinegar enough to cover the whole. Stew until soft.

Spiced Vinegar for Pickles

Take 2 ounces of bruised black pepper, one ounce of bruised ginger, one-half ounce of bruised allspice, and one ounce salt. If a hotter pickle is desired, add one-half drachm of cayenne. Put these in one quart of vinegar, simmer gently in the enameled saucepan until extracted, and pour on the pickles or other vegetables.

The Shakers also used rose hips to flavor foods. The rose hip, the seed pod of the rose, is rich in vitamin C. It is formed after the rose blossoms and is collected in the early fall. Rose hips are cooked lightly before added to recipes. Use fresh rose hips since dried rose hips tend to lose their vitamin C content. A rose hip puree can be made and stored and added to recipes throughout the year. To do this, trim both ends of each rose hip with a pair of scissors; cook them quickly for about twenty minutes in a covered glass, stainless steel, or enamel container (two pounds of rose hips to two pints of water); and then mash them to a pulp with a food mill or through a sieve and strain.

Rose hips may also be preserved as an extract for future use. To make an extract, first chill the hips to inactivate the enzymes that might otherwise cause a loss of vitamin C. Simmer one cup of

Sister Rebecca Hathaway (1872-1958), canning in the Canterbury Syrup Shop. The Syrup Shop, long used to produce Corbett's Sarsaparilla Syrup, was converted in 1919 to a canning kitchen. In this building Sister Rebecca, as Kitchen Deaconess, supervised many of the culinary duties, including the manufacture of confections for sale and the canning of the garden harvest. (Private collection)

previously prepared rose hips in one and a half cups of water for fifteen minutes. Let this mixture stand in a pottery container for twenty-four hours and then strain. Boil the extract, add two table-spoons of lemon juice for each pint, and pour into jars and seal.[30]

Eldress Bertha Lindsay used this recipe:

Rose Hip Jam

Take the fruit of the Sweetbriar wild rose or *Rosa rubiginosa*, also known as *Rosa eglantera*. Wash hips, remove stiff hairs, stems, and calyx. Split open, remove seeds. For each cup of fruit make a syrup of 1 1/2 cups sugar and 1 cup water. Boil 4 min., add fruit and 2 tbsp. lemon juice. Cover, boil 20 min. If fruit is not clear cook uncovered until clear and thick.[31]

Soups

This recipe is a rare one because it contains several herbs, including sorrel, a plant that has acid-flavored leaves and is sometimes used in salads today.

Tomato Soup

Take a saucepan; Put in it 3 Tablespoons of Butter, 4 Onions, 4 Carrots, 1/2 lb. of Ham, a little Sorrel, Parsley, & Sage; Throw all this into the Saucepan—let it hang over, or on a quick fire— then throw in a handful of flour in it, let this cook again. After this throw in as many canned or fresh tomatoes as you wish Soup for; & then a very little Cayenne pepper and powdered sugar. Let all of this cook two hours with frequent stirring. When cooked, see what is wanting, pepper or sugar according to the taste of the people.[32]

Salads and Dressings

Potato Salad

Slice thin six or eight medium-sized boiled potatoes; mince fine two sliver-skin onions, so as to get the flavor and not detect the onions in pieces; mix parsley and the potatoes with the onions, and season with salt and cayenne pepper. Moisten one-third of a teaspoonful of dry mustard with a teaspoonful of hot water; put the yolks of two eggs in same dish, beat together with an egg-beater until well mixed, then drip in a sweet oil, beating it all the time until it thickens like a custard, add one and a half teaspoonfuls of vinegar. Put this dressing over the potatoes and mix all together. The dish can be garnished with celery tops and made very pretty.[33]

The following recipe came from Sister Frances A. Carr and includes herbs sold at Sabbathday Lake:

Shelled Bean Salad

3 small green onions
Shelled beans or string beans
Cheesecloth bag consisting of:
1/8 teaspoon Shaker Thyme
1/8 teaspoon Shaker Sage
1/3 small onion
1/3 bay leaf

French dressing
2 teaspoons chives
2 teaspoons Shaker Chervil
2 teaspoons Shaker Parsley

When you cook the beans add the cheesecloth bag of herbs to the pot. When the beans are done, discard the cheesecloth bag and drain the beans. While the beans are still warm, pour over dressing, onions, and herbs. Allow to cool and serve on lettuce.[34]

The following recipe, taken from a modern cookbook, was a favorite of Eldress Bertha Lindsay:

Tarragon Dressing

$^2/_3$ cup sugar
1 $^1/_2$ cup salad oil
1 cup lemon juice (or $^1/_4$ cup lemon juice and
   $^1/_2$ cup tarragon vinegar, mixed)
1 teaspoon Worcestershire sauce
1 teaspoon dry mustard
1 teaspoon salt
2 tablespoons catsup (homemade if possible)
2 whole cloves
A little grated onion (or 1 teaspoon chives,
   chopped)
1 tablespoon tarragon leaves, chopped

Mix all ingredients in order given. Beat well for 2 minutes. Put in bottle and refrigerate. Should stand overnight. Shake well before using. May be strained before using. Makes 2 $^1/_2$ cups.[35]

Meats and Fish

Of all the culinary herbs that the Shakers sold, sage was probably used the most. The Shakers added it to stuffings for turkey and chicken and flavored various meat dishes with it.

Parsley and mint were favorites for sauces for meats and fish. To make a Shaker mint sauce, which was served by the Shakers with lamb, clean and chop mint leaves and mix with sugar, vinegar, and water. Chill before use. To make a parsley sauce, which was used with fish or poultry, boil stalks of parsley for five minutes in salted water. Drain and cut the leaves from the stalks. Chop the parsley leaves and sauté them in melted butter (a tablespoon of parsley to eight tablespoons of melted butter).

The following recipe came from the Tyringham community and probably dates from about 1850 to 1895. In many nineteenth-century recipes, the mixing instructions were omitted, a practice followed through the twentieth century.

Sausage

For 40 pounds of meat, [add] 1 pound salt, 3 ounces of pepper, 1/3 pint sage, pulverized, [and] 1 cup molasses.[36]

Another version of this recipe also came from Tyringham:

Sausage

To 40 pounds of meat chopped fine add one pound of salt, quarter pound of pepper the same of sage if you like.[37]

Savory Meat

Take cold beef or veal and mince it fine; put an onion in, cut up fine, [add] some sweet marjoram, and a little powdered cloves and moisten it up with beef gravy. Make it into balls; put the yolk of an egg over them and flour them and fry in good sweet lard. This is a good side dish.[38]

This recipe came from *Mary Whitcher's Shaker House-Keeper:*

Baked Fish, Tomato Sauce

Take a fish weighing from four to six pounds. Scrape and wash clean and season well with salt. Make a dressing with five small crackers, rolled fine, one tablespoonful of butter, one teaspoonful of salt, a little pepper, half a tablespoonful of chopped parsley, and water enough to make very moist. Stuff the fish with this preparation, which fasten in with a skewer. Cut slits in the fish and put small strips of salt port into them. Place the fish on a sheet in a baking-pan, and dredge well with flour. Bake one hour, basting often. Serve with a tomato sauce poured around it.

Tomato Sauce: one pint of stewed tomato, one tablespoonful of butter, one of flour, four cloves, a tiny bit of onion. Cook the tomato, clove, and onion together ten minutes. Heat the butter in a small pan and stir the flour into it. Cook, stirring all the time, until smooth and a light brown; then stir into the tomato. Cook two or three minutes longer. Season with salt and pepper and strain.

Vegetables

This recipe came from Eldress Bertha Lindsay, who usually flavored dishes with only salt and pepper, but in recent years, added summer savory to make the beans more digestible.

Baked Beans

2 cups pea beans (or any kind of bean)
2 teaspoons salt
1/4 teaspoon pepper
1 teaspoon baking soda

1 teaspoon (scant) summer savory, dried
2 tablespoons molasses (not black strap)
$^1/_4$ cup maple syrup
1 whole onion, small
1 stick of margarine

Put the beans in a pot to soak overnight in cold water. The next morning, heat to parboiling. Then take them off and drain the beans. In a pot, put salt, pepper, soda, summer savory, molasses, maple syrup, and the whole onion. Add the beans. Pour fresh boiling water over them, a little more than just to cover them. Put the beans into the oven and bake at 225 degrees for six hours. When you take them out, remove the onion and add the stick of margarine.[39]

Sister Frances Carr also used summer savory in this modern recipe for green beans.

Savory Green Beans

1 package frozen green beans [or 1 lb. fresh beans]
1 tablespoon butter or margarine, melted and
  slightly browned
$^1/_2$ teaspoon Shaker savory
Pinch of salt
Pinch of pepper
1 teaspoon lemon juice

Cook the beans as directed on the package.. Add the remaining ingredients together. Pour over the hot beans and toss lightly. Serve at once. Serves 3 to 4.[40]

This recipe is said to have come from the Hancock community in the nineteenth century:

Stewed Beets

Boil them first, & then scrape & slice them. Put them in a stew pan with a piece of butter, rolled in flour, some boiled onions & parsley chopped fine, a little vinegar, salt & pepper. Set the pan on hot coals and let the beets stew for a quarter of an hour.[41]

This recipe came from the Canterbury Sisters Lavinia Clifford and Sarah Woods:

Potato Cakes

Mash your potatoes and mix them with chopped onion, salt, pepper, and herbs. Shape them into balls and dip them in beaten egg, then into bread crumbs. Fry them in hot lard.[42]

Desserts

The Shakers started producing rose water about 1809, but they used it mainly for medicinal purposes. The manufacture of rose

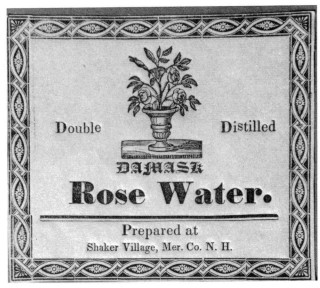

Rose Water label from the Canterbury community. The Shakers double distilled, and sometimes triple distilled, their fragrant waters. (Private collection)

water, made from crushed and distilled rose petals, follows a tradition that can be traced back several centuries. In the early 1900s the Shakers occasionally used rose water water for puddings and cakes. One recipe entitled "Pound Cake," from Hancock, called for cinnamon, mace, nutmeg, brandy, and rose water, with a pound each of butter, eggs (ten), flour (wheat or rice), and sugar. In the twentieth century the Shakers used this flavoring in pies and ice cream.[43]

The following recipe was passed down to Eldress Bertha Lindsay from her older Sisters and was one of her favorites:

Rose Water Apple Pie

1 2-layer pie crust, 9", unbaked
5-7 tart apples (7, if small)
$^1/_2$ cup sugar
Dash salt
1 tablespoon rose water, diluted in
    2 tablespoons water
Dash nutmeg
1 tablespoon cornstarch
2 teaspoons margarine

Mix ingredients. [Today's cook may want to use more sugar

(³/₄ cup) and less rose water (¹/₂ teaspoon to 1 tablespoon)]. Add to pie shell and cover with crust. Cook at 425 degrees 5-10 minutes. Turn oven to 350 degrees and cook 45 minutes.[44]

Rose Water Frosting

4 cups confectioner's sugar, sifted
¹/₄ cup light cream
1 tablespoon rose water

In a medium bowl, combine all the ingredients. Stir until smooth. Spread over cake, cupcakes, or cookies.[45]

According to Sister Frances Carr, the frosting mentioned above is excellent with the following cake. This recipe is said to be an old one that was a specialty of Eldress Prudence Stickney, a Sabbathday Lake Sister who died in the twentieth century.

Mother Ann's Birthday Cake

1 cup butter or margarine
2 cups sugar
3 cups flour
¹/₂ cup cornstarch
3 teaspoons baking powder
1 cup milk
2 teaspoons rose water
12 egg whites, beaten
1 teaspoon salt

Beat butter and sugar into a smooth cream. Sift flour with cornstarch and baking powder. Add flour mixture in small amounts alternately with milk to butter mixture. Beat after each addition. Add rose water. Beat egg whites with the salt. Beat until stiff and lightly fold into the flour mixture. Bake in three 8" cake tins at 350 degrees for 25 minutes.

When cool, fill between the layers with peach jelly and cover the cake with a white icing flavored with rose water.[46]

Beverages

Drinking hot tea was an easy way for the Shakers to ingest the medicinal qualities of many herbs. Most teas are made by either infusion or decoction. The more popular method is by infusion, in which boiling water is poured over the herb and steeped for at least five minutes. The second method is made by bringing both the herb and water to a boil, then reducing it to a simmer for ten to twenty minutes. Some leaves and most herb barks and seeds require decoction with the roots or seeds bruised lightly with a mortar and pestle before simmering.

For many years the Shakers used herbs, such as chicory, sage, balm, dandelion, and different kinds of mint, as substitutes for imported teas and coffees. Herbal teas are wonderfully aromatic and flavorful and can be made from a variety of plants such as spearmint, peppermint, balm, rose geranium, sage, rosemary, bergamot, chamomile, and rose hips. Blends such as rosemary and lavender, pineapple mint and bee balm, marjoram and mint are also fun to try.

To ensure a winter supply, harvest fresh leaves, dry, and store them whole in tightly capped containers. When ready to make a tea, crush the whole leaves. Use one heaping teaspoon for each cup of tea steeped in boiling water for at least five minutes. (Spring water is better and more flavorful for herbal teas.) Do not use metal containers when making teas.

The following is a summer drink used by Eldress Bertha Lindsay:

Herbade

2 cups water
4 tea bags
1 cup mint leaves
1 cup lemon balm leaves
1 cup borage leaves
Juice of 6 lemons
Juice of 4 oranges
5 12-ounce cans ginger ale
1 quart white grape juice

Boil the water. Remove it from the heat, pour it over the herbs and tea, and steep for 1 hour. Add the remaining ingredients. Chill.[47]

This drink was also used by Eldress Bertha Lindsay:

Herb Tea

Add one teaspoon of the following dried herb mix to one cup of boiling water and sweeten with honey.

1 cup mint (not apple)
$1/3$ cup goldenrod leaves (*Solidago odora*)
1 cup borage leaves
1 cup lemon balm[48]

This recipe comes from Sabbathday Lake about 1863:

Rye Coffee

First wash the rye, then boil it until it begins to crack. Drain and dry it in an oven. Brown it as you would other coffee. Grind and when making the coffee clarify with an egg in the usual way. Put in plenty of cream and loaf sugar and it goes very well.[49]

The Shakers in the nineteenth and twentieth centuries experimented with many plants, including sassafras, checkerberry, and spruce, to make refreshing cold drinks.

Currant Shrub

1 lb. currant juice
1/2 lb. sugar
Scald and skim till clear, cool and bottle tight and set away in a cool place.[50]

Rhubarb was sold only by the New Lebanon, New York, and Union Village, Ohio, Shakers. They originally sold it not as a culinary herb, but as a cathartic. The following, however, may be enjoyed today as a cold, refreshing drink.

Rhubarb Sherbet [Shrub]

Boil 6 or 8 stalks of rhubarb ten minutes in a quart of water. Strain the liquor through a tami [cheesecloth] into a jug, with the peel of a lemon cut very thin, and two tablespoonfuls of clarified sugar, let it stand about 5 or 6 hours, and it is fit to drink.[51]

Although the Shakers experienced many years when alcohol was prohibited as a beverage, there were periods when drinking "spirits" was permitted. During those times, the members made a great variety of wines and beers.

Ginger Beer

To one gallon water, put 1 lb. loaf sugar, 1 oz. ginger, 1 oz. cream Tarter; and juice of two lemons with the peel grated into it. Boil it and when cold, add a little yeast; and after standing 12 hours bottle for use.[52]

Spring Beer

For a barrel of 40 gallons, take a 1/2 pint of each of the following:

Princes Pine, Sweet fern, Sarsaparilla Root, Life everlasting, White pine bark, Black Birch bark, Scabish, Feverbush and wintergreen. Then 1/4 lb. of ginger root and hops. To this add 4 gallons of molasses made about as warm as new milk. Add the yeast and place it in an open vessel to ferment, say 6 or 8 hours, then remove the scum and put into a tight cask.[53]

Candy

Peppermint Drops

One pint of granulated sugar, six tablespoonfuls of water, boil five minutes well, take from the fire and add one tablespoonful of granulated sugar fifteen drops of oil of peppermint and one sixth of a teaspoonful of cream of tartar; stir two minutes and drop on tins. Do not butter your tins. If it hardens before it can be dropped, add a very little hot water.

Laura F. K.
Taken from the Household.[54]

The following recipe is from Canterbury and was passed on down to Eldress Bertha Lindsay, who believed that it was two hundred years old. The North Union Shakers had a recipe similar to it. The candy is well worth trying. A candy mold is useful here.

Horehound Candy

3 cups boiling water
3 ounces horehound leaves
6 cups dark brown sugar
1 teaspoon cream of tartar
1 teaspoon butter
1 teaspoon lemon juice

Steep leaves 20 minutes and strain. Add sugar, cream of tartar, and butter. Cook to hard ball stage and add lemon juice. Pour into buttered pan and cut when nearly hard. (Candymakers use oil of marrumbium for flavoring instead of the leaves. This oil is prepared from the plant and is available. It takes but little oil; too much will make the candy bitter.)[55]

10

Domestic Uses of Herbs

M any of the plants that the Shakers grew were used not only for medicinal and culinary purposes, but also for cosmetics, dyes, and other household uses.

The rose, grown originally for its medicinal properties, was also mentioned in many Shaker domestic recipes. The type that the Believers cultivated is known today as the old garden or shrub rose, a species that had gained great popularity from about 1810 to 1830. While old garden roses (a term referring to any rose that existed before the hybrid tea roses were developed in 1867) bloom only once a year, they possess a nostalgic charm and an unmatched fragrance. They come in a variety of colors and forms and are easily maintained landscape shrubs.

Of the approximately seventy-six species that existed in 1820, the Shakers grew and sold only four descendants of the *Rosa gallica:* the damask rose, the red rose, the white rose, and the cabbage rose.[1] The damask rose, or *Rosa damascena,* is said to have come originally from Damascus with the returning Crusaders. It is a graceful, medium to large shrub, growing about three feet high and flowering in many colors from white to deep red. It blooms once a year, and is disease-resistant and hardy. While used medicinally as a mild astringent, as well as a flavoring in foods, it is best known as an aromatic. Historically, this plant was the source of the very best attar of roses (the most fragrant oil). Because of its sweet-smelling petals, it is frequently added to potpourris.

The red rose, also known as the apothecary's rose of Provins, or *Rosa gallica officinalis*, is a stocky bush, two to three feet high. This rose was the Shakers' favorite, and its petals were sold at six of their communities: Watervliet, New Lebanon, Canterbury, Harvard, Union Village, and Sabbathday Lake. The members used it extensively for rose water; they preferred it for its tonic and mildly astringent medicinal properties. This plant is an excellent garden rose, for it has dark green leaves (unlike the more gray color of the foliage of the other three types) and few thorns. The shrub thrives on little attention and poor soil and can be clipped into a hedge. It comes in a wide range of colors from pale pink to dark maroon.

The white rose, or *Rosa alba*, cultivated since Roman times, is a tall, dense, and disease-resistant plant having fragrant, medium-sized flowers in white clusters that are sometimes tinged with pink. The plants have an upright growth habit, good foliage, and are vigorous and long-lived.

The cabbage rose, Provence rose, or *Rosa centifolia*, first appeared in the eighteenth century and was grown by the Union Village, Ohio Shakers. This plant is less orderly than the other three, for it has a drooping habit that sometimes necessitates staking. Its rich scent and pale, dense blossoms, however, make it worth growing. Overall, the plant is graceful with its drooping stems, leaves, and flowers.

All four shrub roses bloom in June. They usually grow from four to six feet tall and four to six feet wide at maturity. While they finish blooming by the middle of July, a bed of shrub roses can be interplanted to mask their less attractive late summer foliage. Foxgloves, delphiniums, lilies, hostas, or santolina are possibilities for this interplanting.

To establish a new bed of roses, it is easier to begin with budded two-year-old field-grown plants. If the bushes are placed in a cool exposure, their blossoms will develop more slowly; however, eight hours of sunlight are recommended. If the plants are provided with good sunlight, humus, water and air drainage, they require little care. Soil should have a pH factor of five or six. Spade the soil deeply, about two feet, and mulch to keep the roots cool.

Shrub roses should be pruned in their second year, immediately after they bloom. When the plant becomes established, it generally produces long, strong shoots near the base in the spring. From these grow side shoots of up to one foot in length which bear the best flowers. After three or four years, one of the two older branches at the base should be removed. Winter pruning to shorten the long stems by one third is also often advisable.

When harvesting the flowers, the pale-colored roses may be picked in bud and allowed to open in water indoors. Others need to develop their deeper tones on the plant and should be picked in full bloom. The blossoms should be picked in the early morning or the evening. If the flowers are meant for a bouquet, it is recommended that the stems be pounded with a hammer to make the blossoms last longer.[2]

In addition to potpourris and sachets, fresh roses have many uses. Eldress Bertha Lindsay, who came to the Canterbury community in 1905, remembered waxing them for gifts by dipping a whole branch in warm wax.[3] The Shakers also made rose oil, distilled from the new petals, a process still popular in the manufacture of perfumes. The soothing therapeutic properties of rose oil are also sought for lotions and fragrant waters. Rose water, a diluted form of the oil, is used for medicinal as well as culinary purposes.

The instructions in the recipes here are as they appeared in their original form. It is important to use plants, either cooked or fresh, that have not been treated with pesticides or fungicides.

Fragrant Waters and Oils

Virtually each community had a distillery where the Shakers made, among other things, fragrant waters. Beginning in 1809 the New Lebanon Believers were making and selling rose water, and other villages soon followed suit. Account books recording the production of rose water at Canterbury indicate that the members there made it for sale, domestic use, and for the infirmary. The North and Church Families combined their rose petals and shared the resulting portions of rose water. The Canterbury Shakers recorded in 1886:

> June 19 gather first roses
> Aug 5 distill
> Church have 50 lbs leaves
> North have 14 lbs leaves
> North have 2 galls R. Water
> Church have 4 galls R. Water
> Office have 3 1/2 galls R. Water[4]

Eight years later the members made some improvements to the trade.

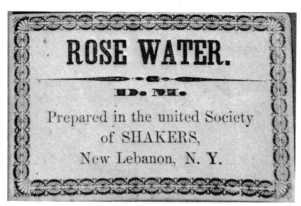

(Private collection)

July 19 Distill Rose Water by steam. The first trial and consider it a success.

> Church have 60 lbs. leaves
> North have 26 ½ lbs. leaves
> North have 2 ½ galls. Rose Water
> Church have 12 galls. Rose Water[5]

Rose Water

Take of roses freshly gathered 6 pound, water 2 gallon. Distill off 1 gallon. Put this into glass bottles. Cover them with so many pieces of paper. Prickle full of holes & set them upon a table which is placed before a window where the sun will shine in upon them. After one month it will be fit for use. The first that blow out might be chilled down in some vessel until you get enough to distill.[6]

A simpler way to make rose water is to obtain rose soluble from a pharmacist. Dilute approximately two and a half teaspoons of the soluble with one pint of distilled water. A drop of red food coloring may be added for color if desired.

Other distilled waters, such as cherry, elder flowers, lavender, peach, peppermint, rose, sassafras, and spearmint, were manufactured through the late nineteenth century at the various Shaker villages. All the fragrant waters were made in a similar way. The following instructions for lavender water starts with oil that is already extracted from the plant:

Lavender Water

Oil Lavender	12 oz.
Cologne Water	½ gall.
Alcohol	1 gall.[7]

Peach orchard at the Enfield, Connecticut, Church Family. Peach water was one of several fragrant waters distilled by the Shakers. (Private collection)

The Shakers' records contain many samples of perfumes and colognes made from scented oils. Although the Believers produced these fragrant oils in large distilleries, it is possible to extract oil from an herb without using such equipment. This is a tedious process, however, so start with the best—rose oil. While it takes approximately two hundred pounds of rose petals to produce one ounce of the attar of roses, it is fun to make a small amount of this high-quality oil at home.

The Hancock Shakers obtained their rose oil in the following way:

Rose Oil

Take a large jar and fill it [with] clean flowers of roses. Cover them with pure water and sit it in the sun in the day time and take in at night for seven days [or] when the oil will float on the top. Take this off with some cotton tied on a stick and squeeze in a phial and stop it up close.

Use either pure spring water or rain water and remember to cover the crock if it looks like rain. The oil or attar looks like a yellowish oily scum and should be removed daily.[8]

Any herb oil can be extracted by following these instructions.

The three following colognes were used by both the Canterbury and Sabbathday Lake Shakers. They come from Sister Mary

Ann Hill, who was born in Maine and entered the Canterbury community at age twelve. In 1859 she was transferred to the Maine village, where she lived until her death in 1890.

Kiss Me Quick

Spirits 1 gallon
ess. Thyme ¼ ounce
ess. Orange flowers 2 ounces
ess. neroli ½ ounce
Attar roses 30 drops
ess. jasmin[e] 1 ounce
ess, balm mint 4 ounces
oil lemon 20 drops
Calamus aromaticus ½ ounce[9]

Homemade Cologne

One forth ounce of oil lavender, one forth ounce of oil bergamot, one eight ounce of oil jessamine, twenty-five drops of oil neroli and one pint of pure spirits of wine. Shake Well.
Taken from the Household, 1880[10]

Cologne, This is equally as good.

one forth ounce of oils of Rosemary and Lemon, one drachm each of bergamot and lavender, eight drachms of oil cinnamon (but I leave the cinnamon out) ten or fifteen drops each of oils of cloves and rose and two quarts of alcohol. Put into a jug bottle, shake well for three or four days.
Taken from the Household.[11]

Another

Oil Neroli 2 Drs
" Rose ½ drs [15 drops]
" Nutmeg 1 drs [30 drops]
" Lemon ½ oz
" Lavender ½ oz
" Bergamot 2 Dra [1 ½ teas.]
" Musk 6 gr [grains (1 ounce = 438 grains)]
Alcohol 1 gall[12]

Cologne for the Sick Room

Oil of Lavender of each 6 drams [a dram = ⅛ oz]
Oil of Lemon of each 6 drams
Oil of Rosemary 2 drams
Oil of Cinnamon 20 drops
Deodorized Alcohol 6 pints
Shake well and let it stand for a few days.[13]

To make your own cologne, try the following recipe.

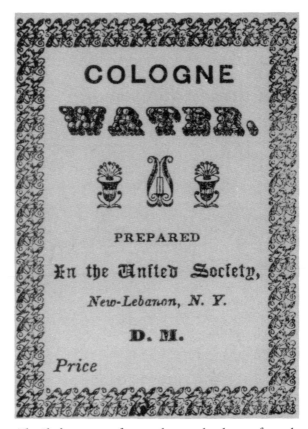

The Shakers manufactured several colognes for sale, using a variety of herbs and spices. (Collection of the United Society of Shakers, Sabbathday Lake, Maine)

Collect a mixture of scented flowers and pack the blossoms in a jar and cover them with the pure ethyl or grain alcohol. Remove the blossoms and strain and squeeze the alcohol back into the jar, and fill the jar again with fresh blossoms. Repeat this procedure each day until the alcohol has reached the desired fragrance; then strain the cologne into bottles and seal tightly. To make the perfume last longer, add a small amount of fixative, such as ambergris, civet, or musk, in the general proportion of fifteen to one.

There are many flowers that can be used for a cologne, including the blossoms of the annual heliotrope, sweet alyssum, mignonette, petunia, sweet pea, phlox, and stock, as well as clematis, perennial dianthus, peony, salvia, and sweet william.

Herbs such as lavender, rosemary, thyme, and lovage may be used as well as iris and daffodil. Try any flower you wish, but remember to keep a record of your experiments.

Cosmetics and Skin Tonics

The Shakers made many of their own cosmetics, which they used for medicinal purposes. In the manufacture of these salves, lotions, and creams, they added herbs and distilled waters. Rose water was particularly popular. This skin tonic was suggested by Eldress Bertha Lindsay of Canterbury:

Rose Water and Witch Hazel Skin Tonic

Mix 2 parts rose water to 1 part witch hazel. The proportions of this refreshing skin tonic can be varied according to skin type.

Rose water was also used by the Shakers in a variety of creams. The following recipe calls for rose water as well as Spermaceti, the fine oil from the sperm whale. Spermaceti was often used in cosmetics and may still be purchased today, although the sperm whale is considered to be an endangered species in most countries. For this reason, using this recipe is not recommended.

Heolane, a cream from the quince seed, was a cosmetic sold by the New Lebanon Shakers:

Ointment of Rose Water

Take of Oil of almonds, two fluid ounces, Spermaceti, half an ounce, White wax one drachm. Melt the whole in a water bath, stirring it frequently; when melted add of Rosewater, two fluid drachms; And stir the mixture continually till it is cold.[14]

Heolane—1 quart

Take 1/3 c. quince seed. Soak in tepid water until the gluten parts from the seeds. Stir once in awhile carefully to avoid discolaration. Strain thru fine sieve or cloth, but do not squeeze. Add 2 full oz. of alcohol, 1 1/2 of glycerine and oils or extracts of perfume according to liking. If oil is used cut it in the alcohol first or it will not mix with the gluten if this is neglected. Thin with water if too thick. Beat it well and bottle tightly. Does not require sealing. Some like oil of Bergamot very much. But the majority prefer Rose Geranium for perfume.[15]

The Hancock Shakers used this hand cream:

Chapped Hands

Take house leek, sweet balsam, Healall, blue balsam blows, coolwort, rock liverwort, water scabish, red plantain, red

clover heads, chamomile flowers, catnep blows, white pop-
pys, Kings clover, ground ivy & put them all in an iron vessel
that will hold 6 qt add 3 pints cold water—simmer gradually
until it boils—strain off the liquor & add 8 oz fresh butter & 1
oz beeswax to it & simmer till the liquor has evaporated then
strain through thick cloth. Anoint the hands with this ointment.[16]

The Shakers sold some of their herbal cosmetics to the World.
In addition to Heolane and Rose Cream, the New Lebanon Shakers
heavily advertised their Shaker Hair Restorer. With the catchy
phrase, "Gray hair may be honorable, / But the natural color is
preferable," the New Lebanon Shakers announced that their hair
restorative was the answer to a "long felt want." Their advertisements stated that "in the great majority of cases gray hair is the
result of disease, necessitating the employment of some remedial
agent." The members claimed that "a few applications [of the
Shaker Hair Restorer] will stop the falling out of the hair, and thus

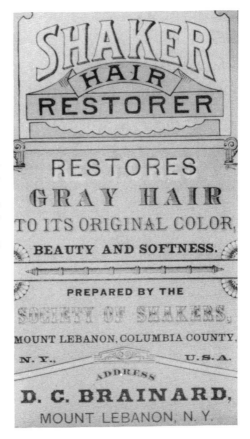

This dual-purpose cosmetic was said not only to help cure baldness but also to restore gray hair to its original color. Products like this one give evidence to the Shakers' ready response to current trends in the World. (Private collection)

prevent baldness."[17] A few years later they included the following quote in their Hair Restorer advertisement:

> "It has been estimated," says the *New York Medical Record,* "that about one-half the adult men of American birth living in our cities are bald-headed." The estimate is not exaggerated, if it is applied to persons above the age of thirty, and it may be rather under the mark.

> The probabilities point toward a race of hairless Americans. The American nation is threatened with the castrophe of a universal alopecia. From the visitors gallery of the Stock Exchange, for example, one views a mob of shining pates, belonging, as a rule, to rather young men. [18]

The following is a recipe for a hair restorer used by the Groveland, New York, Shakers.

Hair Restorative

Put $1/2$ lb. pulv. Lobelia herb in a bottle, add to it equal parts of Whiskey, Brandy and Olive Oil. Bathe the head once a day, it will prevent the loss of hair & is said to restore it.[19]

Soaps and Candles

Mary Ann Hill brought this recipe to Sabbathday Lake from Canterbury in 1859:

Recipe for Toilet Soap

Take six pounds Sal Soda, three pounds unslacked lime, and four gallons water which put together in a kettle and boil till dissolved.

Let it settle, pour off the liquid, add seven pounds clean grease, and then boil to the consistency of honey.

Cast in molds or pans. When dry, it will be fit for use. Can scent with any perfume desired.

P. E., Otto, N.Y., 1863.[20]

Bullard's Oil Soap

Take alcohol 3 quarts soft soap 2 lbs. camphor & Agua ammonia 1 oz, oil lavender $1/2$ oz. mix all but the soap. and when the Camphor is dissolved add the soap. Agitate till incorporated, then filter.[21]

Shaving Soap

A good shaving soap may be made by taking equal parts of:

White wax
Spermaceti
Almond Oil
Melt all together and before cooling, rub in two cakes of
Windsor Soap, which have previously been reduced to a paste
with a small quantity of rose water.

The last, probably, is not unlike a superior shaving soap that has
long been in use, and is known as "rypophagon" soap. A first rate
thing with a very wonderful name.[22]

To Make Candles of A Durable Nature

To ten ounces of Mutton tallow, add a quarter of an ounce of
camphor, four ounces of beeswax, and two ounces of allium;
they will then be very hard, and burn with a clear and
beautiful blaze.[23]

Potpourris

The Shakers also dried their herbs for home use. A common
misconception is that the Shakers made wreaths from their herbs,
but such decoration was banned at the communities for many
years. Even in the late nineteenth and twentieth centuries, when
many of their austere restrictions were loosened, the Sisters did not
characteristically make dried herb wreaths. They did, however,
add dried herbs to their potpourris and sachets. The Shakers made
both moist and dry potpourris. Moist potpourris retain their scent
longer but must be bottled in opaque bottles because the process
discolors the blossoms. Although they are less strongly scented, dry
potpourris are a visual delight.

A moist potpourri is made by first sprinkling layers of partially
dried flower petals, mostly roses, with coarse noniodized salt for
curing. After aging, they are then combined with fixatives, spices,
and perfumed oils. Traditionally, this mixture was placed in a
double-lidded container; the inner lid was perforated to let the
aroma waft into the room, and the outer lid was to close the
container completely.

Rose Jar (using English Damask Roses)

Gather Rose petals in the morning, let them stand in a cool
[place] toss them up lightly to dry, for one hour then put them
in layers, with salt sprinkled over each layer, in a large covered
[jar]. A glass butter dish is a convenient recepital [sic]. Gather
enough to make 4 pints to a quart according to size of your
jar. Stir then transfer to a glass fruit jar in the bottom of which
you placed 2 ounces of allspice, coursely ground, 2 ounces of
stick cinnamon broken coursely. This may now stand six

weeks, closely covered. When it is ready for the permanent jar, which may be as pretty as you please, those with double covers are the best, and very pretty ones in the blue and white Japanese ware, holding over 1 quart can be had for a few shillings. Now have ready 1 ounce each of cloves, allspice, cinnamon & Mace all ground not fine, 1 ounce Orris root bruised and shredded; 2 ounces of Lavender flowers, and a small quantity of any other sweet scented flowers or herbs. Mix all together, and put into the jar in alternate layers with the Rose stock. Add a few drops of the Oil of Rose Geranium or Violet, and pour over the while add 1 gill [4 oz] of good cologne. This will last for years though from time to time you may add a little lavender or Orange flower water or any nice perfume & some seasons, a few fresh rose petals. To use this open one hour every morning and then close.[24]

Dry potpourris are meant to be seen as well as smelled. The aroma is often more delicate, but its visual appeal makes this method most popular. Roses and lavender petals are used for their scent, but other flowers may be added for their color, such as bachelor's buttons, borage, cornflowers, daisies, delphiniums, marigolds, nasturtiums, pansies, peonies, pinks, salvia, violets, yarrow, and yellow primroses. The leaves of herbs such as St. Johnswort, which smell like tangerine, add additional interesting scents. The flowers and leaves of chamomile, costmary, bergamot, and melilot are examples.

While the same ingredients may be included in both the dry and moist potpourris, the former method is simpler, neater, and cleaner. In a dry potpourri the additives, such as spices and rinds, are chopped, not powdered, and they do not cloud the glass container. The petals are mixed with the additives, fixatives, and fragrant oils and placed in a closed container and allowed to cure for six weeks. The mixture is turned occasionally, and, after a week or so, more oil is added if necessary.

To collect ingredients for a potpourri, pick the petals in the morning after the dew is gone, but before noon. Pick only as much as there is space to dry, for the petals need to be spread out in a single layer on a window screen or newspapers in a cool, dark place such as an attic or a closet. Whole buds and leaves may be selected; discard insects and soiled leaves and petals. Wait until the petals are chip dry, about ten days to two weeks, stirring occasionally. Store the petals in a covered container, and they will keep indefinitely in a cool, dry place.

To make any potpourri, mix the petals and spices in the general proportions of one cup of dried petals to one teaspoon of fixative, one teaspoon of spices, and a drop or two of perfuming oil. Pack the mixture in closed containers and allow to age for six to eight weeks, stirring once in a while with a wooden spoon. Choose a pretty, clear, covered container to display the potpourri. Whole, dried blossoms may be affixed to the inside of a glass jar with dabs of beaten egg white. When they have dried on the jar sides, add the potpourri, and top with more whole dried blossoms.

The following instructions were given by Mildred Wells who moved from the Alfred community to Canterbury in 1921. She was the last Canterbury village resident who made and sold potpourri at the Shaker store.

Potpourri

4 oz rose petals
2 oz ground sandalwood
1 oz whole cloves
$^1/_2$ oz cinnamon
$^1/_2$ oz allspice
2 oz crushed orange peel
1 oz powdered orris root
20 drops rose geranium oil
6 drops oil of lavender
Age four to five weeks.[25]

In the twentieth century the Shaker stores were filled with fancy work, a variety of hand-sewn articles made for the World. Some of these articles were sachets that contained fragrant herbs to scent clothes, and others were bags holding moth-repellent herbs. Cloth mice and other cat toys were stuffed with catnip, grown in the Shakers' gardens.

The ingredients for sachets are similar to those for potpourris, but the sachet herbs are pulverized with a mortar and pestle. The Canterbury Shakers made and sold lavender sachets—dainty bags made of various colored organdy, tied with ribbon at the top, and decorated with a sprig of dried flower.

This recipe also came from Mildred Wells of Canterbury.

Organdy Sachets

Lavender flowers
A few drops each of:
  Lavender oil
  Clove oil[26]

Medicines and Medicinal Wines

Many Shaker recipes give a glimpse of the wide variation of herbal cures. The following recipe, which dates back to the 1840s, called for a decoction of rose flowers. The syrup was made by simmering the petals in water for thirty minutes and straining them while hot. It was used as a medicine at Canterbury.

Rose Syrup

Make a strong decoction of rose flowers sweetened very sweet with white sugar, add a little sulfuric acid enough to make sharp look red, and taste well. Dose 1 tablespoonful twice or thrice times a day.[27]

Both the Union Village, Ohio Shakers and the Groveland, New York Shakers issued treatises on wine. Believing that it was important for every family to be able to make their own wine, the Groveland author stated the value of wine as a medicinal agent:

Good wines are agreeable and pleasant to the pallate and do not intoxicate the brain and injure the health as all kind of alcoholic liquors do. Good wines possess *highly valuable and restorative medicinal* . . . properties for refreshing and supporting the sick . . . They cheer and enliven the spirits of the weak and feeble and give strength and comfort both to the body and mind.

. . . every family aught to be able to keep some good wine in the house; not only for medicine but to enable them to treat a friend whenever circumstances might render it advisable to do so . . . it would be advisable for every man and woman to avail themselves of the means and opportunity of acquiring the requisite knowledge for making a variety of good and useful, domestic wines. We have here at the north the means not only for making strong and spirited wines, but also such as are bland, rich, and delicate:

. . . Pure wines do not intoxicate like alcoholic liquors; . . . [they] do not demoralize but they have a direct tendency to elevate and improve the moral condition of society.

. . . When this shall become really a wine growing country, and wines are so plenty that the prices are reduced to something like what they are in Europe, every family can then have one two or more bottles of wines on their table at every meal to supply the place of tea and coffee, which would have a great tendency to improve the health and advance the happiness of the general community.[28]

Blackberry Wine

Measure your berries and bruise them, to every gallon adding one quart of boiling water, let the mixture stand twenty-four hours stirring occasionally. Then strain off the liquor into a cask, to every gallon adding two pounds of sugar; cork tight and let stand till the following October, and you will have wine ready for use.[29]

Home made Grape Wine

Ripe freshly picked cultivated grapes twenty pounds. Put them in a stone jar and pore over them six quarts of water boiling hot soft water when cool squeeze out then thoroughly with the hands and let it stand. three days on the porch with a cloth thrown over it. The jar then out the juice and add ten pounds of white shugger and let it remain a week longer in the jar. Then take off the scum strain and bottle leaving a vent until done fermenting then strain again and bottle tight and lay the bottles on the side in a cool place.[30]

Currant Wine

Take 14 pounds of Currants brake them into 3 gallons of water, let them stand over night, then strain and run the liquor through sand; add 14 pounds of sugar and when well mixed, barrel it having the bung out 14 days, then stop close; if the fermentation continues add a little brandy, rack from the lees about Christmas and add 2 quarts of French brandy to every 10 gallons.[31]

The next few recipes give an idea of the herbal mixtures used by the Shakers, but they are *not* recommended for use today. Recipes for cough medicines abound among the Shaker herbal cures. The following cough remedy came from Canterbury Eldress Hester Ann Adams, who was born in 1817 and entered the Canterbury community in 1826. At age twenty-seven she was appointed to the Ministry of the New Hampshire Bishopric. In 1859, having demonstrated her intellectual skills, she was sent with others by the Lead Ministry to Sabbathday Lake. Her job was to restore "the walls of gospel protection" at the Maine communities, which had serious leadership problems at the time.

Recipe for Cough Candy

    1 lb. Elecampane
    6 oz Slippery Elm Bark
    6 oz Squills
    4 oz Boneset
    1 oz Horehound
    4 oz Liquorice root
    $^1/_2$ gill flax seed [4 oz]

Boil together two hours, have half a pail full when done. Put in 1 pint to 10 lbs [sugar]. N.B. The root and herbs should not be pulverized. Cough Candy should be boiled the same as stick candy. Turn the syrup on the marble slab and crop it off to your liking. No pulling is required.

When your syrup is strained and ready for boiling down, put in your portion of compound liquor and boil together until it will not stick to your teeth.[32]

This cure came from the Hancock community:

For a cough

Dried Hoarhound Leaves 1 oz
Dried Mullein Leaves 1 oz
Marsh Mallow Root 1 oz

Boil in one gallon of water half hour, strain add two pounds of sugar, boil down to a quart, bottle, cork tight & keep in a cool place. Dose from one half to one teaspoonful every two hours.[33]

Cough Syrup

One ounce Sage
One ounce Lemon Balm
1 ounce Comfrey Root
1 ounce Life of Man
1 ounce Saffron
1 ounce Horseradish Root
1 ounce Sarsparilla
3 ounce Burdock Root

Put these in four quarts of water or soft water let it steep four hours then strain, add one pint of molasses, let it scald in.

Dose a wine glass full three times a day before eating.[34]

The following medicinal syrup is made from liverwort, or *Hepatica triloba,* and was made for treating consumption. It was recorded by Elder Freeman White at Canterbury.

To make 5 doz. bottles, Take Liverwort, Skunk Cabbage root, Bugle, Coltsfoot, Cardus & Sassafrass leaves, Bethroot—of each 3 lbs; Solemnseal 5 lbs Bloodroot Balm flowers & Foxglove each $1/4$ lbs. Draw the strength and reduce to 8 or 10 gallons then add 6 oz. Soda skim & add 40 lbs. of sugar, skim again and strain and add 5 quarts of tincture of button snake root.[35]

Clove oil has long been useful for soothing toothaches; the Hancock Shakers used it in the following remedy:

Toothache

Oil Sassafras $1/2$ oz
Oil Cloves 12 oz
Oil Origanum $1/2$ oz

Mix & dip a little cotton or lint into it and apply to the tooth. Renew it a few times & it generally gives relief.

E. Blakeman.[36]

Some of the herbal preparations include items that would hardly be considered to have medicinal value today. These would seem to have been very unpleasant as well, such as this one found at Sabbathday Lake:

Against the Falling Down of the W[omb]

Make a fume of Pigeons feathers, and the sole of a shoe scraped, Rams horns, and white pond lily root, let the patient sit over the smoke of these two or three times and it will give relief.[37]

Other concoctions were made to be taken over a long period of time. They are interesting for their content but, as is the one mentioned above, are certainly *not* recommended

Rheumatism

1 Sassafras, 1 Elecampane, 4 gallons water, 1 lb rusty nails. Boil rapidly down to 1 gallon then add as much as boiled away (3 gal.) 1 quart of good vinegar & let simmer for 10 or 12 hours & strain it thoroughly. When perfectly cold add 1 gal. molasses & 1 gal. brandy. Amalgamate by shaking, bottle & place in a cool cellar.

Use while eating & also at such times & other times as may seem agreeable to the patient.[38]

Should be use for 2 or 3 years in the room of other beverages.

For a wound caused by a nail

Take a lock of black wool and grease it with old grease, and smooth the wound then take a piece of snakeskin and bind.[39]

Herbal medicine was flexible with different herbs tried for a desired result. As the Shakers devised these recipes, they experimented with many combinations and recorded their conclusions. Not all of these attempts, however, were successful as shown in this report:

1863, Sept 29
Experiment Fluid Ext. Buckthorn. We collect 15 lbs berries squeeze out about 6 $1/_2$ pints juice. Having mashed them previously. Let stand 3 days and strain. Add 2 fl. oz. ext. ginger. Grind 2 oz. Allspice—percolate with 6 oz Alcohol and 2 oz water. mix, equals about 8 oz alcohol and in 7 pints. The resulting liquid is awful! This Buckthorn worked and broke the bottle containing it. To take dose 8th part of a minim to be repeated as soon as the patient forgets the taste.

Broken bottles: 30 pint; 40 $1/_2$ pint;
2 half gallons; & 40 $1/_4$ pint.[40]

The Shakers also had several antidotes for dog bites. The following was apparently written for someone who already possessed a good herbal knowledge.

For the Bite of Mad Dogs

The herb grows in moist lands, has square stalks leave like a blue blow. Take of the herb draw it the same as you do tea make it about as strong. Drink it for constant. Drink a quart or more a day—the patient must diet the same as they formerly used to in the inoculation for the Small pox. This to be continued 4 days & every 4th day take a tablespoonful of brimstone, [sulfur]. the days you take the brimstone refrain taking the tea, this has been applyed to several who had been bitten from mad Dogs & not one of them were affected by wounds.[41]

The Hancock Shakers had a recipe that called for only elecampane, or horse heal, mixed with new milk.[42] The roots of elecampane *(Inula helenium),* dug in their second year, were more frequently used in cough medicines.

Bite of a snake

Take strong tobacco Leaf wet it with honey, apply to the bite, the patient must drink a tablespoonfull of the juice of Horehound & plantain pounded together squeezed out once an hour for 4 hours.[43]

Insect Repellants

Many herbs are effective moth repellants and include crushed bay leaves, feverfew, mint, pyrethrum, rosemary, southernwood, tansy, vetiver root, and wormwood. These are strong-scented herbs and are often blended with a dominating flower scent such as lavender.

For a simple moth repellant, collect and crush one quart of dried herbs of your choice, which may include lavender, peppermint, rosemary, santolina, southernwood, spearmint, tansy, thyme, woodruff, and wormwood. Add dried orange, lemon peel, and one teaspoon of either ground cloves, cinnamon, or allspice.

Perfume & Preventative of Moths

Take of cloves, caraway seeds, nutmegs, mace, cinnamon, and Tonquin beans of each one ounce; Then add as much Florintine orris seed as will equal the other ingredients put together. Ground the whole well to powder, & then put it in little bags among your clothes &c.[44]

Eldress Bertha Lindsay, of Canterbury used the following recipe as an insect repellant:

Insect Repellant

Heat a bottle of red wine vinegar to just below boiling. Add enough rosemary to fill the bottle. Pour vinegar over rosemary. Cool. Strain the vinegar and reheat. Repeat the process with new rosemary.[45]

The following is a modern insect repellant which you may also try:

Insect Repellant

Combine equal amounts of fresh spearmint leaves, green onion tops, horseradish (roots and leaves), and cayenne pepper in 2 cups water. Mix in the blender. Add 2 tablespoons of liquid detergent. Keep in refrigerator.[46]

Dyes

Before the advent of commercial and specialized stores, cloth was made and dyed at home in America. The early Shakers manufactured almost all their own cloth and used herbs to dye the material. While the colors of their homemade silks were vibrant, the colors of their cottons, woolens, and linens were more quiet. The Shakers used the bark of butternut (reddish-brown), hemlock, yellow oak, swamp maple, beech, sumac (brown and gray), as well as the plants sorrel (black) and purslain to achieve muted shades of red, orange, brown, blue, gray, and purple.[47] Indigo furnished the deep, permanent blue so highly favored by the World.

Using knitting yarn is the easiest way to experiment with the lovely range of colors that can be achieved by herbal dyeing. For beginners natural or one hundred percent wool yarn is the most satisfactory material for a vegetable dyeing project. (Woven wool works equally as well.)

The wool must be first treated in order to hold the vegetable color permanently. This preliminary step is called mordanting and is necesssary to keep the color from fading. Alum, a white powder that can be bought as potassium aluminum sulfate, is easiest to use. (An adequate substitute for ammonium, alum is available in drugstores.) Different mordants can create different colors from one dye bath. To darken (or sadden) wool, use iron in the mordant; in many cases, the Shakers added rusty nails for this purpose.

To mordant the wool: Divide the wool into skeins of about one ounce apiece and tie them loosely with cotton string, four strings to a skein. (If the ties are too tight, uneven dyeing may result.) Heat four gallons of water in an enameled or stainless steel kettle to hand warmth. Dissolve three ounces of alum and one ounce of cream of tartar in the water. Wet all the wool in warm tap water and submerge it in the kettle. Keep the kettle hot, but not boiling, for one hour. Remove the wool. It is now ready for dyeing. (The wool may either be dried for future use or be put directly into the dry bath. If dried, it must be wet again before submerging into the dye.)

To make a dye bath: Take fresh plant material, enough to fill a two-quart container. (Do not use an aluminum or iron vessel as they may affect the color.) Two quarts of plant material yield about two quarts of dye, an ample amount for half a pound of wool. Cut the plants and cover the pieces completely with water. Simmer for an hour or more. Strain and return the liquid to the kettle.

Submerge a skein of warm wet wool completely into the dye bath. Let the material simmer for about an hour; then rinse it in warm water and hang it to dry in an airy place.

For Red expressly for Carpets—New Lebanon

For one lb of woolen take 3 oz. alum, one oz. cream tartar, 1 lb. Nicaragua [a type of brazilwood used as a yellow dye].

Prepare the liquor in the brass or copper kettle, take a pail of water to a lb. of woolen, put in the tartar & alum, bring to a boil; put in woolen and boil an hour and a half; take it out, air it, and rinse and empty away the liquors; put into the kettle two pails of water to each lb of yarn and the Nicaragua in a bag, Boil an hour & a half, take out the bag, and put in the woolen; boil about an hour, gently stirring it occasionally; it is then to be rinsed & dried. if you wish a scarlet red, add a very little fustic [a source of yellow dye from wood chips] to the Nicaragua.[48]

Black with Sorrel and Logwood

Pull your sorrel, rinse the dirt from the roots, then spread a laying all over the bottom of the kettle, then put in a laying of yarn and if wool put it in loose bags and spread till your kettle is full then fill it with water and make fire enough to wilt the sorrel let it lay all night. Next morning heat up and let it boil a few minutes; heave and air shake out the sorrel have a fresh liquor of logwood [chips make a black, blue, or purple dye] in which handle your [yarn till] … suits this make a good and purment black.[49]

For Coloring Cotton Cloth with Hemlock.
Canterbury N.H.

Use ground Hemlock prepared for tanning leather; Have the dye warm or hot when putting in the cloth.

Heat up to a gentle boiling while coloring, spread a cloth on the top of the kettle letting it cover the grounds to prevent spotting the cloth you are coloring.

Take the cloth out of the dye as often as once in ten minutes to give it the air, 6 or 8 times while coloring. To set the color, wash it in middling strong soap suds. Rinse well, roll in a cloth and iron. This followed, no trouble about spotting it.[50]

The color blue was a favorite among many Shakers. In response to an inquiry from another Shaker village, the Kentucky Shakers wrote an eight-page description of how they made their blue dyes. The recipe is excerpted here to show the care that was given to obtain the perfect color:

Method of colouring Blue
Practiced by the Society of Believers in Kentucky

To set up a dye, put into an iron pot 1 1/2 lb of indigo; add of lye that will bear an egg one part, and of water two parts, sufficient to cover it; let it stand just work 40 hours, keeping it just covered all the while with the lye and water . . .

This done add 1 1/2 lbs. of madder [roots make an orange dye] and one quart of good sweet emptins . . .

To make a bright pale blue . . . We prefer the cold dye altogether for pale blue.

We have two hot dyes and one cold. To make a deep or middling blue . . .

When a dye becomes too weak for cotton we pour it into a tub by itself and let it stand cold and in this situation we use it for colouring wool till the strength is out . . .

We have followed the business for two years, and never yet finished but one dye.

It is said that, necessity is the mother of invention, and so we find it. We obtained the foregoing method of colouring chiefly by trying experiments, in which we have had great success. We have had little or no trouble with our dyes, and they have always been in a prosperous situation [two] young Sisters is the most strength that has ever been applied to them and a part of the time only one; and the income of their work for the World, besides colouring for Believers, who make a very extensive use of blue, has supported their shop with all kinds of stock, and even paid for all their tubs and kettles, and enough to support themselves besides; so that the Society has been at no expense whatever for all their blue.

For sometime past the colouring has been taken care of and done by two active girls; the one that has the chief management is about 15 years of age. She manages her own dyes and keeps them in good order, keeps her own books, sets down her own accounts, receives the yarn &c from customers, delivers it to them again in good order and well dyed, receives her pay for it, and gives good satisfaction both to Believers and the World; and thus by the labour and earnings of these two children, the Society is supported in all their blue besides supporting themselves. What colour then can be cheaper than this.

When the business was first set up, the Trustees of the Society [desired] a strict account might be kept of all the outgoes and incomes of it, which accordingly has been done, and with which they are much pleased, and think it a very profitable branch of business. They think a blue is cheaper than even a bark colour, especially if the root bark is used.[51]

A Selected List of Sources

Rose Plants & References

Historical Roses
1657 West Jackson Street
Painesville, OH 44077

Roses of Yesterday and Today
802 Brown's Valley Road
Watsonville, CA 95076

Joseph J. Kern Rose Nursery
Box 33
Mentor, OH 44060

Tillotson's Roses
802 Brown's Valley Road
Watsonville, CA 95076

The Old Shrub Roses
by Graham S. Thomas
J.M. Dent & Sons

Herb Plants

Sandy Mush Herb Farm
Route 2, Surrett Cove Road
Leicester, NC 28748
704-683-2014

Capriland's Herb Farm
534 Silver Street
Coventry, CT 06238
203-742-7244

Casa Yerba
Star Route 2, Box 21
Day's Creek, OR 97429

Well Sweep Herb Farm
317 Mount Bethel Road
Port Murray, NJ 07865
908-852-5390

Cedarbrook Herb Farm
986 Sequim Avenue South
Sequim, WA 98382
206-683-7733

Meadowbrook Herb Gardens
Route 138
Wyoming, RI 02898
401-539-7603

Nichols Garden Nursery
1190 North Pacific
Albany, OR 97321
503-928-9280

Greene Herb Gardens
Greene, RI 02872

Organizations

Organic Gardening Clubs of America
33 E. Minor Street
Emmaus, PA 18049

The Herb Society of America
300 Massachusetts Avenue
Boston, MA 02115

Potpourri Supplies, Dried Botanics, Essential Oils, Fragrances

Caswell-Massey Co., Ltd.
518 Lexington Avenue
New York, NY 10021

Crabtree & Evelyn
30 E. 67th Street
New York, NY 10021

Haussmann's Pharmacy
534–536 W. Girard Avenue
Philadelphia, PA 19123

Hahn and Hahn, Homeopathic Pharmacy
324 W. Saratoga Street
Baltimore, MD 21201

Herbarium, Inc.
Route 2, Box 620
Kenosha, WI 53140

Botanical Drugs and Spices

Aphrodisia
28 Bleeker Street
New York, NY 10014

Cherchez
862 Lexington Avenue
New York, NY 10021

Kiehl Pharmacy, Inc.
109 Third Avenue
New York, NY 10013

Labels for Jars and Bottles

The Herb Farm Country Store
380 N. Granby Road, Route 189
N. Granby, CT 06060

Dyeing Supplies

Snug Valley Farm
Route 3, Box 394
Kutztown, PA 19530

Straw into Gold
5550-H College Avenue
Oakland, CA 94610

Dye References

The Colour Cauldron
by Su Grierson
Interweave Press, Inc.
306 North Washington Avenue
Loveland, CO 80537

The Dyer's Companion
by Elijah Bemiss
Dover Publications
180 Varick Street
New York, NY 10014

Natural Dyes and Home Dyeing
by Rita J. Adrosko
Dover Publications
180 Varick Street
New York, NY 10014

A Weaver's Garden
by Rita Buchanan
Interweave Press, Inc.
306 North Washington Avenue
Loveland, CO 80537

Advertisements in craft publications such as *Handweaver, Spindle,* and *Dyepot* are the best sources of up-to-date information on natural dye sources.

"These Shall Speak with Touching Power": Shaker Catalogs

A blade of grass—a simple flower
Cull'd from the Dewy lea;
These, these shall speak with touching power,
Of change and health to thee.[1]

Over the years the Shakers issued a variety of catalogs to promote their manufactured goods; these publications advertised the gamut of their products, from furniture to textiles to herbs. These bound and dated volumes were replaced every few years with updated issues when new items came on the market. The Shakers also printed broadsides, similar to our posters today, that advertised products with current prices.

The Shakers' herb catalogs indicated a commitment to the business. The villages who published them—Watervliet, New Lebanon, Canterbury, Harvard, and Union Village—had the most successful industries. Two other communities, Sabbathday Lake, Maine and Enfield, New Hampshire printed only a single catalog; their interest in selling herbs was comparatively late.

From the beginning the Shakers directed their trade to the medical community. They negotiated with leading physicians in the World to endorse their medicines, and they claimed to follow the recommendations of the *U.S. Pharmacopeia.* Their advertisements emphasized a reliance on widely published botanical books, and, for convenience, they listed the herbs alphabetically according to the common as well as botanical names.[2] In later years the Shakers also described the medicinal properties of each herb.

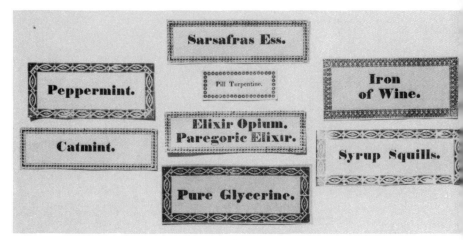

These labels show a typical variety of Shaker medicinal products, from simple herbs to complex preparations. (Private collection)

In 1830 the community of Watervliet published the first dated herb catalog, *Catalogue of Medicinal Plants, and Vegetable Medicines,* followed by others in 1833 and 1837.[3] In 1835 Canterbury produced its first version. In 1836 and 1838 New Lebanon followed suit. The format of Watervliet's 1830 issue was simple. On the cover was an appeal to the public to buy American herbs: "Why send to Europe's bloody shores/For plants which grow by our own doors."[4] That catalog offered 128 herbs, along with pills, syrups, and two medicinal waters. Their 1833 catalog added a selection of twelve extracts, four medicinal ointments, and peach water, which was recommended as a perfume as well as a cure for eruptive diseases.

New Lebanon's first dated catalog was similar in format to Watervliet's, but many of the varieties and prices of the herbs were different. It listed 156 herbs and numerous double-distilled fragrant waters, including cherry, elder flower, peach, peppermint, rose, sassafras, and spearmint. Included in New Lebanon's catalog was an interesting and unique offer to their clients:

> Students of Botany, and others, can be supplied with Herbariums, containing a large collection of specimens of our indigenous plants and cultivated exotics; arranged according to the Linnean System, with correct labels. Prices reasonable.

The herbariums were collections of scientifically arranged dried plants. The herbs were pressed into a book; each plant was identified by its common and Latin name and location.[5] The booklets were early commercial offerings to attract customers and increase sales. The Shaker botanists kept herbariums for their personal use; Harvard's Elisha Myrick frequently referred to putting plants in his herbarium throughout the year.[6]

Canterbury's first catalog was twice the size of those issued by New Lebanon and Watervliet. With all orders directed to Thomas Corbett, this catalog described the medical properties of 150 herbs listed for sale. Compounded medicines included "bone ointment," a preparation made of equal parts of burdock root, low chamomile, comfrey, green tobacco, hemp, henbane, garlic or onions, house leek, melilot, high mallows, nightshade, plantain, sweet elder leaves, St. Johnswort, and yellow dock root.[7] The catalog also gave endorsements by eminent doctors of the World, such as Charles Chadbourne and Dixi Crosby.

Corbett himself endorsed two products, both of his own invention, rocking trusses and vegetable rheumatic pills, the latter being recommended for seamen going "to the West Indies and other tropical climates."[8]

Because of regional availability of the herbs, the varieties and prices differed in the early catalogs of Watervliet, Canterbury, and New Lebanon. Sweet flag, used internally for stomach disorders and externally for blisters and ulcers, was sold by Canterbury for forty-two cents a pound, while Watervliet and New Lebanon sold it for twenty cents less. Sage was priced at fifty cents at New Lebanon, forty cents at Watervliet, and thirty-eight cents at Canterbury. The Shaker physicians frequently negotiated with one another over prices and billing. Often one doctor would request to use one village's bill to pay off another's. When Canterbury Trustee David Parker ordered oils from Union Village, he was told:

> We shall be glad to have your order for a large amount of oils of peppermint and wormseed. Perhaps it might answer you to make an arrangement with Jonathan Wood, New Lebanon. We are indebted there and should like our oil to pay to same. Anything that you can do that would be mutually beneficial we should be glad and thankful for.[9]

By the time the communities of Harvard and Union Village published their first catalogs in the 1840s, their businesses were already prospering. Harvard's first catalog, printed in 1845, listed 197 medicinal herbs with four "sweet" (culinary) herbs and thirteen extracts. This early version offered no compounded medicines such as pills or ointments for sale. Three years later the business had expanded to such an extent that the members bought a new herb press.[10] The next year, when Elisha Myrick, a twenty-five-year-old Believer, took over the concern, he recorded a flourishing trade.

The Shakers made compressed herb packets such as these in an herb press. (Private collection)

> We do our pressing and keep our stock of pressed herbs at the Ministry's barn and pick our herbs and do other work at the yellow house. We distilled 165 gallons of peach water and made 134 pounds of ointment, forty-nine gallons of buckthorn syrup and pressed between February 14, 1849 and February 14, 1850, 10,152 pounds of herbs, roots etc.

> The sales for 1849, including all the herbs, delivered to agents amounted to $4,042.31 net. We raise, gather and prepare this year 5,799 pounds of herbs, barks, roots, etc. which is 800 pounds more than was ever collected before.[11]

When Union Village published their first catalog in 1847, they had an established routine of gathering and distilling herbs:

> July 22. Gathering Oats with a sickle and gathering roots to make extracts.

> August 16. Botanists go to Watervliet to dig Skunk Cabbage.

> Sept 25. Finish'd distilling the mint—and obtain'd 376 lbs.

> Oct 2. Botanical press up and ready for business.

> Oct. 5. Commenc'd distilling the wormseed.[12]

The following year the community was offering 206 herbs and eighteen extracts. With a business second in volume only to New

Lebanon's South Family, which was offering 349 herbs for sale, the members were also experimenting with new varieties of plants. They noted in their 1847 catalog that their physicians had crossed a watermelon and a colocynth, a bitter cucumber and powerful, poisonous native annual plant of Africa and Asia. With the end result they manufactured a new extract used as a cathartic and deobstructant.

> Both the simple and compound extract of colocynth are prepared from the hybrid colocynth, which was originated at Union Village, Ohio, in 1842. This hybrid was produced by planting the seeds of the genuine colocynth, and at the proper time the flowers of the colocynth plant were fecundated with pollen from those of the watermelon . . .

In the 1840s New Lebanon, Canterbury, and Watervliet issued new catalogs. In 1841 the New Lebanon community took the lead by including four culinary herbs—summer savory, sweet marjoram, thyme, and sage—for the first time. In 1848 the village produced another catalog. By 1850 the members reported that they were pressing not less than twenty-one thousand pounds of herbs as well as seven thousand pounds of extracts annually.[13]

The 1840s were prosperous years for the Canterbury Society. The Church Family owned approximately 1,406 acres, 41 dairy cows, 185 sheep, 12 oxen, and 12 horses. The mill system was valued at two thousand dollars, and they reported one year to have ten thousand dollars in cash on hand.[14] In 1848 they purchased a farm along the Merrimack River flood plain, where they raised varieties of herbs such as borage, burdock, poppy, saffron, sage, skunk cabbage, thornapple, valerian, and wormwood. The major crops sold from that site were dandelion, dock, and Indian hemp.[15] Canterbury's 1847 catalog did not include all the herbs listed in its previous publication, but it did have thirteen new plants. For the first time for the village it, too, listed the four culinary herbs: sweet marjoram, summer savory, thyme, and sage. The following year, the Canterbury Shakers issued another version that included the same list of products. In addition, it gave the herbs' common and botanical names and their medical uses. With 152 herbs for sale, this village's output was comparable to Watervliet's.

Watervliet issued catalogs in 1843, 1845, and 1847. By 1847 their publication included advertisements for their own herbal products as well as those made by other companies. This arrangement may have been due to specific relationships the Shakers had with those businesses. One advertisement, for R. F. Hibbard & Company's Wild Cherry Bitters and Carminative Salve, claimed that the herbal ingredients were grown by the Watervliet Shakers. The company had also printed one thousand copies of Watervliet's catalog, which suggests some sort of trade negotiation.[16] The 1848 catalog of New Lebanon also advertised a variety of the World's well-known medicinal products.

> We keep on hand a general assortment of the various preparations introduced by Beech, Thomson, Howard, Smith, and others such as composition powders, hot drops, or No. 6, Wine Bitters, Spice Bitters, Sudorific Drops, Pulmonary Balsam, Neutralizing Cordial, Anodyne Cordial &c, with which the trade can be supplied on reasonable terms.

These efforts were no doubt made in order to expand the business and accommodate all the needs of the customers.

While the Shakers tried to work with other drug companies, confident that their high quality would give them the edge, some businesses frequently misused the Shakers' name. The 1854 catalog from Enfield, Connecticut, contained a statement of warning:

> The society does not consider themselves amenable for the quality of such articles as have never passed their inspection, nor perhaps been within 150 miles of their establishment, although sold under their name; therefore, it would be well for the public who confide in their experience and honesty, to ascertain, before purchasing, whether they are buying the genuine Shaker Preparation, or an imitation, which, perhaps, may sometimes prove equally meritorious and worthy of patronage. We love to see a healthy competition in business, believing it necessary to the well being of society, but object to a piracy of reputation.

Watervliet's catalog of 1860 gave a similar caveat; Union Village, Ohio, addressed the problem as early as 1850:

> We wish the public to understand that, as we never on any occasion obtain any patents for our medicines, or sell any receipts, or sell any medicine of which the materials are secret; any publication purporting to have obtain receipts of us, is a fraudulent attempt to obtain money on our credit.

For some of the villages, the herb business continued to prosper in the 1850s. During this decade the Harvard community produced five catalogs, in 1851, 1853, 1854, 1856, and 1857. In 1851 the Society offered 154 plants, and by 1853 their income from herbs was $3,083.14.[17] During this period it added horseradish to its list of culinary herbs and began selling extracts. The members also sold fruit trees, ornamental shrubs, and seeds. The catalogs reflect a sharp business acumen with clever ads and increased ornamentation. In their 1854 catalog Simon Atherton, who was in charge of the

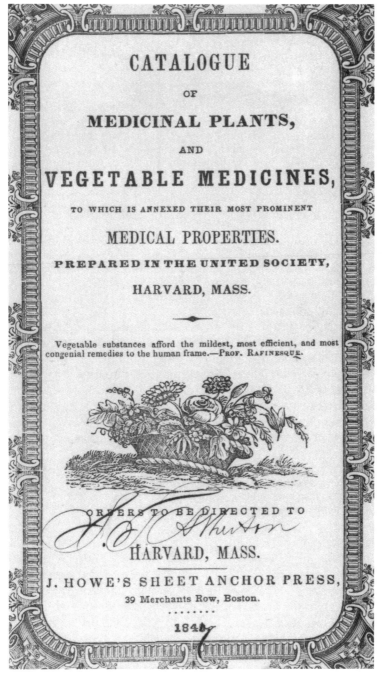

For a number of years, the Harvard Shakers published catalogs with very ornate covers. The image of the basket of flowers, however, appears on catalogs produced by several other Shaker communities. (Collection of Williams College Archives and Special collections)

trade, submitted the following glowing praise of his community's herbs.

> I have the pleasure to enclose to you a copy of a Resolution passed by the Board of Trustees of the Massachusetts College of Pharmacy in reference to some beautifully cured specimens of Herbs. Their honest quality speaks for itself; and a cursory examination only, will satisfy a judge of such commodities, that they were not mowed down with weeds that had usurped their glory and withdrawn their strength, but that they had been watched and nurtured to a state of perfection rarely equalled and never surpassed.

The commercialism and pandering to the World, however, was not approved by all the members of the community:

> Had a visit with Brother Henry DeWitt. He prints all the herb labels & seed bags. Saw him operate on the printing press. He thinks Believers ought to avoid unnecessary embellishments in the printing, and instead of gaudy borders, use plain black lines.[18]

New Lebanon's herb business also expanded in the 1850s. During that time the New Lebanon Shakers issued at least two catalogs. The 1851 version listed 356 herbs along with descriptions of their medical properties. The same four pulverized culinary herbs were offered as well as 181 fluid extracts. The catalog carried an endorsement by Professor Constantine Samuel Rafinesque, a nationally known botanist and author of *Medical Flora, or Manual of Medical Botany of the United States.*

> The best medical gardens in the United States are those established by the communities of the Shakers . . . who cultivate and collect a great variety of medical plants. They sell them cheap, fresh and genuine.

Rafinesque had visited the New Lebanon Shakers twice and had purchased their herbs; it is possible that he and the Shakers had arranged a business agreement for this public statement.

By the 1850s some of the villages had begun to scale down their herb trade. This decline came at a time when many Shakers left the communities due to improved economic conditions in the World and the fading of their religious revival. The death of the last of the original Believers and the burden of caring for large numbers of very young Shakers left a leadership crisis.[19] This population problem was accompanied by a labor question; the Shakers found themselves having to hire more people to help them. Consequently, the added expenses cut into their profits, and competition with the World became more serious.

During this time Union Village issued its last three known catalogs, in 1848, 1850, and 1856. The business did not expand significantly during this time, but the output was impressive. Union Village's 1850 catalog listed more than 250 drug plants, 46 extracts, and 4 culinary herbs.

By the end of the decade the Watervliet members were still carrying on an active trade, pressing 15,100 pounds of herbs a year. In 1860 Chauncey Miller published a twenty-two page catalog which listed 292 herbs, 25 extracts, and 73 varieties of garden seeds for sale. This publication greatly exceeded their 1850 version that had offered 184 herbs. In spite of this high production, the 1860 catalog was Watervliet's last.

In the early 1850s Canterbury's herb sales appeared to be doing well. Trustee John Whitcher reported producing 132 bottles of poppy syrup, 324 gallons of rose water, and 288 gallons of sarsaparilla syrup.[20] In 1852 Blinn recorded that $2,235.79 worth of herbs and $1,050.50 worth of trusses were sold.[21] The following year Trustee David Parker was advertising for herbs to supplement his village's business. On a "Wanted" poster, he asked for the following to be delivered to Canterbury:

> avens root, alder bark, black, bittersweet, blue flag root, bugle, sweet, burdock leaves, root and seed, catmint, coltsfoot, dragon root, dragon's claw or crawley root, dwarf elder root, harvest lice, horsemint, horseradish leaves, lobelia, herb and seed, marigold flowers, motherwort, peppermint, rose flowers, red and white separate, scabish, spearmint, snakehead, stonebrake (purple thoroughwort), sumach leaves, sweet flag root, thoroughwort, vervain, witch hazel leaves, yarrow and finally blackberries.[22]

By the time Canterbury issued its last catalog in 1854, a major change had taken place. The 1848 catalog was issued twice, with orders first directed to Corbett and then to David Parker, Trustee. The 1854 offerings were similar to those in the previous catalog with 152 herbs, 16 extracts, 7 oils, 3 ointments, and 5 syrups. However, orders were now directed to James Kaime. Corbett, who had run the business since 1816, was growing older. A letter to a long-time friend, Chauncey Miller, of Watervliet, revealed a busy man who, despite his responsibilities and age, was not yet ready to relinquish his familiar role:

> Have you dealings with Br. Edward Fowler, New Lebanon, that I could give you in order on him for your balance; as he is owing me about the same I am owing you. I am about settling up and intend to give the trade business up to some

one else. James S. Kaime is the one nominated. I am getting old and find I have too much to do.

If you cannot state an order on Brother Edward I will send you a draft.

Is your Borage a good article. How much have you if we should want. Those barrels of Henbane have come to light, they were lodged in a depot in Boston, where they ought not to have been left or kept. You may sent 50 to 100 lb. Thyme or more if you have it to spare 12 $1/2$ cts. and Horehound 100 lbs @ 10cts. You may direct it to J. S. Kaime, East Concord, N.H. If you have sacks to pack it in we should rather pay for sacks than pay freight on casks or boxes, for such bulky & light articles, so far.

I wish this letter answered by return Mail. Direct T. Corbett, City Hotel Boston as I expect to be there next week on business &c. . . .

I have not the Dr. Warren's pills on hand, but will get some soon as I can, and forward them. Mine are just like them, only not so powerful or harsh.[23]

Corbett's correspondence with Miller at this time shows he was trying to settle his accounts before he turned the business over to Kaime. The two men had bought, sold, and traded herbs for many years, keeping a running total of their transactions. When James Kaime took over the herb business in 1850, he haggled over prices with Chauncey just as Corbett had done.

If you can send me 20 lbs Red rose flowers immediately, you may do so if they are bright & nice. You may also send me 50 lbs solomons seal if it is the large English root. If you can take something of us in exchange for the solomons seal, we will take 200 lbs.

Chamomile at the catalog price, 50 cts. We have usually paid from 7 to 20 cts. If you can send us a small lot, say 50 lbs., [not] to exceed 20 cts, you can do so.

Turnip is not worth more than 10 to 11 cts at most. I should be willing to take one barrel 10 cts if it is a good article.[24]

While 1854 was the last year Canterbury published catalogs, the village continued to sell herbs and medicines. As the sales and manpower decreased, the Sisters contributed their part by making herbal confections. This production, along with the manufacture of witch hazel, Corbett's Sarsaparilla Syrup, and the Cherry Pectoral Syrup, continued until the middle of the twentieth century.

When the Sabbathday Lake community issued its only catalog in the 1860s, it no doubt was looking for new ways to increase its income, selecting a trade it had always carried on in a small way. In the 1840s the members were selling only 83 herbs, purchasing some of them from the Alfred community. In comparison to the other villages, their acreage was small; they planted only one-half acre of sage, their most profitable crop.[25] Their catalog was very simple, devoid of ornamentation. It listed 155 herbs, including four culinary plants, along with a list of medical definitions. Considering their very limited adult work force, the Sabbathday Lake Shakers must have concentrated on only a few herbs, such as sage.

Sabbathday Lake's relatively late start in issuing a catalog was probably due to leadership and membership problems that many other communities were also facing. In 1830, to help save the village, the Lead Ministry in New Lebanon gave the New Hampshire Bishopric the charge of overseeing the two Maine Societies. In 1848 Otis Sawyer, a Minister at Alfred, was asked to move to Sabbathday Lake as Trustee. During his years there, he greatly increased the Society's fortunes. In 1855, after he had proven his skills, Sawyer was appointed Elder; and the Lead Ministry removed the supervisory role of the New Hampshire Bishopric.[26]

Always lonesome for his beloved Alfred, Sawyer was allowed to return home in 1858. After he left Sabbathday Lake, however, the old leadership problems reappeared. It soon became evident that his replacement, Ransom Gillman, had very little business sense. According to Sawyer, "Ransom went into wild speculation in wheat and flour in their new Mill which ended in $15,000 debt."

Soon after, Gillman left the Maine Shakers and retreated to the Second Family at New Lebanon. The problems followed:

> ...the same inordinate ambition led [to] his...[spreading] out too largely in the seed business, which was put in his charge, leading to a loss of a number of thousand dollars.[27]

Gillman then petitioned to be moved to the South Family at New Lebanon, where he stayed until he died. After Gillman left Sabbathday Lake, Charles Vining was given the charge as trustee. Not only were there no improvements for the village, but by 1866 Vining had embezzled the community's remaining funds.[28]

Sabbathday Lake also suffered from a dwindling population. As had its sister communities of Shirley and Alfred, its membership had peaked in the 1820s and steadily declined afterwards. In 1840 28 percent of the 136 members were under the age of sixteen. In 1863 the community had only four Brethren between the ages of eighteen and forty-five.[29] By 1871 their income had declined to such a level that the Sabbathday Lake and Alfred Shakers considered selling their properties and combining their numbers with another community.[30] By 1877 the two villages each had less than seventy members. According to Sawyer, many of the trades had been eliminated in favor of light work done by the Sisters:

> All manufacturing of woodenware was dropped years ago. The tan yard was permitted to run down. The garden seed and herb business was destroyed in consequence of the great competition of extensive establishments west who flooded our state with seeds. The Sisters' fancy work consists of a variety of ladies' work baskets, pin and needle cushions, feather fans and dusters—is the only branch of manufacturing in the Society.[31]

These problems were not exclusive to the Maine communities, many similar situations are found in the records of other villages. In 1881 Sabbathday Lake was persuaded by Dr. A. J. White to manufacture Tamar Laxative. Having first approached New Lebanon with the formula, White was encouraged by that community to contact Sabbathday Lake. The New Lebanon trustees had turned down White because, by this time, their business had reached a plateau, and they were not taking on any new projects. White gave the formula to the Maine village along with "$1,200 worth of materials to be used in its preparation." The Sabbathday Lake Shakers sold this medicine with limited success until the 1890s.[32]

While the Enfield, New Hampshire community had a substantial compound medicine business, there are no known records indicating a sustained, large-scale herb industry at any of the three operating Families.[33] As did the Sabbathday Lake community, Enfield issued only one herb catalog, in the 1860s. This one was identical to Canterbury's 1848 catalog which suggests that the trade might have been a late attempt to raise some much-needed funds. Enfield's Second Family manufactured medicines for many years with the most profitable being Brown's Fluid Extract of Valerian. In 1869 the members reported that there was $1,012 worth of the extract left at their wholesale distributor and $3,880 worth of valerian oil on hand. Nevertheless, the major business ventures for this Family were not medicines or herbs but the manufacture and sale of knitted goods and brooms. The First, Second, and North Families also raised large amounts of dock.

> The Brethren have finished the drying of the Dock root and have shipped some forty-four thousand pounds to the firm of

J. C. Ayer and Co, Lowell, Mass. Of this quantity, the Second Family raised 27,856 lbs, the First Family 11,139 lbs., and the North Family 5,031 lbs.[34]

Enfield's North Family sold some herbs and made Shaker Anodyne but supported themselves mainly from the sale of wooden pails and tubs. In 1869 they sold approximately nine hundred dollars worth of dock, boneset, and various other roots. In 1874 they had sold three thousand pounds of lovage, one thousand pounds of dock, and smaller amounts of chicory and wormwood.[35] The Church Family received much of its income from railroad stock and the sale of brooms and garden seeds. In 1879 it took over the manufacture of Brown's Valerian from the Second Family and Shaker Anodyne from the North Family. Although Enfield sold large amounts of selected herbs and received a steady income from the sale of medicines, a full-scale herb business was not in operation.

The Enfield Church Family was financially solvent up to 1862. The village owed its growth and prosperity from 1820 to 1860 to their Trustee Caleb Dyer, who was assisted by Hyram Baker from 1852 to 1855. Hyram Baker, whose name appears on Enfield's herb catalog, then became the Family Deacon from 1855 to 1874. In 1862 Caleb Dyer was shot and killed by a drunken father who wished to see his daughters who were living at the village. Unfortunately, Dyer retained most of the village's records by memory. After his death, the village had no way of knowing whether the ensuing claims for money were valid; consequently, the community found itself with a fourteen thousand dollar debt.[36] While fighting these claims in court for fourteen years, the Enfield Shakers greatly enlarged their herb business, no doubt to cover some of the expenses.

In 1860 and 1868 the Harvard Shakers issued two more catalogs. In the 1870s they distributed a broadside and a catalog offering 212 herbs. S. S. Pierce, one of 226 customers who were supplied large amounts of herbs from 1879 to 1888, received monthly shipments of thyme, sage, marjoram, sweet savory, and rose water during this time.[37] Harvard's last catalog was issued in 1889 and offered more than two hundred varieties of herbs for sale.

In the 1870s New Lebanon's herb business was still going strong, and the members issued four more annual herb catalogs, in 1872, 1873, 1874, and 1875. Their 1872 wholesale price list of medicinal herbs and roots included 358 herbs. Two years later the Believers were selling 405 varieties.

While dried herbs were the predominate feature of these publications, liquid and solid herbal extracts were also prevalent.

Simon Atherton (1803-1888), as head of the herb business at the Harvard Society for over forty years, oversaw the production of most of the Village's eleven herb catalogs, published between 1845 and 1889. (Collection of the Western Reserve Historical Society, Cleveland, Ohio)

Beginning in 1841, the Shakers began to focus more attention on the business and heavily recommended the extracts. Watervliet's 1850 catalog listed twenty-seven different kinds. In the Enfield, Connecticut 1854 catalog, Jefferson White introduced their list of extracts with the following claims:

> It is a matter of eminent importance to the interested and benevolent physician, to be able to calculate with certainty, on

the effect of any drug or medicine he may administer. This he cannot do, unless he be able to judge of its purity, condition, and carefulness of preparation. Perhaps no class of medicines present so many difficulties, and certainly none which have given such universal dissatisfaction on this point, as vegetable extracts; and some of our best physicians have nearly abandoned their use on this account.

This is not surprising, when we consider the rude and imperfect means generally employed for evaporating, and the want of suitable knowledge and carefulness in the whole process of manufacture. Indeed, it requires much experience and consummate skill, in addition to the most perfect apparatus, to produce extracts that will be uniform and certain in their effects,—as much depends on the freshness of the vegetable operated upon, maturity, season of collection and influence of climate.

To remedy the difficulties complained of, and furnish the profession with the article they so earnestly requested of us— pure and reliable extracts—we have directed our attention to this end, and spared no expense to procure the best information and conveniences for the purpose. Our former experience and observations, of thirty years, have been of value; and the possession of large botanic gardens gives us important advantages in the collection and freshness of the vegetables.

These statements were also made by the New Lebanon Shakers. Their catalogs of the 1860s and 1870s listed 182 extracts, sixty of which were solid extracts.

Appendix I:
Shaker Catalog

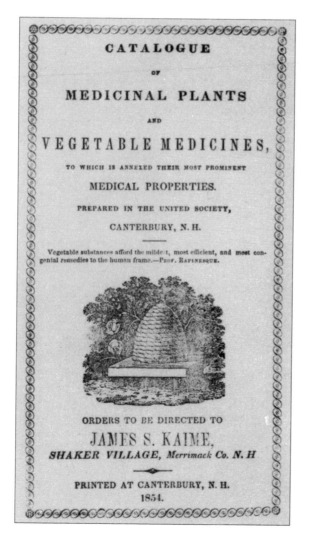

CATALOGUE

OF

MEDICINAL PLANTS

AND

VEGETABLE MEDICINES,

TO WHICH IS ANNEXED THEIR MOST PROMINENT

MEDICAL PROPERTIES.

PREPARED IN THE UNITED SOCIETY,

CANTERBURY, N. H.

Vegetable substances afford the mildest, most efficient, and most congenial remedies to the human frame.—Prof. Rafinesque.

ORDERS TO BE DIRECTED TO

JAMES S. KAIME,

SHAKER VILLAGE, Merrimack Co. N. H

PRINTED AT CANTERBURY, N. H.
1854.

ABBREVIATIONS AND PROPERTIES EXPLAINED.

Acr.   Acrid, biting, caustic,
Alt.   Alterative, which establishes the healthy functions.
Ano.   Anodyne, quieting, easing pain.
A-bil.   Antibilious, correcting the bile.
A-lit.   Antilithic, preventing the formation of gravel or stone.
Ape.   Aperient, laxative or gently cathartic.
A-sep.   Antiseptic, against or preventing mortification.
A-scor. Antiscorbutic, useful in scurvy.
A-spas   Antispasmodic, against spasm, calming nervous irritation.
Aro.   Aromatic, agreeable, spicy.
Ast.   Astringent, shortening the fibres, strengthening.
Bal.   Balsamic, mild, healing, stimulant.
Car.   Carminative, expelling wind.
Cath.   Cathartic, purgative, cleansing the bowels.
Dem.   Demulcent, sheathing, lubricating, preventing irritation.
Deo.   Deobstruent, bettering the secretions, or removing obstruc-
             tions.
Dia.   Diaphoretic, producing insensible perspiration.
Dis   Discutient, dissolving, discussing.
Diu.   Diuretic, increasing the urine.
Eme.   Emetic, causing vomiting.
Emo.   Emollient, softening, causing warmth and moisture.
Err.   Errhine, discharging at the nostrils.
Exp.   Expectorant, producing a discharge from the lungs.
Feb.   Febrifuge, dispelling fever, allaying fever heat.
Her.   Herpetic, curing skin diseases.
Nar.   Narcotic, stupefying, procuring sleep.
Ner.   Nervine, strengthening the nerves.
Pec.   Pectoral, useful in diseases of the lungs.
Ref.   Refrigerent, diminishing animal temperature.
Rub.   Rubefacient, producing heat and redness of the skin.
Sti.   Stimulant, exciting action on the system.
Sto.   Stomachic, good for the stomach.
Sty.   Styptic, preventing bleeding.
Sud.   Sudorific, causing sweat.
Ton.   Tonic, permanently strengthening the system
Ver.   Vermifuge, destroying worms.

TERMS OF DISCOUNT.

Orders over $12·00, and under 25,   15   per cent.
    " $25·00, and under 50,   20   "
    " $50·00, and under 100, 25   "
    " $100·00,   33½   "

CATALOGUE.

Common Names.	Per lb.	Botanical Names.	Properties
Alder buds	$0 25	Alnus serrulata	Deo. Alt. Ast. Ton.
Alder, black, bark	0 50	Prinos verticillatis	Ast. Ver. Ton.
Angelica, leaves	0 33	Angelica atropurpurea	Car. Sto.
do. root	0 50	do. do.	Car. Sto.
Ash, prickly, bark	0 40	Zanthoxylum fraxineum	Sti. Aro.
do. do. pulv.	0 50	do. do.	" "
do. berries	1 50	do. do.	" "
Avan's root	0 50	Geum rivale	Ton. Ast. Sto.
Balm, sweet	0 38	Melissa officinalis	Sto. Dia.
Balm, lemon	0 38	Dracocephalum virginianum	Sto. Dia.
Balm Gilead, buds	1 00	Populus balsamifera	Pec. Bal. Sto.
Bayberry, bark	0 20	Myrica cerifera	Err. Ast. Eme.
do. do. pulv.	0 38	do. do.	" "
Barberry, bark	0 42	Berberis vulgaris	Ton. Ref. Ast.
do. do. pulv.	0 60	do. do.	" "
Beth root	0 75	Trillium erectum	Pec. Alt. Ast. Ton.
do. do. pulv.	1 00	do. do.	" "
Bitter sweet	0 50	Solanum dulcamara	Nar. Her. Deo.
Bitter sweet, false	0 75	Celastrus scandens	A-bil. Dis.
Bitter root, dog bane.	0 75	Apocynum androsæmifolium	Diu. Ver.
do. do. pulv.	1 33	do. do.	" "
Blackberry, root	0 25	Rubus villosus	Ast. Ton
Blood root	0 50	Sanguinaria canadensis	Err. Deo. Dia
do. do. pulv.	0 65	do. do.	" " "
Blue flag, root	0 75	Iris versicolor	Cath. Eme. Dia.
Boxwood, bark	0 50	Cornus florida	Ton. Ast
Buckbean, plant	0 50	Menyanthes trifoliata	Cath. Ton. Deo
Buckhorn malefern	0 50	Osmunda interrupta	Ton. Ast Ver
Buckhorn Syrup	0 40	Rhamnus cathartica	Diu. Cath. Ver
Bugle, sweet	0 50	Lycopus virginicus	Sty. Pec Deo. Ton.
Bugle, bitter	0 50	do. Europeus.	Nar. Pec. Deo. Ton
Burdock, leaves	0 25	Arctium lappa	Sud. Dia Ape.
do. root	0 34	do. do.	Sud. Her. A-scor.
do. seed	0 30	do. do.	Car Ton.
Butternut, bark	0 25	Juglans cinerea	Cath. Deo.
Cancer root, plant	0 50	Epiphegus virginianus	Ast. Ton.
Catmint	0 25	Nepeta cataria	Dia. Sto. Car.
Caraway seed	0 30	Carum carui	Sto. Car. Aro.

3

Common Names.	Per lb	Botanical Names.	Properties.
Cardus, spotted	0 30	Centaurea benedicta	Ton. Dia. Diu.
Cayenne, Afric. gro.	0 50	Capsicum annuum	Sti. Rub. Err.
do. pure pul. No. 1.	1 00	do. do.	" " "
do. do. No. 2.	0 55	do. do.	" " "
Celandine, garden	0 38	Chelidonium majus	Cath. Diu. Dia.
Camomile, low	0 50	Anthemis nobilis	Ton. Sto.
Cherry, black, bark	0 25	Prunus virginiana	Feb. Ast. Ton.
Cicuta, leaves	0 33	Conium maculatum	Nar. Deo.
Clary	0 33	Salvia sclarea	Sto. Diu.
Cleavers	0 33	Galium aparine	Diu. Sud.
Cohosh, black	0 50	Macrotys racemosa	Alt. Deo. Nar.
do. yellow	0 75	Flavus pulvus	Alt. Deo. Nar.
do. red and white	0 75	Actæa rubra et alba	Alt. Deo. Nar.
Coltsfoot, leaves	0 50	Tussilago farfara	Exp. Pec. Dem.
do. root	0 50	do. do.	" " "
Comfrey	0 38	Symphytum officinale	Pec. Dem
Cow parsnip, royal.	2 00	Zizia aurea	A-spas. Ton.
do. root, masterwort	50	Heracleum lanatum	Ner. Car. Diu.
do. seed	0 63	do. do.	Car. Aro.
Cranesbill, American	0 50	Geranium maculatum	Sty. Ast. Ton.
do. pulv.	1 00	do. do.	" " "
Culver's black root	1 00	Leptandra virginica	Cath. Deo.
do. do. do. pulv.	1 34	do. do.	" " "
Dandelion, plant	0 25	Leontodon taraxacum	A-bil. Ast. Ton.
do. root	0 42	do. do.	" " "
Dock, yellow, root	0 38	Rumex crispus	Ton. Deo. Her.
do. broad-leafed	0 33	Rumex obtusifolius	Cath. Deo. Her.
Dragon root	0 38	Arum triphyllum	Dia. Sti. Acr.
Elder, flowers	0 38	Sambucus canadensis	Alt. Sud. Ner.
Elder, dwarf	0 20	Aralia hispida	Dia. Diu. Dem. Ton
Elecampane, root	0 25	Inula helenium	Exp. Ast. Sto.
do. do. pulv.	0 35	do. do.	" " "
Elm, slippery, bark	0 17	Ulmus fulva	Emo. Diu. Dem. Ton.
do. do. extra.	0 25	do. do.	" " "
do. ground	0 25	do. do.	" " "
do. super. flour.	0 50	do. do.	" " "
Feverfew	0 50	Chrysanthemum parthenium	Ner. Sto.
Fern, sweet	0 25	Comptonia asplenifolia	Sto. Ast.
Fleabane	0 42	Erigeron canadense	Sty. Ton. Ast. Diu.
Flax seed, ground	0 20	Lini usitatissimum semina	Dem. Eme.
Foxglove	0 50	Digitalis purpurea	Nar. Diu.

4

Common Names.	Per lb.	Botanical Names.	Properties.
Frostwort	0 30	Cistus canadensis	Ast. Ton.
Fumatory	0 33	Fumaria officinalis	Deo. Dia. Diu.
Garget or poke root	0 25	Phytolacca decandia	Deo. Cath. Aer.
pulv.			
Golden seal, root, gr.	0 60	Hydrastis canadensis	Ape. A-bil. Sto.
do. flour	0 75	do. do.	" "
Gold thread, root	1 25	Coptia trifolia	Sto. Ton.
Hardhack, leaves	0 25	Spirea tomentosa	Ast. Ton.
Harvest lice	0 50	Bidens chrysanthemoides	Ast. Ton.
Hellebore, white, root	75	Veratrum viride	Err. Nar. Aer.
Hemlock, leaves	0 25	Pinus canadensis	Dia. Emo.
do. bark, ground	0 17	" do.	Ast. Ton
do. flour	0 25	" do.	" "
Henbane, bla., leaves	1 00	Hyoscyamus niger	Nar. Ner.
Hollyhock, flowers	0 75	Althea rosea	Ast. Dem.
Horehound, white	0 38	Marrubium vulgare	Ton. Sto. Pec
Horseradish, leaves	0 25	Cochlearia armoracia	Dia. Aer. Sti.
Horsemint	0 25	Monarda punctata	Diu. Cath
Hyssop	0 33	Hyssopus officinalis	Aro. Sti. Dia. Sto
Iceland moss	0 33	Lichen icelandicus	Pec. Dem. Ton.
Indian hemp	1 50	Apocynum cannabinum	Cath. Diu. Dia.
Indian hemp	0 75	Asclepias incarnata	Diu. Dia.
Indigo, wild, root	0 60	Baptisia tinctoria	A-sep. Ton.
John's wort	0 25	Hypericum perforatum	Dia. Ast.
Juniper berries	0 17	Juniperus communis	Diu. Sti.
Life everlasting	0 33	Gnaphalium polycephalum	Sto. Sud.
Lily, white, root	0 50	Nymphea odorata	Pec. Emo. Ast. Ton
do. do. flour	0 75	do. do.	" " "
do. yellow, root	0 50	Nuphar advena	Pec. Emo. Ast. Ton.
do. do. flour	0 75	do. do. flour	" " " "
Liverwort, noble	1 50	Hepatica americana	Pec. Nar.
Lobelia	0 33	Lobelia inflata	Dia. Exp. Eme. Nar.
do. pulv.	0 60	do. do.	" " " "
do seed	1 50	do. do.	" " " "
do do. pulv.	2 00	do. do.	" " " "
Lovage, leaves	0 42	Ligusticum levisticum	Dia. Car. Sto.
do. root	1 00	do. do.	Aro. Dia. Car. Sto.
Lungwort	0 33	Variolaria faginea	Pec. Sto. Dem. Ton
Maidenhair	0 50	Adiantum pedatum	Pec. Ver
Mallow, marsh, leaves	50	Althæa officinalis	Dem. Ast
do. do. root	0 50	do. do.	" "

5

Common Names.	Per lb.	Botanical Names.	Properties.
Mallow, low, leaves	0 25	Malva rotundifolia	Dem. Pec.
Mandrake, root	0 50	Podopiyllum peltatum	A-bil. Diu. Nar.
do. pulv.	0 65	do. do.	" " "
Marigold, flowers	0 75	Calendula officinalis	Sto. Aro.
Marsh rosemary	0 33	Statice caroliniana	Ast. Ton.
Mayweed	0 25	Anthemis cotula	Ton. Dia. Sto.
Marjoram, sweet	0 75	Origanum marjorana	Sto. Aro.
Melilot	0 33	Melilotus officinalis	Dem. Ton.
Moccasin or nerve root	50	Cypripedium pubescens	Ton. Ner. Ano.
do. flour	0 75	do. do.	" " "
Motherwort	0 25	Leonurus cardiaca	Dia. Ner. Sto.
Mountain ash, bark	0 32	Sorbus americana	Ton. Ast.
Mountain mint	0 50	Monarda didyma	Sto. Aro.
Mugwort	0 50	Artemisia vulgaris	Ton. A-bil. Ner.
Mullein, leaves	0 25	Verbascum thapsus	Ano. Dem. Emo.
Nightshade, leaves	1 25	Atropa belladonna	Nar. Dia. Ano. Diu.
Oak of Jerusalem	0 33	Chenopodium botrys	Ver. Sto.
Oak, white, bark	0 17	Quercus alba	Ast. Ton.
Parsley, leaves	0 33	Apium petroselinum	Diu. Dem. Dia.
do. root	0 42	do. do.	" "
Pennyroyal	0 33	Hedeoma pulegioides	Dia. Sti. Sto. Aro.
Peony, root	1 00	Pæonia officinalis	Ner. Ver.
Peppermint	0 25	Mentha piperita	Aro. Sto. Sti.
Pine, white, bark	0 17	Pinus strobus	Dia. Dem. Bal.
Plaintain, leaves	0 33	Plantago major	Ref. Diu. Deo.
Pleurisy, root	0 60	Asclepias tuberosa	Dia. Exp. Sud. Ano.
do. do. pulv.	0 75	do. do.	" " "
Poplar, bark, gr.	0 15	Populus tremuloides	Ton. Ast. Aro.
do. do. flour	0 20	do. do.	" " "
Poppy, flowers	1 50	Papaver somniferum	Sti. Nar. Ano.
do. leaves	0 50	do. do.	" " "
do. capsules	0 50	do. do.	" " "
Raspberry, leaves	0 25	Rubus strigosus	Ast. Ton.
do. do gro.	33	do. do.	" "
Rose flowers, red	1 25	Rosa gallica	Ast. Ton
do. do. white	1 25	do. alba	" "
do. water, gallon.	2 25	do. aqua	Fragrant.
Rue	0 50	Ruta graveolens	Sti. A-spas Diu. Sto
Saffron	4 50	Carthamus tinctorius	Dia. Sto. Aro.
Sage	0 40	Salvia officinalis	Aro. Sto. Bal.
do. ground	0 50	do. do.	" " "

6

Common Names.	Per lb	Botanical Names.	Properties.
Sarsaparilla, root	0 50	Aralia nudicaulis	Alt. Dia. Dem. Deo
do. do. pulv	0 60	do. do.	" " "
Sassafras, bark	0 33	Laurus sassafras	Sti. Sto. Aro
Savin, leaves	0 34	Juniperus communis	Sti. Aer. Dia
Savory, summer	0 25	Satureja hortensis	Car. Sti. Sto. Aro.
do. ground	0 62	do. do.	" " "
Scabish	0 33	Œnothera biennis	Dem. Sto.
Scullcap, blue	0 75	Scutellaria lateriflora	Ton. Sud.
do. do. ground	1 00	do. do.	" "
Scurvy grass	0 25	Cochlearia officinalis	A-scor. Sti.
Silk weed	0 33	Asclepias syriaca	Exp. Diu. Ano.
Skunk cabbage, root	0 50	Ictodes fœtida	Exp. A-spas. Ner. Aer.
do. do. flour	0 60	do. do.	" "
Snakeroot, Canada	0 50	Asarum canadense	Sti. Ton. Aro. Ner.
Snakehead, bitter, herb	33	Chelone glabra	A-bil. Ton.
Solomon seal, root	0 50	Convallaria multiflora	Pec. Dem. Bal.
Southernwood	0 50	Artemisia abrotanum	Ton. Ner.
Spearmint	0 25	Mentha viridis	Sto. Aro. Sti
Spikenard, root	0 33	Aralia racemosa	Alt. Bal. Sto.
Spice, or fever bush	0 25	Laurus benzoin	Feb. Aro. Sti.
Stone brake	1 00	Eupatorium purpureum	A-lit. Dia.
Sumach, leaves	0 25	Rhus glabrum	Ast. Ton.
do. berries	0 25	do. do.	Ast. Ref.
Sweet flag, root	0 33	Acorus calamus	Sti. Ton. Aro. Sto.
Tansy, double	0 25	Tanacetum crispum	Ton. Sto. Ver.
Thorn apple, leaves	0 33	Datura stramonium	Nar. Aer.
do. do. root	0 50	do. do.	" "
do. do. seed	0 50	do. do.	" "
Thoroughwort	0 25	Eupatorium perfoliatum	Eme. Sud. Ton.
Thyme	0 75	Thymus serpyllus	Sto. Aro.
Uva ursi	0 25	Arbutus uva ursi	A-lit. Ast. Ton.
Vervain	0 25	Verbena hastata	Sud. Ton.
Valerian, English	0 60	Valeriana officinalis	Ner. Ano. Sto.
do. do. pulv	0 75	do. do.	" "
Water pepper, aromat	25	Polygonum punctatum	Sud. Sti. Aer.
Whitewood, bark	0 40	Liriodendron tulipifera	Sto. Aro.
Wintergreen	0 25	Chimaphila umbellata	Diu. Sti.
Witch hazle, leaves	0 42	Hamamelis virginica	Ast. Her.
Wormwood	0 33	Artemisia absinthium	Ton. Sto. A-bil.
Wormseed	0 50	Chenopodium anthelminticum	Ver
Yarrow	0 25	Achillea millefolium	Aro. Ast. Sto.

7

Extracts.

Common Names.	Per lb
Butternut	0 50
Cicuta	1 00
do. best	2 00
Clover	1 00
Cow parsnip	1 50
Dandelion	0 75
do. best	1 50
Garget, or poke	1 50
Hardhack	0 50
Henbane	1 50
do. best	3 00
Nightshade	2 00
do. best	3 00
Oak, white	0 75
Sarsaparilla	1 50
Thorn apple	1 00
Thoroughwort	1 00
Valerian, Engl. best	3 00
Wintergreen	1 50
Wormwood	1 50

Extracta.

Botanical Names	Properties.
Juglans cinerea	Cath. Alt.
Conium maculatum	Nar. Deo.
do. do.	" "
Trifolium pratense	Pec. Aer.
Heracleum lanatum	Cath. Car. Diu.
Leontodon taraxacum	Ton. Deo. Diu
do. do.	" " "
Phytolacca decandra	Cath. Deo. Alt.
Spiræa tomentosa	Ast. Ton.
Hyoscyamus niger	Nar. Ano. Ner.
do. do.	" " "
Atropa belladonna	Nar. Ano.
do. do.	" "
Quercus alba	Ast. Ton.
Aralia nudicaulis	Alt. Dia. Deo.
Datura stramonium	Nar. Ano.
Eupatorium perfoliatum	Ape. Ton. Sud.
Valeriana officinalis	Ner. Ano. Sti.
Chimaphila umbellata	Diu. Sti.
Artemisia absinthium	Ton. Sto. A-bil.

Oils.

Cedar	0 80
Checkerberry	6 00
Fir	0 80
Goldenrod	10 00
Snakeroot, Canada	14 00
Wormwood	7 00
Wormseed	4 00

Olea.

Juniperus virginiana	Sti. Diu.
Galtheria procumbens	Aro. Diu. Sto.
Pinus balsamea	Sti. Ton. Aro.
Solidago odora	Aro. Dia.
Asarum canadense	Aro. Ner.
Artemisia absinthium	Sto. A-bil.
Chenopodium anthelminticum	Ver.

8

Ointments.

Bone, or Kittredge	1 25
Savin	0 75
Thorn apple	0 75

NET PRICES OF

Syrups Compound.

Black Cohosh, per gall.	3 00
in bottles, per doz.	4 25
Liverwort, per gall.	3 00
in bot. per doz	4 25
Poppy, per gall.	3 00
in bot. per doz	4 25
Sarsaparilla, per gall.	5 00
in bot. per doz.	5 50
Wild Cherry Pectoral, in bottles, per doz.	4 00

Sundries.

Rheumatic Vegetable Pills, per doz.	3 00
Anti-bilious Pills, do.	3 00
Compound Emetic, half pint bottles, per doz.	4 00
Nitrous Salts, per lb.	0 42
Chemical Liniment, per doz. bottles	4 00
Ginger, pure, gr.	0 20

Various other kinds of Extracts and Ointments made to order, strictly according to the Pharmacopœia, or to the directions given, if the simples can be obtained.

The common names in this Catalogue are such as are generally used in the New England States. The botanical names are from Eaton's Manual of Botany, last edition.

Orders attended to at all seasons; but customers are requested to forward them in the spring, if new articles are wanted, and thus give time for collection in the proper season.

Orders for such native plants as are not found in the Catalogue, if forwarded with their botanical names, will be attended to with care and fidelity.

Botanical practitioners are hereby informed that the various simples and compounds introduced by Beach, Howard, Thompson, Smith, and others, are prepared with fidelity and care, and sold on terms corresponding with prices in the general Catalogue.

Any of the above articles pulverized to order for a fair compensation.

☞ The best extracts are cold expressed, and evaporated by the sun. Those not marked *best*, are by a higher heat. The sun heat is very important on account of not destroying the essential oil.

Appendix II:
Medicinal Herb Catalogs

This information was extracted from Mary L. Richmond, "By the Shakers," *Shaker Literature, A Bibliography, I* (Hanover, N.H.: 1977), pp. 25-61.

As Mary Richmond noted, many other Shaker publications and medicines probably exist. Those mentioned here show a representation of the full range of Shaker herbal industries. The listing of materials from some communities is inadequate; North Union, Ohio, industries are completely unrepresented and those of some other communities are represented by only one product.

Alfred, Maine

Catalogue of Medical Plants, Prepared in the United Society, Alfred, Maine. [n.p., n.d.]. Broadside.

Canterbury, New Hampshire

Catalogue of Medicinal Plants and Vegetable Medicines. Prepared in the United Society, Canterbury, N.H. . . . Orders to be Directed to T. Corbett, Shaker Village, Merrimack Co., N.H. Printed at Shaker Village: 1835. Cover title. 16 pp.

____Prepared in the United Society of "Shakers," Merrimack County, N.H.. [Printed at Canterbury, N.H.: n.d.]. Broadside.

Catalogue of Medicinal Plants and Vegetable Medicines, to which is Annexed their most Prominent Medical Properties. Prepared in the United Society, Canterbury, N.H. . . . Orders to be Directed to Thomas Corbett, Shaker Village, Merrimack Co., N.H. Printed at Canterbury, N.H.: 1847. Cover title. 8 pp. illus.

___Orders to be directed to Thomas Corbett, Shaker Village, Merrimack, N.H. Printed at Canterbury, N.H.: 1848. Cover title. 8 pp.

___Orders to be Directed to David Parker, Shaker Village, Merrimack Co., N.H. Printed at Canterbury, N.H.: 1848. Cover title. 8 pp.

___Orders to be Directed to James Kaime, Shaker Village, Merrimack Co., N.H. Printed at Canterbury, N.H.: 1854. Cover title. 8 pp.

Enfield, Connecticut

Catalogue of Medicinal Plants, Barks, Roots, Seeds and Flowers, with their Therapeutic Qualities and Botanical Names. Also, Pure Vegetable Extracts, and Shaker Garden Seeds, Raised, Prepared and Put up in the Most Careful Manner, by the United Society of Shakers, Enfield, Conn. All orders addressed to Jefferson White, Thompsonville, Conn., Wholesale Agent for the Shaker Society, will meet Prompt Attention. First Established in 1802, being the Oldest Seed Establishment in the United States. Hartford [Conn.]: Elihu Geer, Stationer and Steam Printer, 1854. Cover title. 24 pp.

Fresh Herbs, Raised, Gathered, and Put up by the United Society. . . Shakers . . . Enfield, Conn. Address Jefferson White (Seedsman and Herb Agent) Thompsonville, P.O., Conn. (on or before July annually). Pressed and Neatly Put Up in Packages, from 1 oz. to 1 lb. each as Ordered. [n.p. 185_]. Broadside.

Enfield, New Hampshire

Catalogue of Medicinal Plants and Vegetable Medicines to which is Annexed their most Prominent Medical Properties, Prepared in the United Society, at Enfield, N.H. Orders to be Directed to Hiram C. Baker, Shaker Village, Enfield, N.H., Concord, N.H. From L. L. Mower's Printing Engine, [186_?]. Cover title. 7 pp.

Hancock, Massachusetts

Harvard, Massachusetts

Catalogue of Medicinal Plants and Vegetable Medicines, to which is Annexed their most Prominent Medical Properties. Prepared in the United Society, Harvard, Mass. Orders to be Directed to [blank space for name to be supplied] Harvard, Mass. Boston: J. Howe's Sheet Anchor Press, 1845. Cover title. 8 pp.

___Boston: H.L. Devereux, Printer, 1849. Cover title. 8 pp.

Catalogue of Herbs, Roots, Barks, Extracts, Ointments, Powdered Articles, &c., &c. Prepared in the United Society, Harvard, Mass. . . . Orders to be Directed to Simon T. Atherton, South Groton, Mass. Boston: H. L. Devereau & Co., Printers, 1851. Cover title. 8 pp.

Catalogue of Herbs Roots, Barks, Powdered Articles, &c., &c. Prepared in the United Society, Harvard, Mass. Orders addressed to Simon T. Atherton, South Groton, Mass. will meet with Prompt Attention. Boston, Mass.: Cross & Freeman, Printers, 1853. Cover title. 8 pp.

___Boston: J. E. Farwell & Co., Printers, 1854. Cover title. 8 pp.

_____Boston: J. E. Farwell & Co., Printers, 1856. Cover title. 14 pp.

_____Boston: Printed by Evans & Company, 1857. Cover title. 16 pp.

_____Boston: Printed by Fred Rogers, 1860. Cover title. 16 pp.

_____Boston: C. C. P. Moody, Printer, 1868, Cover title. 15 pp.

Catalogue of Roots, Herbs, Barks, Powdered Articles &c. Prepared in the United Society, Harvard, Mass. Orders Addressed to Simon T. Atherton, Groton Junction . . . Boston: C. H. Shepard, Printer, 1873. Cover title. 15 pp.

_____&c. Prepared in the United Society, Harvard Mass. Post Office Address, S. T. Atherton, Ayer (formerly Groton Junction) Mass. 187_. [n.p. 1875?]. Broadside.

Reduced Price List. Herbs, Roots, Barks, Powdered Articles, Etc., Prepared in the United Society, Harvard, Mass. Post Office Address, S. T. Atherton, Ayer (formerly Groton Junction), Mass. 1889. [n.p.188_?]. Broadside.

Shaker Herbs [n.p., n.d.] Broadside. Illus.

Reduced Price List. Catalog of Herbs, Roots, Barks, Powdered Articles, Rosewater, Etc. Prepared in the United Society, Harvard, Mass. Post Office Address: John Whitely, Successor to S. T. Atherton, Ayer, Mass. [n.p. 1889?]. Cover title. [7] pp.

New Lebanon, New York

Annual Catalog of Herbs, Medicinal Plants, with their Therapeutic Qualities and Botanical Names; Also Extracts, Ointments, Essential Oils, Double Distilled and Fragrant Waters, Raised, Prepared and Put Up in the Neatest Style, and Most Careful Manner, at the Botanic Garden, New Lebanon, Columbia County, N.Y. [n.p., n.d.]. [12] pp.

Catalogue of Medicinal Plants and Vegetable Medicines, Prepared in the United Society, New Lebanon, N.Y. Albany: Printed by Hoffman and White, 1836. 8 pp.

_____To which is Affixed their most Prominent Medical Properties. Prepared in the United Society, New Lebanon, N.Y. . . . Orders to be Directed to [blank for name to be supplied] New Lebanon, N.Y. Albany: Printed by Packard and Van Benthuysen, 1837. Cover title. 8 pp.

_____Bought of Charles F. Crosman, Agent for the United Society, New Lebanon, N.Y. The Following Medicinal and Vegetable Medicines. [n.p. 1838]. Caption title. [3] pp.

_____New York: New Franklin Printing Office, 1841. Cover title. 12 pp.

Catalogue of Shaker Herbs, Roots, and Medicinal Plants. . . . Raised, Manufactured and Put up by the Shakers of New Lebanon . . . New York: 1848. 10 pp.

Catalogue of Medicinal Plants, Barks, Roots, Seeds, Flowers and Select Powders, with their Therapeutic Qualities and Botanical Names. Also Ointments, Waters, &c. Raised, Prepared, and Put Up in the most Careful Manner, by the United Society of Shakers, at New Lebanon, N.Y. . . . For Sale by W. A. Leckler, 71 Maiden Lane, New York. E. B. Hyde & Co. [n.p., n.d.]. [24] pp.

_____Orders Addressed to Edward Fowler . . . Albany: Van Benthuysen, 1860. Cover title. 35 pp.

_____Orders Addressed to Edward Fowler . . . Albany: Van Benthuysen, Printer, [n.d.]. Cover title. 34 pp.

_____Orders Addressed to [blank space for name to be supplied] will Meet with Prompt Attention . . . Albany: Van Benthuysen, Printer, [n.d.]. Cover title. 32 pp.

_____Orders Addressed to [blank space for name to be supplied] will Meet with Prompt Attention . . . New Lebanon, N. Y: W.H. Hill, Printer, [n.d.]. 23 pp.

Prices of Fluid Extracts, Manufactured by the Shakers, Mount Lebanon, N.Y. [n.p., 1867]. Caption title. [3] pp.

_____1868. 3 pp.

Shakers' Wholesale, Price List Of Medicinal Herbs, Roots, &c., &c. Nett [sic] Prices Cash. To Wholesale Dealers Only, Corrected March 1872. Mount Lebanon, N.Y. [n.p., 1872]. Broadside.

_____Corrected to June 1872. To Wholesale Dealers Only, Mount Lebanon, N.Y. [n.p., n.d.]. Broadside.

Druggist's Hand-book of Pure Botanic Preparations, &c. Sold by the Society of Shakers, Mt. Lebanon, N.Y, Albany, N.Y.: Weed, Parsons & Company, Printers, 1873. 58 pp. (Cover title: Catalogue of Medicinal Plants, Barks, Roots, Seeds, Flowers & Select Powders, with their Therapeutical Qualities & Botanical Names . . .).

. . . Shakers' Price List of Medicinal Preparations, Mount Lebanon, Columbia Co., N.Y. Herbs, Roots Barks, and Powders, Net Prices. Fluid and Solid Extracts, Discount According to the Amount Purchased. [n.p., 1874]. Caption title [4] pp.

_____[n.p., 1874]. [4] pp.

_____Albany, N.Y: Weed, Parsons & Company, 1875. 58 pp.

Shakers' Fluid Extracts, Prepared by the Society of Shakers, Mount Lebanon, N.Y. Albany: Printed by C. Van Benthuysen, [n.d.]. Cover title. [8] pp.

Revised Prices Current of Pure Medicinal Extracts, Prepared by the Shakers, Mount Lebanon, Columbia County, N.Y. Benjamin Gates. [n.p.,n.d.]. Cover title. [4] pp.

Price List Adopted January 1st, 1919. Shaker Medical Department, Mount Lebanon, Columbia County, N.Y. [n.p., 1918]. Broadside.

Sabbathday Lake, Maine

Catalogue of Medicinal Plants Prepared in the United Society of "Shakers." New Gloucester, Cumberland County, Maine: [n.d.]. Broadside.

Catalogue of Herbs, Roots, Barks, Powdered Articles, &c., Prepared in the United Society, New Gloucester, Maine. Orders Addressed to Charles Vining, West Gloucester, Maine, will meet with Prompt Attention. Portland [Maine]. B. Thurston, Printer, 1864. 15 pp.

Shirley, Massachusetts

South Union, Kentucky

Tyringham, Massachusetts

Union Village, Ohio

Catalogue of Medical Plants and Extracts; to which are Affixed their most Prominent Medical properties. Also Essential Oils, and Double-Distilled Fragrant Waters. Prepared and for Sale by the United Society of Shakers at Union Village, Ohio. . . Union Village, O: Day Start Print., Jan. 1847. 8 pp.

Annual Wholesale Catalogue of Herbs, Medical Plants; Also Extracts, Essential Oils, Double-Distilled and Fragrant Waters. Prepared, and for Sale by the United Society of Shakers, at Union Village . . . Orders addressed to Peter Boyd, Union Village, near Lebanon, Ohio, will meet with Prompt Attention. Union Village, Ohio: Printed by G. H. Vandever, 1850. 11 pp.

_____Printed at Union Village, Warren County, Ohio: 1856.

Catalogue of Medical Plants, Extracts, Essential Oils, Etc. Prepared and for Sale by the United Society of Shakers, at Union Village, O. [Lebanon, O.: n.d.]. [4] pp.

Watervliet, New York

Catalogue of Medicinal Plants and Vegetable Medicines, Prepared in the United Society, Watervliet, N.Y. [quotation]. Orders to be Directed to [blank for name to be supplied] Watervliet, N.Y., Albany, N.Y.: Printed by Packard and Van Benthuysen, 1830. Cover title. 8 pp.

_____Prepared in the United Society, Watervliet, N.Y. [quotation]. Orders to be Directed to [blank for name to be supplied] Watervliet, N.Y., Hudson [N.Y.]: Printed by Ashbel Stoddard, 1833. Cover title. 8 pp.

_____and Vegetable Medicines, To which is affixed their most Prominent Medical Properties. Prepared in the United Society, Watervliet, N.Y. . . . Orders to be Directed to [blank for name to be supplied] Watervliet, N.Y., Albany: Printed by Packard and Van Benthuysen, 1837. Cover title. 8 pp.

_____Albany [N.Y.]: Printed by C. Van Benthuysen and Co., 1843. Cover title. 12 pp.

Catalogue of Herbs, Medicinal Plants, and Vegetable Medicines, with their Theapeutic [sic] Qualities and Botanical names; Also, Extracts, Ointments, Essential Oils, Double Distilled and Fragrant Waters; With a List of Garden Seeds . . . Raised, Prepared and put Up in the most Careful Manner, by the United Society of Shakers, Watervliet, N.Y. Orders to be Directed to Buckingham and Copley, Post Office, Albany, N.Y. Albany: Printed at the Office of the Evening Atlas, 1845. 11 pp.

_____Fragrant Waters, Raised, Prepared, and Put Up in the most Careful Manner, by the United Society of Shakers, Watervliet, N.Y. Orders to be Directed to Buckingham and Copley, Albany, Post Office N.Y. New York: Piercy and Hovel, Printers, 1847. Cover title. 7 pp.

_____Raised, Prepared and Put Up in the most Careful Manner, by the United Society of Shakers, Watervliet (near Albany,) N.Y. Orders to be Directed to Chauncey Copley, Albany P.O., N.Y. Albany: Printed by Charles Van Benthuysen, 1850. 11 pp.

Catalogue of Medicinal Plants, Barks, Roots, Seeds and Flowers, with their

Therapeutic and Botanical Names. Also, Pure Vegetable Extracts, and Shaker Garden Seeds, Raised, Prepared, and Put Up in the most Careful Manner, by the United Society of Shakers, Watervliet (near Albany,) N.Y. All Orders Addressed to Chauncey Miller, Shaker Village, (Albany P.O.), N.Y. [n.p.,n.d]. Cover title. [22] pp.

Whitewater, Ohio

Appendix III:
Seed Catalogs

This information was extracted from: Mary L. Richmond, "By the Shakers," *Shaker Literature, A Bibliography, I* (Hanover, N.H., 1977), pp. 25-61.

Alfred, Maine

Garden Seeds, Raised at Alfred, Me. & sold by John Wooley . . . [n.p., 182_?]. Broadside.

Catalogue of Garden Seeds, Raised by the United Society, at Alfred, Maine. Sold by Nathan Freeman . . . 184_. Among which are the following: [n.p., 184_?]. Broadside.

Canterbury, New Hampshire

Garden Seeds. Raised at Canterbury, New Hampshire 181[0] and Sold by [Francis Winkley]. [n.p., 181_?]. Broadside.

Enfield, Connecticut

Catalogue of Flower Seeds, Cultivated by the United Society—Shakers—Enfield, Conn. Address Jefferson White, Thompsonville P.O., Conn. Hartford, Conn.: Elihu Geer, [n.d.]. Broadside.

Garden Seeds, Fresh and Genuine, Raised by the United Society (Shakers), Enfield, Conn. Jefferson White, Thompsonville P.O., Conn. Seedsman and Agent. [Hartford, Conn.: Elihu Geer, n.d.]. Broadside.

_____Raised by the United Society--Shakers, Enfield, Conn. Address Nathan Damon, Thompsonville, Conn., Seedsman and Agent. [Hartford: Elihu Geer, n.d.]. Broadside.

_____Raised by the United Society--Shakers, Enfield, Conn. Address Jefferson White, Thompsonville P.O., Conn. (on or before July annually), Seedsman and Agent. Hartford: Elihu Geer [n.d.]. Broadside.

_____For Sale by David Young, Seedsman, Americus Geo. [rgia]. [Hartford, Conn.: Elihu Geer, n.d.]. Broadside.

_____Enfield, Conn. Address to Nathan Damon, Thompsonville, Conn., on or before July annually. Seedsman and Agent. [Hartford, Conn.: Elihu Geer, n.d.]. Broadside.

_____For Sale by Clark, George & Co., Seedsmen and Druggist, Mobile, Alabama [Hartford, Conn.: Elihu Geer, n.d.]. Broadside.

Garden Seeds, Raised at Enfield, (Conn.) [blank space for name to be supplied] [n.d., n.p.]. Broadside.

Enfield, New Hampshire

Garden Seeds, Raised at Enfield, New-Hampshire, and sold by [blank for name to be supplied]. The following, which are [blank for Box number] [n.p. 180_?]. Broadside.

_____[n.p.1808]. Broadside.

_____[n.p.1809]. Broadside.

_____[n.p.1810]. Broadside.

Hancock, Massachusetts

Garden Seeds, Raised at Hancock, and Put Up in Papers, with the Retail Price Printed on them, For Sale by [blank for name to be supplied]. Among which are the Following: [n.p., 1813?]. Broadside.

Garden Seeds Raised at Hancock, Berkshire Co., (Mass.) and Put Up in Papers, with the Retail price Printed on them: For Sale, By [blank space for name to be supplied] Among which are the Following: [n.p., 1819?]. Broadside.

_____[n.p., 1819?]. Broadside.

_____[n.p., 1824?]. Broadside.

Garden Seeds, Raised at Hancock, Berkshire County, Mass. And Neatly Put Up in Papers, having the name and Retailing Price of the Seed Printed on them, and the Letters D. G. for Sale by [blank for name to be supplied]. [n.p. 1826?]. Broadside.

_____[n.p., 1827-1828?]. Broadside.

. . . Catalog of Garden Seeds, Raised and Sold by the United Society, Pittsfield, Berkshire Co., Mass. [n.p. 183_?]. Broadside.

. . . Catalog of Garden Seeds, Raised and Sold by the United Society, Pittsfield, Berkshire Co., Mass. [n.p. 183_?]. Broadside.

_____[n.p., 183_?]. Broadside.

Harvard, Massachusetts

New Lebanon, New York

Fresh Garden Seeds. A General Assortment of such as are in Common Use, Lately Received for the Quakers' [sic]. [n.p., 1814]. Broadside.

Just Received. A New Assortment of Choice Garden Seeds, Raised and Put up in the Best Manner by the United Society of Shakers, at New Lebanon, Columbia County, New-York, and ... Marked with the Letters D.M. For Sale [blank space to be filled in]. Albany, N.Y.: Van Benthuysen, Printers, [n.d.]. Broadside.

Shakers' Garden Seeds, Raised at New Lebanon, Columbia County, N.Y. [n.p.,n.d.]. Broadside.

_____[Albany, N.Y.: Van Benthuysen 184_?]. Broadside.

Descriptive Catalog of Vegetable Seeds Raised at New Lebanon, N.Y. with Directions for their Cultivation. All Orders should be Directed to D. C. Brainnard, Mt. Lebanon, N.Y.: [n.p.] Chickering & Axtell, Steam Printers, 1870. Cover title. [19] pp.

_____New York: Lange, Little & Hillman, 1873. Cover title. 23 pp.

Brainard's Shaker Catalog and Amateur's Guide to the Flower and Vegetable Garden. D. C. Brainard, Mount Lebanon, New York.: Albany, Weed, Parsons & Company, Printers, 1874. 96 pp. Illustrated.

[Shakers' Annual Catalog of Vegetable Seeds and Rural Register. Mt. Lebanon, N.Y.] [n.p., 1874] [pp. 25-26 _Catalogue of the Emma B. King Library, Shaker Museum (Old Chatham, N.Y., 1970), item 80.]_

Shakers' Catalogue and Amateur's Guide to the Flower and Vegetable Garden. Charles Sizer, Mt. Lebanon, N.Y., Albany, N.Y.: Weed Parsons & Co., 1875. 84 pp. Illustrated.

Rural Register and Almanac for 1876 from D. C. Brainard, Mt. Lebanon, N.Y. For the Southern and Middle States. Albany [N.Y.]: Weed, Parsons & Company, Printers, 1876. Cover title. 63 pp.

Shakers' Descriptive and Illustrated Catalogue and Amateur's Guide to the Flower and Vegetable Garden. From Charles Sizer. Mt. Lebanon, N.Y.: Mount Lebanon Printing Press of the United Society of Shakers [Washington Jones, Book and Job Printer], 1876. 84 pp. illus.

Shakers' Descriptive and Illustrated Catalogue of Flower and Vegetable Seeds for 1881. Address D. C. Brainard Ag't, Mt. Lebanon, N.Y. [Rochester, N.Y.: Rochester Dem. and Chron. Print.], 1881. 60 pp. illus.

_____From William Anderson, Mount Lebanon, N.Y.: Mt. Lebanon, N.Y.: Printing Press of Washington Jones, Book and Job Printer, 1881. 84 pp. illus.

Shakers' Descriptive and Illustrated Annual Catalogue and Amateur's Guide to the Flower and Vegetable Garden. Mount Lebanon, N.Y. Established 1795. Mount Lebanon, N.Y.: Washington Jones, Book and Job Printer, 1882. 84 pp.

_____Mt. Lebanon: Printing Press of the United Society [Washington Jones, Book and Job Printer], 1883. 84 pp.

Shaker Seed Co.'s Wholesale Price List of Garden Seeds. January 1st, 1885.

Shaker Seed Co., Mount Lebanon, Columbia Co., N.Y. If You Want a Splendid Garden, Plant Shaker Seeds; They are the Best. Pittsfield [Mass.]: Berkshire County Eagle Print., [1884]. 14 pp.

_____January 1st, 1886. Shaker Seed Co., Mt. Lebanon, Pittsfield, Mass.: Berkshire County Eagle, [1885]. Cover title 13 pp.

_____January 1st, 1887. [n.p., 1886]. 23 pp. illus.

The Shaker Seed Co's Annual Price List for Market Gardeners. Pittsfield, Mass.: Eagle Job Print., 1886. Cover title [4] pp.

Shaker Seed Co. [n.p., 1886]. [76] pp.

_____Mount Lebanon, N.Y.: 1888. 98 pp. illus.

Shaker Seed Co.'s Wholesale Price List of Seeds, Grown and for Sale by the Shaker Seed Co., Mt. Lebanon, N.Y. For Dealers Only. [n.p., 1887]. Caption title [4] pp.

The Shaker Seed Co.'s Special Price List of Vegetables and Other Seeds for Grangers. [Mt. Lebanon, N.Y.: n.d.] [4] pp.

_____of Vegetables and Other seeds for Market Gardeners. Mt. Lebanon, N.Y.: Shaker Seed Co., [1888?]. [4] pp.

Shakers' Genuine Garden Seeds. From New Lebanon (Columbia County), N.Y. Post Office Address, William Anderson, Mount Lebanon, Columbia County, N.Y. Albany: Weed, Parsons & Co., Printers [188_?]. Broadside.

. . . Bought of Levi Shaw. [Mt. Lebanon, N.Y.: 188_?]. Broadside.

Catalogue of Choice Vegetable Seeds. Shaker Seed Co. D.M. Mount Lebanon, N.Y.: [n.d.]. Broadside.

New Tomato "Livingston's Beauty." Shaker Seed Company, Wholesale and Retail Dealers in Garden Seeds. Mt. Lebanon, N.Y.: Buffalo, Clay and Richmond, [n.d.]. Broadside.

For Sale by Shaker Seed Co., Mount Lebanon, N.Y. Read the Verdict! Cleveland's Alaska Pea...Sold only under the Seal of the Originators. [n.p., n.d.]. Cover title [6] pp.

"Garden Seeds Warranted Fresh and Genuine, Raised by the United Society of Shakers. Strattan and Warner, Sole Agents," in Annual Herbalist's Catalogue of Medicinal Plants...(New York: n.d. 48 pp.) pp. [46]-48.

Sabbathday Lake, Maine

Shirley, Massachusetts

Garden Seeds Raised at Shirley, Massachusetts, and Sold by [blank space for name to be supplied] among which are the Following: [n.p., 180_?]. Broadside.

_____[n.p., 181_?]. Broadside.

_____and Sold by 182_. [Blank space for the name to be supplied]. Among which are the Following: [n.p., 182_?]. Broadside.

_____and Sold by 183_. [blank space for name to be supplied]. Among which are the Following: [n.p.], Carter Andrews, & Co., Print., [183_?]. Broadside.

Garden Seeds, Fresh and Genuine, Raised and Put Up by the United Society. Shirley Village, Mass. Boston: Franklin Printing House, [1855]. Broadside.

_____Fitchburg, Mass.: [186_?]. Broadside.

South Union, Kentucky

Garden Seed. Raised at South Union, Ky. [n.p. 18__?]. Broadside.

Garden Seed. Raised by the Shakers, at South Union, Ky. Crop of 1850. [n.p., 1849]. Broadside.

Garden Seed. Crop of 1853. Grown by the Shakers, at South Union, Ky. [n.p., 1853]. Broadside.

_____Crop of 1856. Cultivated by the Shakers, at South Union, Ky. [n.p., 1856]. Broadside.

_____Crop of 1858. Cultivated by the Shakers, at South Union, Ky. [n.p., 1858]. Broadside.

_____Crop of 1861. Cultivated by the Shakers, at South Union, Ky. [n.p., 1861]. Broadside.

Garden Seed. Grown by the Shakers, at South Union, Ky. Crop of 1866. [n.p., 1866]. Broadside.

_____Crop of 1868. [n.p., 1868]. Broadside.

_____Crop of 1869. [n.p., 1869]. Broadside.

_____Crop of 1870. [n.p., 1870]. Broadside.

_____Crop of 1871. [n.p., 1871]. Broadside.

Shakers' Catalogue of Garden Seeds, Grown at South Union, Ky. Crop of 1866. [n.p., 1866]. Broadside.

_____Crop of 1876. [n.p. 1876]. Broadside.

Catalogue of Shaker Garden Seeds. Grown at South Union, Ky. Crop of 1867. [n.p. 1867]. Broadside.

_____Crop of 1868. [n.p., 1868]. Broadside.

_____Crop of 1869. [n.p., 1869]. Broadside.

_____Crop of 1870. [n.p., 1870]. Broadside.

_____Crop of 1871. [n.p., 1871]. Broadside.

Catalogue of Garden Seeds. Cultivated by the Shakers at South Union, Ky. Bowling Green, Ky.: Gazette Print., 1884. Cover title [4] pp.

_____From the Shakers at South Union, Ky. Crop of 1873. [n.p. 1873]. Broadside.

_____From U. E. Jones, South Union, Ky. Crop of 1872. [n.p., 1872]. Broadside.

_____Grown by the Shakers at South Union, Ky. Crop of 1875. [n.p., 1875]. Broadside.

_____Grown by the Shakers at South Union Ky., for the Spring of 1877. [n.p., 1877?]. Broadside.

Garden Seeds. Crop of 1872. [n.p., 1872]. Broadside.

Crop of 1873. [n.p. 1873]. Broadside.

Just Received, a New Assortment of Choice Garden Seeds, Raised and Put Up in the Best Manner by the United Society of Shakers, at South Union, Jasper Valley, Logan County, Ky., and Marked with the name, and the Retail Price of the Seeds, and the Letters E.M.S.U. For Sale [blank space for name to be supplied]. Bowling Green, Ky.: Gazette (?) and Advertiser Office, [n.d.]. Broadside.

Tyringham, Massachusetts

Seeds, Garden Seeds, Raised at Tyringham, Berkshire County, Mass. And Put Up in Papers with the Retailing Prices of the Seeds on them. For Sale by [blank space for name to be supplied] Among which are the Following:-- [n.p., 182_?]. Broadside.

Catalogue of Garden Seeds, Raised by the United Society of Shakers in Tyringham, Berkshire County, Mass. Lee, Mass.: French and Royce, Printers, 185_. Broadside.

Union Village, Ohio

Watervliet, New York

. . . Bought of Chauncy [i.e., Chauncey] Miller. No Seed Warranted and no Damages Allowed above the Price of the Seeds when Sold, [n.p, 187_]. Broadside.

. . . Bought of Philip Smith. N.B. While We Exercise the Greatest Care to have all Seeds Pure and Reliable, it is Hereby Agreed...that We do Not Warrant Same, and are Not in any Respect Liable or Responsible for Seeds Sold by Us, for any Damage Arising from any Failure thereof in any Respect. [n.d., 188_]. Broadside.

_____Shakers, Albany. Co., N.Y. 1880

_____Address Chauney [ie. Chauncey] Miller, Albany, N.Y. Shaker Trustee or W. S. Carpenter, 468 Pearl Street, New York, N.Y. [n.p., n.d.]. Broadside.

List of Garden Seeds Raised by the Society of Shakers, near Albany, N.Y. Orders Addressed to Chauncy [i.e. Chauncey] Miller, Shakers, Albany, N.Y., Dealer in Brooms, Brushes, prepared Sweet Corn, Medical Herbs, Roots & Extracts, and All Other Articles manufactured by the Society. [n.p., n.d.]. Broadside.

_____Orders addressed to Philip Smith, Shakers, N.Y., . . . [n.p.,n.d.]. Broadside.

Whitewater, Ohio

Catalogue of Garden Seeds Raised by the United Society of Shakers. At Whitewater Village, Hamilton Co., O. [n.p.,n.d.]. Broadside.

Notes

Acknowledgments

[1] The reader will notice throughout the book that the word *World* (capitalized) is the term the Shakers used to identify everyone outside their respective communities.

Who Are the Shakers?

[1] Elder Henry Blinn lists the travelers as Mother Ann Lee, Father William Lee, Father James Whittaker, Elder John Hocknell, Richard Hocknell, James Shepard, Mary Partington, Nancy Lee, and Abram Stanley. See Henry Clay Blinn, *Mother Ann Lee* (East Canterbury, N.H., 1901).

[2] For a detailed look at the communities' demographics, see Priscilla J. Brewer, *Shaker Communities, Shaker Lives* (Hanover, N.H., 1986), pp. 207-238.

Chapter 1

[1] Charles Nordhoff, *The Communistic Societies of the United States* (Harper & Bros., N.Y., 1875; reprint, New York: Dover Publications, 1966), p. 161.

[2] Brewer, in *Shaker Communities*, p. 245, brought up the idea that members of the Ministry may also have been given particularly well-made articles as tokens of esteem. Studies Mary Boswell conducted at Shaker Village, Inc. for an exhibit called "Blessed in Our Basket," which included artifacts from several communities, corroborate this theory.

[3] John Whitcher, *A Brief History or Record of the Commencement & Progress of the United Society of Believers, at Canterbury, County of Merrimack. And. State of New Hampshire*, vol. 1, 1782-1871, Canterbury, N.H., Shaker Village, Inc., Canterbury, N.H. (hereafter SVI) #21, p. 39.

[4] Dorothy M. Filley, *Recapturing Wisdom's Valley: the Watervliet Shaker Heritage* (Albany, N.Y.: Albany Institute of History and Art, 1975), p. 69.

[5] Henry Clay Blinn, *Historical Notes Having Reference to the Believers in Enfield, N.H.*, vol. 1, 1782-1847, Enfield, N.H., SVI #761, p. 29.

[6] Nordhoff, *Communistic Societies*, pp. 154-155.

[7] Benjamin Silliman, "Remarks Made on a Short Tour between Hartford and Quebec in the Autumn of 1819," *Christian Monthly Spectator,* (1820), pp. 41-53.

[8] Quoted by Flo Morse, *The Shakers and the World's People* (New York: Dodd, Mead & Co., 1980), p. 87.

[9] Whitcher, *Brief History,* p. 39.

[10] Blinn, *Historical Notes,* p. 12. After a fire destroyed Jewett's house in 1792, the Believers met in the nearby home of Nathaniel Barker.

[11] Caleb Dyer, *A Historical Narrative of the Rise and Progress of the United Society of Shakers,* 1782-1858, Enfield, N.H., Shaker Museum, Old Chatham, N.Y. (hereafter Shaker Museum), #16,622, pp. 82-83.

[12] Blinn, *Historical Notes,* pp. 81-84. A snath is a long, bent handle; it is part of a scythe, an implement used for mowing or reaping.

[13] Dyer, *A Historical Narrative,* p. 97.

[14] Wendell Hess, *The Enfield, New Hampshire Shakers, A Brief History* (n.p., 1988), p. 54.

[15] Julia Neal, *By Their Fruits: The Story of Shakerism in South Union, Kentucky* (Chapel Hill, N.C.: University of North Carolina Press, 1947), pp. 10, 15.

[16] Edward Deming Andrews, *The People Called Shakers* (New York: Dover Publications, 1963), p. 84.

[17] Andrews, *The People Called Shakers,* p. 72.

[18] Henry Clay Blinn, ed., *The Manifesto* 29 (1889), p. 114.

Chapter 2

[1] Isaac N. Youngs, *A Concise View of the Church of God and of Christ on Earth Having its foundation In the faith of Christ's first and Second Appearing,* 1856-1860, Andrews Collection, Winterthur Museum, Winterthur, Del., (hereafter Andrews Collection), SA 760, p. 276-282.

[2] Amy Bess Miller, *Shaker Herbs, A History and Compendium* (New York: Clarkson N. Potter, Inc., 1976), p. 32.

[3] By 1830, the proportion of children under fifteen in the eastern communities had reached 15.2 percent; the proportion of young adults aged fifteen to twenty-nine had increased to 26.7 percent. See Brewer, *Shaker Communities,* p. 115; Miller, *Compendium,* p. 50. Seth Bradford of Enfield recorded that in 1846 four Shakers traveled from the Shaker community to Norwich, Vermont (more than twelve miles) "after Indian hemp root." Seth Bradford, *A Diary or Memorandum,* November 1850, Enfield, N.H., copy of manuscript in Museum at Lower Shaker Village, Enfield, N.H. (hereafter LSV), n.p.

[4] Sister Marsha Bullard, "Shaker Industries," *Good Housekeeping* 43 (1906), p. 37.

[5] Isaac Hill, "The Shakers," *The Farmers Monthly Visitor* 2 (1840), p. 115.

[6] Miller, *Compendium,* p. 183.

[7] *Catalogue of Medicinal Plants, Barks, Roots, Seeds, Flowers and select powders with their Therapeutic qualities and botanical names; Also, Pure Vegetable Extracts. Prepared in Vacuo. Ointments, Inspissated Juices, Essential Oils, Double Distilled and Fragrant Waters &c &c. Raised, Prepared and put up in the most careful manner by the United Society of Shakers at New Lebanon, N.Y.,* 1851, Western Reserve Historical Society (hereafter WRHS), Microfiche Collection, Cleveland, Ohio, pp. 32-33.

[8] Letter of Horace Jennings, 1860, quoted in Miller, *Compendium,* p. 50. Jennings was a peddler from Searsburg, Vermont.

[9] Miller, *Compendium,* p. 24.

[10] William Proctor, "New Lebanon: Its Physic Gardens and Their Products," *The American Journal of Pharmacy* 18 (New Lebanon, N.Y., 1852), p. 89.

[11] *A Manual of Botany for the Northern States* was written by Amos Eaton of the Rensselaer Institute in 1817; *Medical Flora or Manual of the Medical Botany of the United States in North America* was written by Constantine S. Rafinesque and was published in two volumes in Philadelphia by Atkinson-

Alexander in 1828 and in 1830.

[12] Bradford, *A Diary*, n.p.

[13] Benson J. Lossing, "A Visit to the Shakers at New Lebanon," *Harper's New Monthly Magazine* 86 (1857; repr. 1957), Shaker Museum, p. 173.

[14] Proctor, "New Lebanon," p. 89.

[15] Proctor, "New Lebanon," p. 89.

[16] Lossing, "A Visit to the Shakers," p. 172-173.

[17] Elisha Myrick, *Herb Department Diary*, December 1853-1857, Harvard, Mass., Andrews Collection, ASC 837, n.p., December, 1855.

[18] Myrick, *Herb Department Diary*, April, 1854.

[19] Myrick, *Herb Department Diary*, Dec. 31, 1853; Dec. 31, 1854.

[20] Myrick, *Herb Department Diary*, July and Dec., 1853.

[21] Elder Benjamin B. Dunlavy, "Trip of the Ministry of Pleasant Hill and South Union to the Eastern Societies," *Journal*, WRHS, Reel 39 VB 228, p. 26.

[22] Henry Elkins, *Fifteen Years in the Senior Order of the Shakers* (Hanover, N.H.: Dartmouth Press, 1853), p. 97.

[23] Myrick, *Herb Department Diary*, July and Dec., 1853.

[24] Hill, "The Shakers," p. 115.·

[25] Myrick, *Herb Department Diary*, Feb. 28, 1853.

[26] Myrick, *Herb Department Diary*, Aug. 13, 1853.

[27] Myrick, *Herb Department Diary*, Dec. 31, 1853.

[28] Edward Deming Andrews, *The Community Industries of the Shakers* (New York: University of the State of New York. Reprint of the New York State Museum Handbook, 15, 1933), p. 92.

[29] Andrews, *Community Industries*, p. 92.

[30] It was recorded that in 1831 a box of herbs valued at $30.68 was shipped to Paris, and thirteen boxes of herbs valued at $896.65 were shipped to Charles Whitlaw, a botanist in London. See Andrews, *Community Industries*, p. 91.

[31] Andrews, *Community Industries*, p. 274; Youngs, "Concise View," pp. 276-282.

[32] Miller, *Compendium*, pp. 94, 100.

[33] Record of Hervey L. Eades, 1836-1868, quoted in Miller, *Compendium*, p. 109.

[34] Andrews, *Community Industries*, p. 67.

[35] Miller, *Compendium*, p. 9.

[36] These herbs are listed in the *Catalogue of Medicinal Plants Prepared in the United Society of "Shakers,"* 1840, New Gloucester, Me., WRHS Microfiche Collection.

[37] Sabbathday Lake issued one bound herb catalog; in that catalog, dated 1864, 155 herbs were for sale.

[38] Miller, *Compendium*, p. 65.

[39] Miller, *Compendium*, p. 62.

[40] Margaret F. Somer, *The Shaker Garden Seed Industry* (Old Chatham, N.Y.: The Shaker Museum Foundation, 1972), p. 15.

[41] Dyer, *A Historical Narrative*, p. 95.

[42] Hill, "Enterprise of the Shakers," *The Farmers Monthly Visitor* 9 (1839), p. 141.

[43] Hill, "The Shakers," p. 115.

[44] Hill, "The Shakers," p. 115.

[45] Hill, "The Shakers," p. 115.

[46] Thomas Hammond, *Diary* 1851, Harvard, Mass., WRHS, Reel 48.

[47] Henry Clay Blinn, *Church Record*, 1784-1879, Canterbury, N.H., SVI #764, p. 200.

[48] Andrews, *Community Industries*, p. 89.

[49] Hill, "The Shakers," p. 115.

[50] Hill, "The Shakers," p. 115.

[51] Henry Clay Blinn, ed., *The Manifesto* 22 , Published by United Societies (1892), p. 187.

52 *Notebook,* 1793-1866, Canterbury, N.H., SVI #273; Blinn, *Church Record,* p. 64.

53 Letter of Ministry Canterbury to Ministry New Lebanon, 1829, WRHS, Reel 17 IV A 3.

Chapter 3

1 Inside cover of a South Union, Kentucky, seed box.

2 Somer, *The Shaker Garden Seed Industry,* p. 10; "A Brief History of the Raising of Garden Seeds Among Believers &c.," WRHS, p. 256; *Records of the Church at Watervliet, N.Y., Comprising the principal events relative to said Church, in connection with other Families and Societies since the year 1788,* I, WRHS Microfilm Reel 44 VB 279.

3 Andrews, *Community Industries,* pp. 66, 69; Edward Deming Andrews and Faith Andrews, *Work and Worship: The Economic Order of the Shakers* (New York: New York Graphic Society, 1974), p. 53; Henry Clay Blinn, *A Historical Record of the Society of Believers,* 1792-1848, Canterbury, N.H., SVI #763, p. 130, 46, 34.

4 Somer, *Garden Seed Industry,* p. 11; Miller, *Compendium* , p. 94; Andrews, *Community Industries,* p. 70; *Record of the Church at North Union Containing the Rise and Progress of the Church Commencing in the Year 1822 and Brought Forward to the Present 1843 . . .,* 1843, North Union, Ohio, WRHS VB 177.

5 Bradford, *Diary,* n.p.

6 Corinne W. Willard, *Garden Writers Bulletin,* "Shaker Highlights," Sept./Oct. 1964.

7 Andrews and Andrews, *Work and Worship,* p. 53.

8 Andrews and Andrews, *Work and Worship,* p. 55.

9 Andrews, *Community Industries,* p. 81.

10 Melon seeds were the only exception. "Declaration of Intent to Sell No Seeds Mixed with Seeds 'of the world,' " 1819, New Lebanon, N.Y., SVI Ms. 454.

11 According to Seth Bradford, the Enfield, New Hampshire Shakers grew seeds for their sister community in Connecticut in 1839. Bradford, *Diary,* n.p.

12 Neal, *By Their Fruits,* p. 105.

13 *Records of the Church at Union Village, Ohio,* 1842, WRHS Reel 40, VI 230.

14 Miller, *Compendium,* pp. 14, 61-62, 86; Andrews and Andrews, *Work and Worship,* p. 54; James J. Pettengill, Jr., "Accounts," I, 1812-1852, Enfield, N.H., New Hampshire Historical Society (hereafter NHHS), p. 36.

15 Andrews and Andrews, *Work and Worship,* p. 53; *Church Family Record,* 1788 Vol. 1, Watervliet, N.Y., WRHS Reel 44 VB 279, p. 7; Blinn, *Church Record,* p. 79.

16 Andrews and Andrews, *Work and Worship,* p. 54; Miller, *Compendium,* p. 36. After 1854 the herb business became the more profitable of the two. That year New Lebanon's seed sales decreased to $9,000 while herb sales climbed to $15,000. The most profitable year for the herbs was 1855, with the Church Family selling enough to make $23,006.99. This income varied considerably over the years, but the seed sales never surpassed herb sales after 1854. "Inventory Book of Money and Stock Held at the Beginning of Each Year," 1839-1864, New Lebanon, N.Y., WRHS, Reel 9 11B-38.

17 Blinn, *Church Record,* p. 217.

18 Linda Deatrick, "The Shaker Seed Industry; More than a Business. It was a Philosophy," *Shaker Messenger,* I (1979), p. 5.

19 Correspondence from Deacons Canterbury to Deacons Sabbathday Lake, 1828-1838, Collection of the United Society of Shakers, Sabbathday Lake, Me. (hereafter SDL).

20 Letter of William Willard and Israel Sanborn to Rufus Bishop, New Lebanon, N.Y., 1839, WRHS Reel 17.

21 Blinn, *Church Record,* p. 179.

22 Charles F. Crosman, *The Gardener's Manual: Containing Plain and*

Practical Directions for the Cultivation and Management of Some of the Most Useful Culinary Vegetables: to which is Prefixed a Catalogue of the Various Kinds of Garden Seeds raised in the United Society at Enfield, Conn.; with a Few General Remarks on the Management of a Kitchen Garden, 1835, Albany, N.Y., WRHS Microfiche Collection #370, n.p.

[23] Somer, *Garden Seed Industry,* p. 33.

[24] Andrews and Andrews, *Work and Worship,* pp. 53; Stephen W. Miller, *Marketing Community Industries, 1830-1930, A Century of Shaker Ephemera* (New Britain, Conn., 1988); Andrews and Andrews, *Work and Worship,* p. 55; Dyer, *A Historical Narrative,* p. 92.

[25] David Austin Buckingham, *A Journal or a Daily Account of Passing Events, Kept for the Benefit of the Church, First Order,* January 1, 1848-May, 1854, Watervliet, NY, WRHS Reel 44 VB 280.

[26] Willard, "Shaker Highlights," *Garden Writers Bulletin,* Sept/Oct., 1964.

[27] Blinn, *Historical Record,* pp. 304, 310.

[28] Blinn, *Historical Notes,* pp. 81-82.

[29] Somer, *Garden Seed Industry,* p. 15; Andrews and Andrews, *Work and Worship,* p. 60; Miller, *Compendium,* p. 53.

[30] Dyer, *Journal;* "Inventory Book"; "Primarily Tax Records for Shaker Communities of Canterbury, N.H., Enfield, N.H., Union Village, Ohio, Enfield, Conn.," 1915-1939, SVI Ms. 37.

[31] "Account Book," n.d., Canterbury, N.H., SVI #1304; "Account Book of Expenses and Receipts for Produce . . .," 1944-1949, Canterbury, N.H., SVI #1021.

Chapter 4

[1] Interview with Happy Griffith and Sonya Swierczynski, June 27, 1990.

[2] Interview with Amy Bess Miller, July 24, 1990, and with Tom Weldon, August 29, 1990.

[3] Interview with Martha Vadnais, August 20, 1990.

[4] Interview with Debbie Larkin Pope, August 20, 1990.

[5] Interview with Dory Hudspeth, September 16, 1990.

[6] Interview with Sister Frances Carr, Brother Arnold Hadd, and Sister Meg Haskett, July 10, 1990. *A Catalogue of Shaker Herbal teas, culinary herbs, vinegars, Potpourris & other interesting items,* n.d., Sabbathday Lake, Me., United Society of Shakers.

Chapter 5

[1] *The Gardener's Manual containing Plain Instructions for the planting, preparation, and Management of a Kitchen Garden, with practical directions for the cultivation and management of some of the most useful Culinary Vegetables,* 1843, New Lebanon, N.Y., WRHS Microfiche Collection #674, p.8.

[2] *Gardener's Manual,* p. 1.

[3] *Gardener's Manual,* pp. iii, iv.

[4] *Gardener's Manual,* p. iii.

[5] *Gardener's Manual,* p. 5.

[6] *Gardener's Manual,* p. 5.

[7] James Holmes, *The Farmer's Second Book. A collection of Useful Hints for Farmers and many valuable Recipes, Collected and compiled,* West Gloucester, Me., 1853, WRHS Microfiche Collection #413, p. 24..

[8] *Gardener's Manual,* p. 5.

[9] Crosman, *The Gardener's Manual,* n.p.

[10] *Gardener's Manual,* p. 5.

[11] Holmes, *Farmer's Second Book,* p. 24.

[12] Charles E. Kellogg, "We Seek, We Learn," *Soils, The Yearbook of Agriculture* (Washington, D.C.: U.S.D.A., U. S. Printing Office, 1957), p. 3.

[13] Letter of M. Dubec to Garrett K. Lawrence, 1822, WRHS Reel 117.

[14] Holmes, *Farmer's Second Book*, p. 46.

[15] Holmes, *Farmer's Second Book*, p. 51.

[16] Holmes, *Farmer's Second Book*, pp. 53-56.

[17] Frank G. Viet, Jr. and John J. Hanway, "How to Determine Nutrient Needs," *Soils, The Yearbook of Agriculture*, (Washington, D.C.: U.S.D.A., U. S. Printing Office, 1957), p. 173.

[18] Holmes, *Farmer's Second Book*, pp. 53-56.

[19] *Gardener's Manual*, pp. 6-8.

[20] *Gardener's Manual*, p. 6.

[21] Holmes, *Farmer's Second Book*, pp. 22-23.

[22] James Holmes, *A Collection of Useful Hints for Farmers and Many Valuable Recipes*, 1849, West Gloucester, Me., WRHS Microfiche Collection #410, p. 74.

[23] Holmes, *Farmer's Second Book*, p. 101.

[24] *Gardener's Manual*, p. 6.

[25] *Gardener's Manual*, p. 6.

[26] *Gardener's Manual*, p. 7.

[27] Mary Kerwin, conversation with Galen Beale, August 12, 1990, Canterbury, N.H.

[28] *Gardener's Manual*, p. 7.

[29] *Gardener's Manual*, pp. 7-8. According to the *Manual*, rollers were made of wood and were eighteen inches in diameter and four feet long. Rollers are no longer used today; modern seeders have built-in devices that tamp down the seeds. The same effect can be accomplished by lightly packing down the soil on top of the seeds with a foot or hoe. This step ensures that the seeds have good contact with the ground and will cause better germination.

[30] *Gardener's Manual*, p. 7.

[31] Jefferson White, *Gardener's Manual: Containing Plain and Practical Directions for the Cultivation and Management of some of the Most Useful Culinary Vegetables: to which is Prefixed a Catalogue of the Various Kinds of Garden seeds Raised in the United Society of Shakers at Enfield, Ct., first Established in 1802 ... With a Few General Remarks on the management of a Kitchen Garden*, 185_, revised Hartford, Conn., WRHS Microfiche Collection #439, p. 8.

[32] *Gardener's Manual*, p. 8.

[33] Crosman, *Gardener's Manual.*

[34] Crosman, *Gardener's Manual.*

[35] Crosman, *Gardener's Manual.* The sulfur was used as a fungicide, and the soot may have been used as an insecticide. Today, soaking seeds is not recommended as they can easily rot. The Shakers may have figured that out, for in the 1843 manual, the soil, and not the seed, was recommended for soaking.

[36] *Gardener's Manual*, p. 8.

[37] Holmes, *Farmer's Second Book*, p. 42.

[38] *Gardener's Manual*, p. 8.

[39] *Gardener's Manual*, pp. 8-9.

[40] Crosman, *Gardener's Manual.* Nicotine has an adverse affect on both harmful and helpful insects. Frequently, nicotine insecticides may contain hydrated lime and sulfur, which can damage foliage. Tobacco is, however, useful in a compost pile, as it provides potash, but any compost containing tobacco should not be applied to members of the solanaceae family.

[41] *Gardener's Manual*, p. 11.

[42] *Gardener's Manual*, p. 10.

[43] Hill, "The Enterprise of the Shakers," pp. 86-87.

[44] *Gardener's Manual*, p. 11. Unless otherwise stated, the following remedies come from this source and page.

[45] Holmes, *Farmer's Second Book*, pp. 137-139.

[46] *The Shaker Manifesto* 8 (1878), p. 20.

[47] *The Shaker Manifesto,* (1878), p. 20.
[48] Kerwin, conversation with Beale.
[49] *Gardener's Manual,* p. 12.
[50] White, *Gardener's Manual,* pp. 19-20.
[51] White, *Gardener's Manual,* p. 20.
[52] White, *Gardener's Manual,* p. 15.
[53] White, *Gardener's Manual,* p. 15.
[54] Crosman, *Gardener's Manual.*

Chapter 6

[1] Anna White and Leila S. Taylor, *Shakerism: its Meaning and Message* (Columbus, Ohio: Fred J. Heer, 1904), p. 353.

[2] Youngs, *Concise View,* p. 268-276.

[3] Benjamin Youngs, *Testamony of Christ's Second Appearing, exemplified by the Principles and Practice of the True Church of Christ. History of the Progressive Work of God, extending from the Creation of Man to the 'Harvest,' comprising the Four Great Dispensations Now Consummating in the Millenial Church. Antichrist's Kingdom, or Churches, contrasted with the Church of Christ's First and Second Appearing, the Kingdom of the God of Heaven . . . ,* 4th edition (Albany, N.Y.: 1856), p. 632.

[4] White and Taylor, *Shakerism,* p. 23.

[5] Henry Clay Blinn, *Historical Notes Having Reference to the Believers in Enfield, N.H.,* vol. 2, 1847-1902, Enfield, N.H., SVI #761, p. 69.

[6] Youngs, *Concise View,* pp. 269-270.

[7] Miller, *Compendium* p. 109.

[8] Harold H. Levine, *Folk Medicine in New Hampshire* (n.d.; reprint, Concord, N.H.: Mass. Medical Society, 1941), pp. 3-4. Other studies of early medicine include: Roblay Dunglison, M.D., *History of Medicine from the Earliest Ages to the Commencement of the Nineteenth Century* (Philadelphia: Lindsay Blakiston, 1872); Guenter P. Risse, *Medicine Without Doctors: Home Health Care in American History* (New York: Science History Publishers, 1977); Richard H. Shryock, *Medicine and Society in America, Historical Essays, 1660-1860* (New York: N.Y. University Press, 1960).

[9] Maurice Kaufman, *American Medical Education, The Formative Years, 1765-1910* (Westport, Conn.: Greenwood Press, 1976), pp. 64-65.

[10] Levine, *Folk Medicine,* pp. 16-17.

[11] Quoted in Spencer Klaw, "Belly-my-Grizzle," *American Heritage* 28 (1977), p. 99.

[12] Samuel Thomson, *A New Guide to Health or Botanic Family Physician* (Boston: J. Q. Adams, 1832).

[13] Samuel Thomson, *A New Guide to Health or Botanic Family Physician* (Boston: J. Q. Adams, 1835), p. 149.

[14] Klaw, "Belly-my-Grizzle," *American Heritage,* p. 98.

[15] In 1809 Thomson was charged for manslaughter when a patient whom he had treated died. He was put in jail but was later exonerated.

[16] Klaw, "Belly-my-Grizzle," *American Heritage,* p. 105.

[17] Klaw, "Belly-my-Grizzle," *American Heritage,* pp. 104-105.

[18] Blinn, *Historical Notes,* vol. 2, pp. 219-220.

[19] Martha J. Anderson, "History of Dietetic Reform as Practiced at the North Family, Mt. Lebanon and Canaan, Columbia County, New York," *Food, Home and Garden,* (1894), pp. 6-7.

[20] Miller, *Compendium,* p. 37.

[21] Susan H. Myrick, *The Physician's Journal or an Account of the Sickness in the Society at Harvard,* 1831-1842, Harvard, Mass., WRHS Reel 30 FB-41.

[22] Eldress Betsy Smith, *Travel Journal,* 1854, South Union, Ky., quoted in Miller, *Compendium,* p. 36.

[23] P[helmon] Stewart, "Poland Mineral Springs, Medicinal Water," [broadside],

West Gloucester, Me., SDL.

[24] Quoted in "The Shaker Medicinal Spring Water," 1881, Boston, Mass., WRHS Microfiche Collection #840, pp. 2, 3, 5, 6.

[25] The Harvard Shakers built Rural Home originally as a dwelling house for the North Family. When they experienced insolvency, they sold it. It was later advertised as a hotel. Maggie Moody Stier, conversation with Galen Beale, July 10, 1990. The South Family of Enfield, New Hampshire, managed their stone office as a hotel for several years. Hess, *The Enfield, New Hampshire Shakers.* The communities of South Union, Kentucky, and New Lebanon, New York, also ran similar operations.

[26] John Steel, *An Analysis of the Congress Spring with Practical Remarks on the Medical Properties,* revised and corrected by John L. Perry, M.D. (New York: Wm. W. Rose, 1856), pp. 24-33.

[27] Blinn, *Church Record,* p. 192.

[28] Blinn, *Church Record,* p. 198.

[29] Blinn, *Historical Notes,* pp. 349, 238; Otis Sawyer, *Church Family Journal,* I, 1872-1878, Alfred, Me., SDL.

[30] Letter of Ministry Canterbury to Ministry New Lebanon, 1827,WRHS Reel 117.

[31] Letter of Grove Wright to Grove Blanchard, August 19, 1860, WRHS IV A 20, quoted Brewer, *Shaker Communities,* p.61.

[32] Blinn, *Historical Record,* p. 130.

[33] Blinn, *Historical Record,* p. 130.

[34] Blinn, *Historical Record,* p. 163.

Chapter 7

[1] Miller, *Compendium* p. 28.

[2] These women may have been well versed in matters of folk medicine, but it is doubtful that any of them could read. When the Sisters who founded the Canterbury Society signed the covenant in 1792, each one made the mark of an "X" instead of her name. In the 1804 covenant, the women signed their names. It is unknown if by this time they had learned to read as well as write.

[3] Blinn, *Church Record,* p. 268.

[4] Blinn, *Historical Record,* p. 133.

[5] Blinn, *Historical Record,* p. 145.

[6] Blinn, *Historical Record,* p. 139.

[7] Blinn, *Historical Record,* p. 139.

[8] Blinn, *Historical Record,* pp. 241-246.

[9] John Whitcher, *A Brief History,* p. 14.

[10] Blinn, *Church Record,* p. 106.

[11] Hill, "The Shakers," pp. 114-118.

[12] Bertha Lindsay and Lillian Phelps, *Industries and Inventions of the Shakers* (Concord, N.H.: Hazen Printing Co., 1968), p. 8.

[13] Blinn, *Historical Record,* p. 161.

[14] Blinn, *Church Record,* p. 270.

[15] Whitcher, *A Brief History,* pp. 150, 126.

[16] Blinn, *Historical Record,* p. 239.

[17] "A Report of the Examination of the Shakers of Canterbury and Enfield, before the New Hampshire Legislature, at the November Session," (Concord, N.H.: Ervine B. Tripp, 1848), New Hampshire State Library, p. 57.

[18] Blinn, *Church Record,* p. 315.

[19] Whitcher, *A Brief History,* p. 272.

[20] Whitcher, *A Brief History,* p. 273.

[21] Whitcher, *A Brief History,* p. 98. Hannah Goodrich came from the Hancock community to lead the New Hampshire Bishopric with Job Bishop of New Lebanon.

[22] Myrick, *Physician's Journal,* n.p.

[23] Myrick, *Physician's Journal,* n.p.

[24] Buckingham, *Journal,* p. 11.

[25] Jessie Evans, et al., *Family Journal or Current Events,* n.d., Canterbury, N.H., SVI #34, p. 122; Irving Greenwood, "Notebook of Information on machinery, buildings, equipment, property, etc.," n.d., Canterbury, NH, SVI #28, p. 7; "Dates of Buildings," 1889, Canterbury, N.H., SVI p. 21.

[26] Blinn, *Historical Record,* p. 210.

[27] June Sprigg, *By Shaker Hands* (New York: Alfred A. Knoph, 1979), p. 134.

[28] Brewer, *Shaker Communities,* p. 150.

[29] Blinn, *Historical Record,* pp. 58, 54.

[30] "Report of the Examination," p. 60.

[31] "Report of the Examination," p. 61.

[32] Brewer, *Shaker Communities,* p. 142.

[33] *Records of the Church at Union Village, Ohio,* 1842, WRHS Reel 40 VI 230, p. 251. In the mid-nineteenth century black-faced minstral shows were sweeping the country. A black Shaker skit was often included in the programs. William Tripure and a "Mrs. Tripure" were members of a troupe known as the "Case Family" which appeared in the late 1840s in the areas around Shaker villages in New York, Ohio, and Massachusetts. Mary L. Richmond, *Shaker Literature: A Bibliography* (Hanover, N.H.: University Press of New England, 1977), p. 61.

[34] "Report of the Examination," pp. 13, 14.

[35] Barnabus Hinckley, *Diary,* 1836-1837, New Lebanon, N.Y., Andrews Collection ASC 831, n.d.

[36] Wheeler, John, M.D., "Obituary Notice of R. P. J. Tenney, M.D." 1877. Daniel T. Neal, p. 10.

[37] Whitcher, *A Brief History,* pp. 66, 67.

[38] Blinn, *Church Record,* p. 237.

[39] Jessie Evans, *Diary,* 1916, Canterbury, N.H., SVI #1985.15, n.p.

[40] Bertha Lindsay, Monologue on the Infirmary, Tape Recording, Canterbury, N.H., SVI.

[41] Jessie Evans, *Diary,* 1892, Canterbury, N.H., SVI.

Chapter 8

[1] Inside wrapper of Corbett's Shaker Compound Cherry Pectoral Syrup, n.d., Private Collection.

[2] Otis Sawyer and John Vance, *Church Record,* Vol. 2, 1879-1886, Alfred, Me., SDL, p. 218.

[3] Sawyer and Vance, *Church Record,* p. 203.

[4] Hill, "The Shakers," pp. 117-118.

[5] Nordhoff, *Communistic Societies,* p. 160.

[6] "Shaker Community Wines. A Treatise on Pure Wines and its Beneficial Uses. Shaker Community Wine Growers . . . ," n.d., Union Village, Ohio, WRHS Reel 117 XI B 29.

[7] Corbett's Wild Cherry Pectoral Syrup was made from the bark of the wild cherry tree and the tinctures of antimony, cicuta, bloodroot, ipecac, and morphine. See "A Repository of Medical Recipes," 1883, Shaker Museum, p. 16.

[8] James Vail, "Record Book," 1841-1857, New Lebanon, N.Y., WRHS Microfilm Collection.

[9] Youngs, *A Concise View,* p. 279.

[10] Lossing, "A Visit to the Shakers," pp. 174-175.

[11] "To Druggists, Apothecaries, and All Others Dealing in or Using Medical Extracts prepared by the Shakers," [broadside], n.d., New Lebanon, N.Y., WRHS Microfiche Collection, #374.

[12] Phyllis Shimko, *Sarsaparilla Bottle Encyclopedia* (Aurora, Ore., n.p., 1969), p. 11.

[13] Wooster Beach, *The Family Physician* (New York, 1845), SVI, p. 674; George

B. Wood, M.D., and Franklin Bache, M.D., *The Dispensatory of the United States of America*, 7th edition (Philadelphia: J. P. Lippencott, 1847), p. 116.

[14] Stewart H. Holbrook, *The Golden Age of Quackery* (New York: McMillan, 1959), p. 45. The alcohol content of these early concoctions varied greatly; some contained up to 25 percent alcohol; Corbett's Sarsaparilla was 10 percent alcohol. Shimko, *Sarsaparilla Bottle Encyclopedia*, p. 19.

[15] Blinn, *Historical Record*, p. 161.

[16] "Compound Concentrated Syrup of Sarsaparilla. Prepared Directly by B. Hinkley, Physician in the United Society of Shakers, New Lebanon, N.Y.," [broadside, 185-], Williamiana Collection, Williams College Library, Williamstown, Mass., (hereafter Williams College).

[17] [Peter Boyd or Charles Summer], *A Brief History of the Shaker Community of Union Village, O. (188-)*, WRHS Microfiche Collection #577, p. 4.

[18] Briggs, "The Canterbury Shakers," pp. 310-311.

[19] James B. Woodman, "Presidential Address," *New England Journal of Medicine* 226 (1942), p. 639.

[20] *The Shakers' Manual* (Concord, N.H.: Canterbury Shakers, 1852), p. 11.

[21] *The Shakers' Manual*, p. 9.

[22] "Dates of Buildings," 1889, Canterbury, N.H., SVI, p. 25; "Notebook with 'Wanted' Poster, 1852, on Back Cover," September 20, 1861, Canterbury Church Family, N.H., Shaker Museum, #13,084/9785M4; *Historical Record of the Church Family*, 1890-1930, Canterbury, N.H., SVI #33, p. 288; Thomas Corbett, "Formula for making Shakers' Compound Syrup of Sarsaparilla," n.d., Canterbury, N.H., SVI #168, pp. 4-8.

[23] "A collection of Interesting Facts and Recipes Book," 1864-1884, Canterbury, N.H., Shaker Museum, #13,084; "Formulas, Lists and Costs of Ingredients Primarily Dealing with the Shakers' Compound Concentrated Syrup of Sarsaparilla, But Other Compounds Mentioned. 12 Items," n.d., Canterbury, N.H., SVI #168; "Deeds," 1824-1913, Canterbury, N.H., SVI #247.

[24] *The Shakers' Manual* (1879), p. 3; Whitcher, *A Brief History*, p. 87; *The Shakers' Manual* (1879, p.3; [John McClintock], "The Canterbury Shakers, " *The Granite Monthly* (1880), p. 147.

[25] *The Shakers' Manual* (1879), p 4.

[26] Whitcher, *A Brief History*, pp. 152-153; "Deeds," SVI #247; Whitcher, *A Brief History*, pp. 273-274.

[27] Blinn, *A Historical Record*; United States Census, 1870. Hogsheads were large casks of varying capacities; the Canterbury Shakers listed theirs as containing nine hundred gallons. "Collection of Interesting Facts"; Shimko, *Sarsaparillla Bottle Encyclopedia*.

[28] "Collection of Interesting Facts"; "Account Book," 1894-1913, Canterbury, N.H., SVI #17; "Cash Account Book," 1884-1931, Canterbury, N.H., SVI #19, pp. 47, 117, 324; Jessie Evans, *Diary*, April 13, 1914, Canterbury, N.H., SVI #1984.13, Blinn, *Historical Record*, p. 288.

[29] "Shaker Medicines, Shaker Knit Goods and Religious Publications: Also a Variety of Fancy Articles," n.d., Canterbury, N.H., WRHS Microfiche Collection; "Collection of Interesting Facts,"; "Hart & Shepard, Manufacturers of Athletic and Fancy Goods. Holiday Goods a Specialty," n.d., Canterbury, N.H., Shaker Museum #245; "Account Book."

[30] Richmond, *Shaker Literature*, pp. 5-6.

[31] "Facts Concerning Brown's Shaker Pure Extract of English Valerian (*Valeriana officinalis*) made at Enfield, N.H.," n.d., Enfield, N.H., WRHS Microfiche Collection #235.

[32] "Brown's Shaker Pure Extract of English Valerian (Valeriana officinalis) . . . Prepared by the United Society of Shakers, for Sale by all Druggists, price 25 Cents per Bottle," 1879?, Enfield, N.H., Shaker Museum #239; Nicholas Briggs, "Forty Years a Shaker," *The Granite Monthly* 52 (1920), pp. 463-474; Nicholas

Briggs, "Forty Years a Shaker," *The Granite Monthly* 53 (1921), pp. 19-32, 56-65, 113-121.

[33] Blinn, *Historical Notes,* p. 107. The "fresh, green roots" were said to be stronger and more effective than the dried root. "Brown's Shaker Pure Extract."

[34] "Facts Concerning Brown's Shaker Pure Extract"; *The Shakers' Manual* (Concord, N.H., 1851).

[35] Blinn, *Historical Notes;* "Facts Concerning Brown's Shaker Pure Fluid Extract"; "Brown's Shaker Pure Extract"; "Primarily Tax Records."

[36] Andrews and Andrews, *Work and Worship,* p. 60.

[37] "Conferences held at the Office," 1885-1888, Canterbury, N.H., SVI #24, p. 107; Edward Deming Andrews and Faith Andrews, *Fruits of the Shaker Tree of Life: Memoirs of Fifty Years of Collecting and Research* (Stockbridge, Mass.: Berkshire Traveller Press, 1975), pp. 161-162.

[38] *The Shaker Quarterly* 11 (1971), inside cover.

Chapter 9

[1] Letter to Ministry Canterbury from Ministry New Lebanon, writing from South Union, Kentucky, 1862, SVI.

[2] Brewer, *Shaker Communities,* p. 106.

[3] Bertha Lindsay, *Seasoned with Grace: My Generation of Shaker Cooking,* ed. Mary Rose Boswell (Woodstock, Vt.: The Countryman Press, 1987), p. xx.

[4] Blinn, *Historical Record,* p. 214.

[5] Blinn, *Historical Record,* p. 145.

[6] Letter of Benjamin S. Youngs to Molly Goodrich, Feb. 10, 1811, WRHS IV A 19, quoted in Brewer, *Shaker Communities,* p. 34.

[7] *Domestic Journal of Important Occurrences,* 1780-1860, New Lebanon, N.Y., WRHS V B 60-61, Sept. 1, 1800, quoted in Brewer, *Shaker Communities,* p. 39.

[8] Blinn, *Historical Record,* p. 214.

[9] Lindsay, *Seasoned with Grace,* p. xxii.

[10] Ephraim Prentiss, "Report of Interesting Experience with the Boys of whom he was a caretaker," 1835-1837, Watervliet, N.Y., WRHS VII B 258, quoted in Brewer, *Shaker Communities,* p. 107.

[11] Brewer, *Shaker Communities,* p. 108.

[12] Blinn, *Church Record,* pp. 252-253.

[13] Youngs, *Concise View,* p. 291-292. quoted in Brewer, *Shaker Communities,* p. 131.

[14] Blinn, *Historical Record,* pp. 22-23.

[15] Martha J. Anderson, "Social Life and Vegetarianism," 1893, Mount Lebanon, N.Y., as quoted in Marcia Byrom Hartwell, "Shaker Foods: The Shaker Vegetarian Experiment," *The Shaker Messenger* 10 (1988), p. 16.

[16] Miller, *Compendium,* pp. 213, 133, 224.

[17] Blinn, *Historical Record,* p. 280.

[18] Blinn, *Church Record,* p. 40.

[19] Brewer, *Shaker Communities,* p. 131.

[20] Blinn, *Church Record,* p. 101; Whitcher, *A Brief History,* p. 299.

[21] Marcia Byrom Hartwell, "Comparison of Shaker Food to that of the Outside World's (19th Century)," *The Shaker Messenger* 5 (1983), p. 10.

[22] Briggs, "Forty Years a Shaker," p. 20.

[23] A list of the herbs appeared on the back cover of *The Shaker Quarterly* 11 (1971).

[24] Lindsay, *Seasoned with Grace,* pp. 2, 24, 90.

[25] Lindsay, *Seasoned with Grace,* p. 2, xvi. At the time of Rebecca Hathaway's death, the membership at Canterbury consisted of fewer than sixteen Sisters between the ages of forty-six and eighty-three; Sister Ethel Hudson, conversation

with Mary Rose Boswell, November 13, 1985.

[26] Sister Frances Carr, *Shaker Your Plate: Of Shaker Cooks and Cooking* (Hanover, N.Y.: University Press of New England, 1985), p. 16.

[27] Sister Frances Carr, conversation with Galen Beale, January 11, 1986, Sabbathday Lake, Me.; Carr, *Shaker Your Plate*, pp. 46–48.

[28] Lavinia Clifford and Sarah Woods, *Cookbook* (Canterbury, N.H.,n.d.).

[29] *The Shakers' Manual* (Canterbury, N.H.: Canterbury Shakers, 1879), from the collection of Williams College.

[30] William H. Hylton, ed., *The Rodale Herb Book* (Emmaus, Pa.: Rodale Press Book Div., 1974), p. 54.

[31] Eldress Bertha Lindsay, handwritten recipe, n.d., Canterbury, N.H., SVI.

[32] "Recipes," n.d., WRHS Reel 117 XI B 27.

[33] *Mary Whitcher's Shaker House-Keeper.*

[34] Carr, *Shaker Your Plate*, p. 62.

[35] Amy Bess Miller and Persis Fuller, *Best of Shaker Cooking* (New York: Clarkson N. Potter, 1970), p. 396.

[36] "Recipes," n.d., WRHS Reel 117 XI B 13.

[37] "Recipes," n.d., WRHS Reel 117 XI B 11.

[38] Clifford and Woods, *Cookbook.*

[39] Lindsay, *Seasoned with Grace*, p. 45.

[40] Carr, *Shaker Your Plate*, p. 116.

[41] This recipe was found in a late nineteenth-century cooking manuscript attributed to the Hancock, Massachusetts community. See Hartwell, "Shaker Fruits of the Earth," p. 15.

[42] Clifford and Woods, *Cookbook.*

[43] Marcia Byrom Hartwell, "Shaker Foods: Roses and Rosewater," *The Shaker Messenger* 10 (1987), pp. 22–23.

[44] This recipe was passed down to Bertha Lindsay, Lead Eldress of the United Society of Believers, who came to the Canterbury community in 1905. The date of the recipe is unknown. See Lindsay, *Seasoned with Grace*, p. 89.

[45] Carr, *Shaker Your Plate*, p. 133.

[46] Carr, *Shaker Your Plate*, p. 129.

[47] Eldress Bertha Lindsay, conversation with Galen Beale, Canterbury Shaker Village, N.H., 1983.

[48] Lindsay, conversation with Beale.

[49] Tabitha Lapsley, "Miscellaneous Receipts, Extracted from C. Mary Whitcher," 1863, Sabbathday Lake, Me., SDL, n.p.

[50] Lapsley, "Miscellaneous Receipts," n.p.

[51] *The Gardener's Manual*, pp. 22–23.

[52] Lapsley, "Miscellaneous Receipts," n.p.

[53] Lapsley, "Miscellaneous Receipts," n.p.

[54] Sister Mary Ann Hill, "Recipe Book," 1857, Canterbury, N.H., SDL, n.p.

[55] Eldress Bertha Lindsay, scrapbook, n.d., Canterbury, N.H., SVI, quoted in Lindsay, *Seasoned with Grace*, p. 120.

Chapter 10

[1] John Lindley described seventy-six species and sub-species. William H. Hylton, ed., *The Rodale Herb Book* (Emmaus, PA: Rodale Press Book Div., 1974), p. 544.

[2] This information about planting and harvesting is from Graham S. Thomas, *The Old Shrub Roses* (London: J. M. Dent & Sons Ltd., 1983).

[3] Bertha Lindsay, interview by Galen Beale, May 12, 1986.

[4] A Collection of Interesting Facts

[5] A Collection of Interesting Facts.

[6] WRHS Reel 117.

[7] "Recipe Book," 1859, Pittsfield, Mass., WRHS Reel 117 XI B22.

[8] "Recipe Book," (Pittsfield, Mass., 1859), WRHS Reel 117, XI B511.

[9] David Serette, ed., *The Shaker Herbalist* 1 (United Society of Shakers, SDL, 1975), p. 8; Sister Mary Ann Hill, "Recipe Book," 1857, Canterbury, N.H., SDL.

[10] Hill, "Recipe Book."

[11] Hill, "Recipe Book."

[12] WRHS Reel 117 XI B-22.

[13] WRHS Reel 117 XI B-9.

[14] WRHS Reel 117 XI B-22.

[15] "Recipe for 1 quart of Healolene," n.p. SVI Located in Canterbury, N.H., n.d., SVI #950.

[16] "Recipe Book," p. 151.

[17] "The Shaker Hair Restorer," [broadside], 1886, Mount Lebanon, N.Y., WRHS Microfiche Collection.

[18] "The Shaker Hair Restorer."

[19] "Receipts of *Material Medica*," May 1842, Groveland, N.Y., WRHS Reel 117.

[20] Hill, "Recipe Book."

[21] WRHS Reel 117 XI B-5.

[22] WRHS Reel 117 XI B-7.

[23] WRHS Reel 117 XI B-24.

[24] "Rose Jar Recipe (using Damask Roses)," transcribed from *Popular Science News*, in "Recipe Book," 1880, WRHS Reel 117 XI B-7.

[25] Mildred Wells, "Recipe," n.d., Canterbury, N.H., private collection.

[26] Mildred Wells, "Recipe."

[27] "Infirmary Recipes," 1840?, Canterbury, N.H., SDL.

[28] "A Manual of Wine Making," WRHS Reel 117 XI B-29.

[29] WRHS Reel 117.

[30] "Recipes," 1856, SDL.

[31] WRHS Reel 117 XI B-6 II.

[32] Sister R. Mildred Barker, "Eldress Hester Ann Adams' 'Oh Praised Be God . . .,' " *Shaker Quarterly* 11 (1971), p. 131; Hester Ann Adams, "Memorandum Book," 1839, Canterbury, N.H., SDL, pp. 11-12.

[33] "Recipe Book," p. 250.

[34] Julia Briggs, "Recipe Book," 1872, SDL.

[35] "Formulas, Lists and Costs of Ingredients."

[36] "Recipe Book."

[37] "A Book of Recipes against Diseases," n.d., Sabbathday Lake, Me., SDL.

[38] "Book of Formulas, chiefly of medicine," 1858-1878, Shaker Museum #9785.M4/G/13,340.

[39] WRHS Reel 117.

[40] "Diary on Medical Preparations," 1862, n.p., Shaker Museum #4456 9788 M4 G.

[41] WRHS Reel 117 XI B-13.

[42] "Recipe Book."

[43] WRHS Reel 117 XI B-13.

[44] WRHS Reel 117.

[45] Eldress Bertha Lindsay, conversation with Galen Beale, May 15, 1983, Canterbury, N.H.

[46] Mary Kerwin, conversation with Galen Beale, August 6, 1990, Canterbury, N.H.

[47] Susan Love, *The Cheap Family Dyer*, 1858, Groveland, N.Y., WRHS Reel 117 XI B-4.

[48] Briggs, "Recipe Book."

[49] WRHS Reel 117 XI-B.

[50] WRHS Reel 117 XI B-28.

[51] WRHS Reel 117.

Chapter 11

[1] *Catalogue of Medicinal Plants, Barks, Roots, Seeds, Flowers and Select Powders, with their Therapeutic Qualities and Botanical Name; Also, Pure Vegetable Extracts, Prepared in Vacuo; Ointments, Inspissated Juices, Essential Oils, Double Distilled and Fragrant Waters &c, &c. Raised, Prepared and Put Up in the Most Careful Manner by the United Society of Shakers at New Lebanon, N.Y. . . . Orders Addressed to Edward Fowler will meet with Prompt Attention*, 1851, Albany, N.Y., WRHS pp. 32-33. Throughout this chapter refer to the listing of catalogs in the appendix.

[2] The Shaker physicians relied on the latest edition of Amos Eaton's *Manual of Botany 1776-1847 for North America* (Albany, N.Y.: Websters & Skinn, 1829). This book, the first of its kind to be printed in English in America, was published in 1817. There were seven editions to this book; when Eaton died in 1842 his work was superseded by Asa Gray's botany book of 1848. In 1853 Elisha Myrick recorded in his diary that Gray made a visit to Harvard.

[3] An undated catalog from New Lebanon exists; it probably pre-dates the first catalog published by Watervliet.

[4] In 1837 New Lebanon's catalog cover read: "Why send to Europe's distant Shores/For plants which grow by our own Doors." Ten years later Union Village's catalog cover stated: "Why send to the Atlantic Shores/For plants . . ." In 1850 the quote was abandoned altogether.

[5] Mildred Wells of Canterbury remembered gathering herbs with the children and making herbariums with them. Making the books helped teach the children botany. Conversation with Galen Beale, May 15, 1983, Canterbury, N.H.

[6] Myrick, *Diary* (1853-57).

[7] Sister Marguerite Frost, "Notes on Shaker Herbs & Herbalists," *The Herb Grower Magazine* 5 (1951), p. 89.

[8] Frequently the Shakers manufactured medicines targeted for a special group. The Enfield, New Hampshire, Shakers recommended that their Syrup Arnikate of Tannin, which they claimed to be a preventative against cholera and dysentery, was especially useful to those venturing West in response to the gold rush. "Shaker Medicines, Approved by the Regular Faculty. Compound syrups, Extracts, Pills &c. Prepared in the Society of Shakers, by Jerub Dyer, Enfield, N.H.," n.d., Boston, broadside in collection of NHHS.

[9] Miller, *Compendium* p. 102.

[10] Miller, *Compendium*, p. 71.

[11] "Shaker Herbs," broadside, n.d., Williams College.

[12] *Records of the Church at Union Village, Ohio*, n.d., Union Village, Ohio., WRHS Reel 40 VB-230-231, pp. 253, 376, 356.

[13] Andrews, *The Community Industries*, p. 98.

[14] [Town Tax?] "Inventory," 1816-1848, Church Family, Canterbury, N.H., SVI #117.

[15] "Account Book," 1852-1856, Concord, N.H., Shaker Museum, #8069.

[16] Miller, *Compendium*, p. 16.

[17] "Account Book of Herb Department," 1853, Harvard, Mass., Andrews Collection #1101.

[18] Eldress Betsy Smith, *Travel Journal*, 1854, South Union, Ky., quoted in Miller, *Compendium*, p. 37.

[19] Brewer, *Shaker Communities*, pp. 141, 147.

[20] Whitcher, *Brief History*, p. 223.

[21] Blinn, *Church Record*, pp. 106, 108.

[22] "Notebook," Shaker Museum, #13,084/9785M4.

[23] Letter of Thomas Corbett to Chauncey Miller, January 13, 1850, WRHS Reel 17 FB 6.

[24] Letter of James Kaime to Chauncey Miller, February 19, 1852, WRHS Reel 17 IV A-6.

[25] Elder Otis Sawyer, "Small Book," October 16, 1861, Sabbathday Lake, Me., SDL; "Journal," May 18, 1877, Church Family, Sabbathday Lake, Me., SDL.

[26] Brewer, *Shaker Communities*, p. 98.

[27] Sawyer and Vance, *Church Record*," p. 444.

[28] Sawyer and Vance, *Church Record*, pp. 145, 231.

[29] Brewer, *Shaker Communities*, pp. 217, 215, 174.

[30] Brewer, *Shaker Communities*, pp. 181-182.

[31] Otis and Vance, *Church Record*, p. 218.

[32] "Tamar Account Book," 1882, Sabbathday Lake, Me., Sister Francis Carr, "The Tamar Fruit Compound, A Maine Shaker Industry," *Shaker Quarterly* 2 (1962), pp. 39, 41.

[33] "Inventory Book for Church, Second, and North Families," 1864-1882, Enfield, N.H., SVI #171.

[34] Blinn, ed., *The Shaker Manifesto* (Canterbury Shakers: 1889), p. 114.

[35] "Inventory Book."

[36] The authors are indebted to Wendell Hess for his information on Hyram Baker. Letter of Wendell Hess to Galen Beale, March 21, 1986. The fourteen thousand dollar figure was agreed upon in court. The actual amount was probably far greater. See Sawyer and Vance, "Church Record," p. 268.

[37] "Account Book," 1879-1888, Church Family, Harvard, Mass., manuscript in Fruitlands Museums Library, Harvard, Mass. (hereafter Fruitlands).

Bibliography

Abbreviations

Andrews Collection: Edward Deming Andrews Memorial Shaker Collection, Henry
Francis du Pont Winterthur Museum.
Fruitlands: Fruitlands Museums Library, Harvard, Massachusetts.
NHHS: New Hampshire Historical Society, Concord, New Hampshire.
LSV: Lower Shaker Village, Enfield, New Hampshire.
Shaker Museum: The Shaker Museum, Old Chatham, New York.
SDL: United Society of Believers, Sabbathday Lake, Maine.
SVI: Archives, Shaker Village, Inc., Canterbury, New Hampshire.
WRHS: Western Reserve Historical Society, Cleveland, Ohio.

Anonymous. *Account Book.* Canterbury, N.H., 1894-1913. Shaker Village, Inc., Archives,
Canterbury, N.H., no. 17 (hereafter SVI).
_____. *Account Book.* Canterbury, N.H., 1894-1922. SVI, no. 19.
_____. *Account Book.* Canterbury, N.H., n.d. SVI, no. 1304.
_____. *Account Book.* Church Family, Harvard, Mass., 1879-1888. Fruitlands Museums
Library, Harvard, Mass. (hereafter Fruitlands).
_____. *Account Book.* Concord, N.H., 1852-1856. The Shaker Museum, Old Chatham,
N.Y., no. 8069 (hereafter Shaker Museum).
_____. *Account Book of Expenses and Receipts for Produce* ... Canterbury, N.H.,
1944-1949. SVI, no. 1021.
_____. *Account Book of Herb Department.* Harvard, Mass., 1847-1854. Edward Deming
Andrews Memorial Shaker Collection, Henry Francis duPont Winterthur Museum,
Winterthur, Del., no. 1101 (hereafter Andrews Collection).
_____. *Accounts of the Church, Second, and North Families.* Enfield, N.H., 1864-1882.
SVI, no. 171.
_____. *A Biography of the Life and Tragical Death of Elder Caleb M. Dyer, together
with the Poem and Eulogies at his Funeral, July 21, 1863.* Manchester, N.H.: Gage,
Moore & Co., 1863.
_____. *Book of Formulas, chiefly of medicine.* n.p., 1858-1878. Shaker Museum, no.
9785.M4/G/13,340.

_____. *A Book of Recipes against Diseases.* Sabbathday Lake, Me., n.d. Collection of the United Society of Shakers, Sabbathday Lake, Me. (hereafter SDL).

_____. "A Brief History of the Raising of Garden Seeds Among Believers &c.," *Records of the Church at Watervliet, N.Y., Comprising the principal events relative to said Church, in connection with other Families and Societies since the year 1788,* Vol. I. Western Reserve Historical Society Shaker Collection, Cleveland, Ohio, Reel 44 VB 279 (hereafter WRHS).

_____. *A Brief History of the Shaker Community of Union Village, Ohio,* n.d. WRHS Microfiche Collection 577.

_____. "Brown's Shaker Pure Extract of English Valerian (*Valeriana officinalis*) . . . Prepared by the United Society of Shakers, for Sale by all Druggests, price 25 Cents per Bottle." Enfield, N.H., 1879? Shaker Museum, no. 239.

_____. "Cash Account Book." Canterbury, N.H., 1884-1931. SVI, no. 19.

_____. "A Collection of Interesting Facts and Recipe Book." Canterbury, N.H., 1864-1884. Shaker Museum, no. 13,084.

_____. "Compound Concentrated Syrup of Sarsaparilla. Prepared Directly by B. Hinkley, Physician in the United Society of Shakers, New Lebanon, N.Y." 185_. [Broadside.] WRHS Microfiche Collection 577 4.

_____. "Conferences held at the Office." Canterbury, N.H., 1885-1888. SVI, no. 24.

_____. "Dates of Buildings." Canterbury, N.H., 1889. SVI.

_____. "Deeds." Canterbury, N.H., 1824-1913. SVI, no. 247.

_____. *Descriptive Catalogue of Vegetable Seeds Raised at New Lebanon, N.Y. with Directions for their Cultivation.* New York: Lange, Little & Hillman, 1873.

_____. *Diary on Medical Preparations.* n.p., 1862. Shaker Museum, no. 4456/9788 M4 G.

_____. "Facts Concerning Brown's Fluid Extract of English Valerian. The Every-Day Book, containing Useful and Entertaining Matter with Instructions for the Preservation of Health." Boston: Edward Brinley, n.d. Shaker Museum, no. 19,232.

_____. "Facts Concerning Brown's Shaker Pure Extract of English Valerian (*Valeriana officinalis*) made at Enfield, N.H." WRHS Microfiche Collection 235.

_____. "Formulas, Lists and Costs of Ingredients, Primarily Dealing with the Shakers' Compound Concentrated Syrup of Sarsaparilla, But Other Compounds Mentioned. 12 Items." Canterbury, N.H., n.d. SVI, no. 168.

_____. *The Gardener's Manual containing Plain Instructions for the planting, preparation, and management of a Kitchen Garden, with practical directions for the cultivation and management of some of the most useful Culinary Vegetables.* New Lebanon, N.Y., 1843. WRHS Microfiche Collection 674.

_____. "Hart & Shepard, Manufacturers of Athletic and Fancy Goods. Holiday Goods a Specialty." Canterbury, N.H., n.d. The Shaker Museum, no. 245.

_____. *Historical Record of the Church Family.* Canterbury, N.H., 1890-1930. SVI, no. 33.

_____. "Infirmary Recipes." Canterbury, N.H., 1840?, SDL.

_____. "Inventory Book." New Lebanon, N.Y., 1839-1864. WRHS Reel 9.

_____. "Inventory Book for Church, Second, and North Families." Enfield, N.H., 1864-1882. SVI, no. 171.

_____. *Mary Whitcher's Shaker House-Keeper.* Boston: Weeks & Potter, 1882. SVI, no. 754.

_____. "Notebook." Canterbury, N.H.. n.p., n.d. SVI, no. 273.

_____. "Notebook with 'Wanted' Poster, 1852, on Back Cover." Canterbury Church Family, N.H., September 20, 1861. Shaker Museum, no. 13,084/9785 M4.

_____. *NSA Aglime Book.* Washington, D.C.: National Stone Association, 1986.

_____. "Primarily Tax Records for Shaker Communities." Canterbury, N.H., 1915-1939. SVI, no. 37.

_____. "Recipe for 1 quart of Healolene." n.p., n.d., SVI, no. 950.

_____. Recipes from various communities, WRHS Reel 117.

_____. "Record Book." New Lebanon, N.Y., 1841-1857. WRHS.

_____. *Records of the Church at Union Village, Ohio.* 1842. WRHS Reel 40, VI 230.

_____. "A Report of the Examination of the Shakers of Canterbury and Enfield, before the New Hampshire Legislature, at the November Session." Concord, N.H.: New Hampshire State Library, Ervin B. Tripp, 1849.

_____. "A Repository of Medical Recipes." 1883. Shaker Museum, p. 16.

_____. "Shaker Community Wines. A Treatise on Pure Wines and its Beneficial Uses. Shaker Community Wine Growers ... " Union Village, Ohio, n.d. WRHS Reel 117, XI B 29.

_____. "Shaker Hair Restorer." Mount Lebanon, N.Y., 1886. [Broadside] WRHS Reel 117.

_____. "Shaker Medicines, Approved by the Regular Faculty. Compound syrups, Extracts, Pills &c. Prepared in the Society of Shakers, by Jerub Dyer, Enfield, N.H." Boston: Devereaux & Co., n.d. Broadside in collection of New Hampshire Historical Society Library, Concord, N.H. (hereafter NHHS).

_____. "Shaker Medicines, Shaker Knit Goods and Religious Publications: Also A Variety of Fancy Articles." Canterbury, N.H., n.d. WRHS Microfiche Collection.

_____. The Shaker Quarterly 7 (1967).

_____. The Shakers' Manual. 1847.

_____. The Shakers' Manual. 1851.

_____. The Shakers' Manual. 1852.

_____. The Shakers' Manual. 1879.

_____. "Shaker Medicinal Spring Water," Harvard, Mass., 1881. WRHS Microfiche Collection 840 2-6.

_____. Soils, The Yearbook of Agriculture. The USDA, Washington, D.C., U.S. Printing Office, 1957.

_____. "Tamar Account Book." Sabbathday Lake, Me., 1882, SDL.

_____. "To Druggists, Apothecaries, and All Others Dealing in or Using Medical Extracts prepared by the Shakers." New Lebanon, N.Y., n.d. [Broadside]. WRHS Microfiche Collection 374.

_____. [Town Tax?] "Inventory." Church Family, Canterbury, N.H., 1816-1848. SVI, no. 117.

Anderson, Martha J. "History of Dietetic Reform as Practiced at the North Family, Mt. Lebanon and Canaan, Columbia County, New York." Food, Home and Garden. 1894, pp. 6-7.

Anderson, Russell. "Agriculture Among the Shakers, Chiefly at Mount Lebanon." Agricultural History 24 (1950), pp. 113-20.

Andrews, Edward Deming. The Community Industries of the Shakers. Reprint of New York State Museum Handbook 15. Albany, N.Y.: University of the State of New York, 1933.

_____. The People Called Shakers. New York: Oxford University Press, 1953.

_____ and Faith Andrews . Fruits of the Shaker Tree of Life: Memoirs of Fifty Years of Collecting and Research. Stockbridge, Mass.: The Berkshire Traveller Press, 1975.

_____. Work and Worship: The Economic Order of the Shakers. Greenwich, Conn.: New York Graphic Society, 1974.

Barker, Sister Mildred R. "Eldress Hester Ann Adams "Oh Praised Be God ..." The Shaker Quarterly 11 (1971), pp. 131-134.

Beach, Wooster. The Family Physician. Published by the author. New York, 1945. SVI, p. 674.

Bigelow, Tom and John Knies. "Letterpress Printing at Canterbury," The Canterbury Shakers (1986), p. 5.

Blinn, Henry Clay. Church Record. Canterbury, N.H., 1784-1879. SVI, no. 764.

_____. A Historical Record of the Society of Believers. Canterbury, N.H., 1792-1848. SVI, no. 763.

_____. Historical Notes Having Reference to the Believers in Enfield, N.H., 2 vols. Enfield, N.H., 1782-1847. SVI, no. 761.

_____. ed. The Manifesto 19 (1889), p. 114.

_____. ed. The Manifesto 22 (1892), p. 187.

_____. Mother Ann Lee. East Canterbury, N.H.: The Canterbury Shakers, 1901.

[Boyd, Peter or Charles Summer]. A Brief History of the Shaker Community of Union Village, O. 188_. WRHS Microfiche Collection 577 4.

Bradford, Seth T. A Diary or Memorandum Dept. . . . in the Horticulture Line . . . Enfield, N.H. November, 1850. Copy in Museum at Lower Shaker Village, Enfield, N.H. (hereafter LSV).

Brewer, Priscilla J. Shaker Communities, Shaker Lives. Hanover, N.H.: University Press of New England, 1974.

Briggs, Julia. "Recipe Book," n.p. 1872, SDL.

Briggs, Nicholas A. "The Canterbury Shakers." *The Granite Monthly* 8 (1885), pp. 310-11.

_____. "Forty Years a Shaker." *The Granite Monthly* 52 (1920), pp. 463-74.

_____. "Forty Years a Shaker." *The Granite Monthly* 53 (1921), pp. 19-32, 56-65, 113-21.

_____. Nicholas A. *The Shaker*, 1876-1877.

Buckingham, David Austin. "Epitomic History of the Watervliet Shakers," *The Shaker* (1877), p. 49.

_____. *A Journal or a Daily Account of Passing Events, Kept for the Benefit of the Church, First Order.* Watervliet, N.Y., Jan. 1, 1848-May, 1854. WRHS Reel 44, VB 280.

Bullard, Sister Marsha. "Shaker Industries." *Good Housekeeping* 43 (1906), pp. 33-37.

Carr, Sister Frances. *Shaker Your Plate: Of Shaker Cooks and Cooking.* Sabbathday Lake, Me.: United Society of Shakers, 1985.

_____. "The Tamar Fruit Compound, A Maine Shaker Industry," *Shaker Quarterly* 2 (1962), pp. 39, 41.

Coleman, Eliot, *The New Organic Grower.* Chelsea Green, Vt., n.p. 1989.

Corbett, Thomas. "Formula for making Shakers' Compound Concentrated Syrup of Sarsaparilla." Canterbury, N.H., n.d. SVI, no. 168.

Correspondence from various communities. SVI.

Crosman, Charles F. *The Gardener's Manual Containing Some Plain and Practical Directions for the Cultivation and Management of Some of the Most Useful Culinary Vegetables to which is Prefixed a Catalogue of the Various Kinds of Garden Seeds raised in the United Society at New Lebanon, Pittsfield and Watervliet with a Few General Remarks on the Management of a Kitchen Garden.* Albany, N.Y.: 1835. WRHS Microfiche Collection 370.

Deatrick, Linda. "The Shaker Seed Industry; More Than a Business. It Was a Philosophy." *Shaker Messenger.* 1 (1979), p. 5.

Draper, Nathaniel, Francis Winkley, et al. *A Remonstrance Against the Testimony and Application of Mary Dyer.* Concord, N.H.: Isaac Hill, 1818.

Dunglison, Roblay, M.D. *History of Medicine from the Earliest Ages to the Commencement of the Nineteenth Century.* Philadelphia: Lindsay-Blakiston, 1872.

Dunlavy, Elder Benjamin B. "Trip of the Ministry of Pleasant Hill and South Union to the Eastern Societies." *Journal.* WRHS Reel 39 V B 228.

Dyer, Caleb. *A Historical Narrative of the Rise and Progress of the United Society of Shakers.* Enfield, N.H. 1782-1858. Copy at The Shaker Museum, no. 16,222.

Elkins, Hervey. *Fifteen Years in the Senior Order of Shakers: A Narration of the Facts concerning That Singular People.* Hanover, N.H.: Dartmouth Press, 1853.

Evans, Jessie. *Diaries.* Canterbury N.H., 1879-1931. SVI, nos. 1984. 13-15, 1985.6-43.

_____ et al. *Family Journal or Current Events.* Canterbury, N.H., n.d. SVI, no. 34.

Filley, Dorothy M. *Recapturing Wisdom's Valley: the Watervliet Shaker Heritage, 1775-1975.* Albany, N.Y.: Albany Institute of History and Art, 1975.

Francis, Samuel W., M.D. *Memoir of the Life and Character of Prof. Valentine Mott.* Middleton, N.H.: W.J. Middleton, 1865.

Frost, Marguerite, "Notes on Shaker Herbs & Herbalists," *The Herb Grower Magazine* 5 (1951), p. 89.

Greenwood, Irving. "Expenses for Sarsaparilla." Canterbury, N.H., 1879. SVI no. 247.

_____. "Notebook of Information on machinery, buildings, equipment, property, etc." Canterbury, N.H., n.d. SVI, no. 28.

Hammond, Thomas. *Diary.* Harvard, Mass., 1851. WRHS Reel 48.

Hartwell, Marcia Byrom. "Comparison of Shaker Food to that of the Outside World's (19th Century)." *The Shaker Messenger* 5 (1983), p. 10.

_____. "Roses and Rosewater." *The Shaker Messenger* 10 (1987) pp. 23, 25.

_____. "Shaker Fruits of the Earth." *The Shaker Messenger.* 10 (1988), p. 15.

_____. "The Shaker Vegetarian Experiment." *The Shaker Messenger* 10 (1988), p. 16, 31.

Heard, D. Hamilton, ed. *History of Merrimack and Belknap Counties, N.H.* Philadelpha: J.W. Lewis & Co., 1885.

Hess, Wendell. "Caleb Marshall Dyer: Shaker Trustee," *Shaker Messenger* (1985) pp. 8-9.

_____. *The Enfield, N.H. Shakers, a Brief History.* 1988.

Hill, Isaac. *Farmers Monthly Visitor* 9 "The Enterprise of the Shakers," (1839), p. 141.

_____. *Farmers Monthly Visitor* 2 "The Shakers," (August 31, 1840), pp. 114–118.

Hill, Mary Ann. *Recipe Book.* Canterbury, N.H.: 1857, SDL.

Hinckley, Barnabus. *Diary.* New Lebanon, N.Y., 1836–1847. Andrews Collection, no. ASC 831.

Holbrook, Stewart H. *The Golden Age of Quackery.* New York: MacMillan Co., 1959.

Holmes, James. *A Collection of Useful Hints for Farmers and Many Valuable Recipes.* West Gloucester, Me., 1849. WRHS Microfiche Collection 410.

_____. *The Farmer's Second Book. A Collection of Useful Hints for Farmers and many valuable Recipes.* West Gloucester, Me., 1853. WRHS Microfiche Collection 413.

_____. *The Farmer's Third Book. A Collection of Useful Hints for Farmers and Gardeners, and many valuable Recipes.* Sabbathday Lake, Me., 1856. WRHS Microfiche Collection 414.

Hylton, William H., ed. *The Rodale Herb Book.* Emmaus, Pa.: Rodale Press Book Division, 1974.

Isaacson, Doris A., ed. *Maine, A Guide: "Down East,"* 2nd edition. Rockland, Me.: Courier-Gazette, Inc., 1970.

Kaufman, Maurice. *American Medical Education, The Formative Years, 1765-1910.* Westport, Conn.: Greenwood Press, 1976.

Kemp, James F. "The Mineral Springs of Saratoga." Albany, N.Y.: State University of N.Y., 1912.

Klaw, Spencer. "Belly-my-Grizzle." *American Heritage* 28 (1977), pp. 96–105.

Landreth, Burnett. "Early History of the American Seed Business." *Seed World* 14 (1923), pp. 13–14.

Lapsley, Tabitha. *Miscellaneous Receipts, extracted from Mary Whitcher.* Sabbathday Lake, Me., 1863. SDL.

Levine, Harold B. "Folk Medicine in New Hampshire." *Journal of New England Medicine.* Boston: Massachusetts Medical Society, Concord, N.H., 1941, reprint.

Lindsay, Eldress Bertha. Monologue on the Infirmary. Canterbury, N.H.. Tape recording, SVI.

_____. "Recipe." Canterbury, N.H., n.d., SVI.

_____. "Scrapbook." Canterbury, N.H., n.d., SVI.

_____. *Seasoned with Grace: My Generation of Shaker Cooking.* Woodstock, Vt.: The Countryman Press, 1987.

_____ and Lillian Phelps. *Industries and Inventions of the Shakers.* Concord, N.H.: Hazen Printing Co., 1968, p. 8.

Lomas, G.A., ed. *The Shaker,* 1871-1872, 1876-1877.

_____. *The Shaker Manifesto,* 1878-1881.

Lossing, Benson T. "A Visit to the Shakers at New Lebanon, N.Y." *Harper's New Monthly Magazine* 86 (1857), pp. 165–177.

Love, Susan. *The Cheap Family Dyer.* Groveland, N.Y., 1858. WRHS Reel 117, XI B-4.

[McClintock, John]. "The Shakers." *The Granite Monthly* 3 (1880), pp. 145–147.

Miller, Amy Bess. *Shaker Herbs, A History and A Compendium.* New York: Clarkson N. Potter, Inc., 1976.

_____ and Persis Fuller. *Best of Shaker Cooking.* New York: Macmillan Publishing Co., Inc., 1970.

Morse, Flo. *The Shakers and the World's People.* New York: Dodd, Mead & Co., 1980.

Myrick, Elisha. *Herb Department Diary.* Harvard, Mass., 1853-1857. Andrews Collection, no. ASC 837.

Myrick, Susan H. *The Physician's Journal or an Account of the Sickness in the Society at Harvard.* Harvard, Mass., 1831-1842. WRHS Reel 30, FB 41.

Neal, Julia. *By Their Fruits: The Story of Shakerism in South Union, Kentucky.* Chapel Hill, N.C.: University of North Carolina Press, 1947.

Neal, Mary Jane, ed. *Journal of Eldress Nancy; Kept at South Union, Kentucky, Shaker Colony, August 14, 1861-September 4, 1864.* Nashville, Tenn.: The Parthanon Press, 1963.

Nordhoff, Charles. *The Communistic Societies of the United States.* New York: Harper and Bros., 1875. New York: Dover Publications, Inc., 1966, reprint.

Pettingill, James J., Jr. *Accounts.* Enfield, N.H., 1812-1852. I NHHS.

Piercy, Caroline B. *The Shaker Cook Book: Not by Bread Alone.* New York: Crown Publishers, Inc., 1953.

Proctor, William. "New Lebanon: Its Physic Gardens and Their Products." *The American Journal of Pharmacy* 18 (1852) p. 89.

Richmond, Mary L. *Shaker Literature: A Bibliography,* 2 vols. Hanover, N.H.: University Press of New England, 1977.

Risse, Guenter P. *Medicine Without Doctors: Home Health Care in American History.* New York: Science History Publishers, 1977.

Sawyer, Otis. *Small Book.* Sabbathday Lake, Me., October 15, 1861. SDL.

———— and John Vance. *Church Record.* 2 vols. Alfred, Me., 1879-1886. SDL, p. 218.

Serette, David, ed. *The Shaker Herbalist* 1 (1975).

Shimko, Phyllis. *Sarsaparilla Bottle Encyclopedia.* Aurora, OR: n.p., 1969.

Shryock, Richard H. *Medicine and Society in America, Historical Essays, 1660-1860.* New York: New York University Press, 1960.

Silliman, Benjamin. "Remarks Made on a Short Tour between Hartford and Quebec in the Autumn of 1819." *Christian Monthly Spectator* (1820), pp. 41-53.

Somer, Margaret Frisbee. *The Shaker Garden Seed Industry.* Old Chatham, N.Y.: The Shaker Museum Foundation, Inc., 1972.

Sprigg, June. *By Shaker Hands.* New York: Alfred A. Knoph, 1979.

Starbuck, David R., ed. *An Historical Survey.* Durham, N.H.: University of New Hampshire Press, 1981.

———— and Margaret Supplee Smith, eds. *Historical Survey of Canterbury Shaker Village.* Boston: Boston University, 1979.

Steel, John. *An Analysis of the Congress Spring with Practical Remarks on the Medical Properties.* Revised and corrected by John L. Perry, M.D. New York: William W. Rose, 1856.

Stewart, P[hilemon]. "Poland Mineral Springs, Medicinal Water." West Gloucester, Me.. [Broadside], SDL.

Thomas, Graham S. *The Old Shrub Roses.* London: J.M. Dent & Sons Let., 1983.

Thomson, Samuel. *The Constitution, Rules and Regulations for the Friendly Botanic Society,* 12th edition. Portsmouth, N.H.: n.p., 1812.

————. *A New Guide to Health or Botanic Family Physician.* Boston: J. Q. Adams, 1832.

————. *A New Guide to Health or Botanic Family Physician.* Boston: J. Q. Adams, 1835.

————. *Thomsonian Materia Medica or Botanic Family Physician.* Albany, N.Y.: J. Munsell, 1841.

Vail, James. *Record Book.* New Lebanon, N.Y., 1841-1857. WRHS.

Wells, Mildred. *Recipes.* Canterbury, N.H., n.d. Private collection.

Wheeler, John, M.D. "Obituary Notice of R. P. J. Tenney, M.D." *Transactions of the N.H. Medical Society.* Pittsfield, N.H.: Daniel T. Neal, 1877. New Hampshire State Library.

Whitcher, John. *A Brief History or Record of the Commencement & Progress of the United Society of Believers, at Canterbury, county of Merrimack, and State of New Hampshire.* Canterbury, N.H., 1782-1871. SVI, no. 21.

Whitcher, Mary. *Mary Whitcher's Shaker House-Keeper,* 1882, SVI 754.

White, Anna and Leila S. Taylor. *Shakerism: its Meaning and Message.* Columbus, Ohio: Fred J. Heer, 1904.

White, Jefferson. *Gardener's Manual: Containing Plain and Practical Directions for the Cultivation and Management of some of the Most Useful Culinary Vegetables: to which is Prefixed a Catalogue of the Various Kinds of Garden seeds Raised in the United Society of Shakers at Enfield, Ct., first Established in 1802 . . . With a Few General Remarks on the management of a Kitchen Garden.* Hartford, Conn., 185 . WRHS Microfiche Collection 439.

Willard, Corinne W. "Garden Writers Bulletin." 1964.

Wood, George B., M.D. , and Franklin Bache, M.D. *The Dispensatory of the United States of America,* 7th edition. Philadelphia: J. B. Lippincott, 1847.

Woodman, James B. "Presidential Address." *New England Journal of Medicine* 226 (1942), p. 639.

Yepson, Roger B., Jr., Ed., *The Encyclopedia of Natural Insect & Disease Control.* Emmaus, Pa.: Rodale Press, 1984.

Youngs, Benjamin. *Testamony of Christ's Second Appearing, exemplified by the Principles and Practice of the True Church of Christ. History of the Progressive Work of God, extending from the Creation of Man to the "Harvest," comprising the Four Great Dispensations Now Consummating in the Millenial Church. Antichrist's Kingdom or Churches, contrasted with the Church of Christ's First and Second Appearing, the Kingdom of the God of Heaven,* 4th edition. Albany, N.Y., 1856.

Youngs, Isaac N. *A Concise View of the Church of God and of Christ on Earth Having its foundation In the Faith of Christ's first and Second Appearing.* New Lebanon, N.Y., 1856-1860. Andrews Collection, SA 760.

Index

Adams, Eldress Hester
 Ann, 191
Alden, Ebenezer, 42
Alfred, Maine, xviii, xxiv
 catalogs, 223, 229
 establishment, 12
 seed business, 30, 38-40
American Reformed
 System, 104
Atherton, Simon, xx, 208,
 216
Auchmoody, Jack, 46
Avery, Elizabeth, 115
Avery, Elder Giles, 133

Babbit, Abiathar, xx, 29
Babbit, Tabitha, xviii, 122
Baker, Hyram, 215
Barnes, John, 12
Barrett, Salome, 122
Beech, Wooster, 104
Bennett, D. M., 140
Beverages, 173-175
 herb tea, 174
 herbade, 174
 currant shrub, 175
 ginger beer, 175
 rye coffee, 174-175
 spring beer, 175
Bishoprics, 2, 7, 17-18
Blinn, Elder Henry, 4, 43-
 44, 102, 111-113, 118-
 119, 155-156, 159, 211

Botanic Family Physician,
 105
Boyd, Peter, xx, 139-140
Bradford, Seth, 24
Briggs, Nathaniel A., 146
Briggs, Nicholas, 33, 148, 151,
 154
Brinley, Edward, 146, 148
Brown, Lyman, 135
Brown, Samuel, 120-121, 152
Brown's Fluid Extract of
 English Valerian, 136,
 146, 151-153, 214-215
Bruce, Elder Arthur, 149

Candy, 175-176
 horehound candy, 176
 peppermint drop, 175-176
Canterbury, New Hamp-
 shire, ix, xv, xviii-xxii,
 xxiv
 Compound of Wild
 Cherry Pectoral Syrup
 and Sarsaparilla
 Lozenges, xxi, 136, 212
 catalogs, 204-207, 211-212,
 223, 229
 establishment, 8
 health care, 111
 herb business, 31-33
 income-producing
 activities, 9
 physic gardens, 29

re-created herb gardens,
 46-52
 seed business, 36, 39-41,
 43-44
 size, 9
 West Family, 9
Carr, Anna, 116
Carr, Frances, 59, 61 164,
 168, 171, 173
Catalogs, 203-217, 223-234
 Catalogue of Medicinal
 Plants and Vegetable
 Medicines, 204
 endorsements, 205
 warnings, 208
 See also Alfred, Maine;
 Canterbury, New
 Hampshire; Enfield,
 Connecticut; Enfield,
 New Hampshire;
 Hancock, Massachu-
 setts; Harvard,
 Massachusetts; New
 Lebanon, New York;
 Sabbathday Lake,
 Maine; Shirley,
 Massachusetts; South
 Union, Kentucky;
 Tyringham, Massachu-
 setts; Union Village,
 Ohio; Watervliet, New
 York; Whitewater,
 Ohio

259

Ceeley, Sally, 161
Chadbourne, Charles, 125–126, 205
Chauncey, Israel, 10
Church Family Ministry, 2
Clifford, Hiram, 128
Clifford, Lavinia, 161, 165, 171
Clough, John, 125–126
Cooley, Ebenezer, 10
Condiments, 165–168
  horseradish, 165–166
  piccalilli, 166
  rose hip jam, 167–168
  spruced vinegar for pickles, 166
  tomato catchup, 166
Converts, 2, 5
Corbett, Jesse, 117–118
Corbett, Josiah, 117
Corbett, Thomas, xix, 20, 27, 31, 34, 132, 117–119, 122, 126, 159, 162,205, 211–212.
  Corbett's Sarsaparilla Syrup, xx–xxi, 139–143, 145–146, 148–149, 212
Cosmetics and Skin Tonics, 184–186
  chapped hands, 184–185
  hair restorative, 186
  heolane, 184
  ointment of rose water, 184
  rose water and witch hazel skin tonic, 184
Couch, Isaac, xix, 121
Creating Shaker Herb Gardens, 63–100
  culinary garden, 74–75
  cultivation, 90
  design, 70–71
  dividing plants, 84–85
  flowering garden, 78–79
  fragrant garden, 80–81
  growing four culinary herbs, 97–99
  harvesting and storing, 94
  hotbeds, 87–88
  improving soil, 65, 70, 81
  medicinal garden, 76–77
  mulches, 90–91
  pest control, 91–94
  preparing the garden for winter, 97
  preparing soil, 81–84
  starting seeds indoors, 85–87

starting seeds outdoors, 89–90
  tea garden, 72–73
  transplanting, 88–89
Crook, Ida, xxii
Crooker, Martha, 129
Crosby, Asa, 141
Crosby, Dixi, 141–142, 205
Crosby, Josiah, 126
Crosman, Charles F., 42, 64

Culinary herbs, 160, 207, 208, 210

Dean, John, 108
"Death of Old Alcohol," 158
Desserts, 171–173
  Mother Ann's Birthday Cake, 173
  rose water apple pie, 172–173
  rose water frosting, 173
DeWitt, Henry, 210
Dietary trends, 155–158, 161
Drake, Molly, 112
Dunlavy, Benjamin, 58
Dyer, Caleb, 10, 31, 43, 215
Dyer, Jerub, 147, 150–151
Dyes, 195–198
  black, 196
  blue, 197–198
  coloring cotton, 196–197
  red, 196
  to make a dye bath, 196
  to mordant the wool, 195

Elders and Eldresses
  See Families
Elkins, Mercy, 112
Enfield, Connecticut, xviii, xx–xxi, xxiv
  catalogs, 208, 216–217, 224, 229–230
  seed business, 31, 39, 43
  size, 8
Enfield, New Hampshire, xviii–xix, xxii, xxiv
  catalogs, 214, 224, 230
  English Valerian, xx, xxi, 10, 145
  physic gardens, 29
  prosperity, 11
  re-created herb gardens, 52–53
  seed business, 31, 36, 38, 40, 44
  village gardener program, 54

Evans, Ezekiel, 120
Evans, Elder Frederick, 1, 134, 160
Evans, Jessie, 130, 149
Every-Day Book, 146
Extract House, 137

"Facts Concerning Brown's Shaker Pure Fluid Extract of English Valerian," 153
Families, 2
  gathering, 12
  governance, 2, 4–5
  naming, 2
Farmer's Second Book, 92
Fitch, A. Perley Company, 154
Foster, Stephen, 59
Fowler, Edward, 23, 25, 28, 121, 211
Fowler, Mary, 117
Fragrant Waters and Oils, 179–184
  colognes, 182–184
  homemade cologne, 182
  kiss me quick, 182
  lavender water, 180–181
  peach water, 181
  rose oil, 181
  rose water, 180
Friendly Botanic Society, 105
Frost, Eldress Marguerite, 116
Fruitlands Museums, xxii

Garden Seeds, 35–44
  advertising, 37
  agents, 38
  Civil War impact, 43
  commissions, 38
  competition, 42–44
  Gardener's Manual, 41–42
  individual packaging, 36–37, 39
  origin/Watervliet, 35, 39
  overlapping, 40–41
  printing, 42–43
  support for one another, 37–38
  transportation, 38
Gardener's Manual, xx, 64–66, 85, 89, 91–92, 94, 97
Gates, Benjamin, 19, 138, 150–151
Gillman, Ransom, 213

Goodrich, Mother Hannah, 121
Gorham, Maine, xix, xxiv, 2
Graham Diet, 159, 161
Graham, Sylvester, 159
Greenwood, Irving, 149
Griffith, Happy, 52-54
Groveland, New York, xx, xxiv, l6
seed business, 30

Hancock, Massachusetts, xviii, xxii, xxiv
catalogs, 230
re-created herb gardens, 55-56
seed business, 31, 38
size, 7
Hall, Francis, xxii
Harlow, Calvin, 7
Harlow, Eliab, xix, 23, 34, 115, 121, 128
Harvard, Massachusetts, xviii-xx, xxiv
catalogs, 205, 208-210, 215-216, 224-225
herb business, 31
physic gardens, 29
seed business, 46
size, 18
spring, 109-110
Hathaway, Rebecca, 154, 163, 167
Hawkins, Daniel, 37
Herb business, 19-34
botanists, 20-21
catalog, 29, 31
collecting by children, 19-20
herb press, 25-27, 32
medical community acceptance, 22
planting gardens, 23-24
physician responsibility, 24
process, 19, 25
purchasing from World, 28
quality, 21
sale of seeds, 29-31
shipment, 27, 29
trade model/New Lebanon, 24
uses, 21
Hibbard, R. F., and Company, 207
Hill, Mary Ann, 181-182, 186
Hill, Isaac, 21, 27, 32, 68, 118, 133

Hinckley, Barnabas, 107, 121, 128
Hocknell, John, 2
Hollister, Alonzo, 28
Holman, Dr., 108
Holmes, James, 64
Houston, Andrew, xx, 29
Howe's, S. D., Shaker Compound Extract of Sarsaparilla Syrup, 140
Hudson, Ethel, ix, 46
Hudspeth, Dory, 59
Hunt, Lucy, 129-130
Hydropathy, 108-113, 164

Infirmaries, 124-125
Insect repellants, 194-195
perfume and preventative of moths, 194

Jennings, Horace, 23
Jethro, 23
Jewett, James, 10
Jewett, John, 112
Jewett, Sarah, xviii, 122
Johns, Harriet, 130
Johnson, Ted, 59
Joslin, Joseph, 156

Kaime, James, 126, 148, 211-212
Kendall, Hannah, 8
Kendall, Sarah, 12, 107
King, Emma, xxii

Land acquisition, pattern of, 2
Landreth, David, 36
Lankester, Elizabeth, 118
LaSalette Order of Roman Catholic brothers, 52
Lawrence, G. K., 23, 67, 115, 128, 139, 141, 159
Lead Ministry, xix-xx, xxii, 2, 3, 7 22, 213
Lee, Mother Ann, xiii-xiv, xvii-xviii, 1, 7, 10, 101-102, 115-116, 130
Lindsay, Eldress Bertha, ix-xi, xxii, xxiii, 46, 73, 109, 160, 163, 165, 167- 168, 170, 172, 174, 176, 179, 194
Lossing, Benjamin, 137

Mace, Aurelia, 62
Massachusetts Charitable Mechanics Association, 145

Maynard and Noyes, 148-149
McNear, Alice, 130
Meacham, David, 136
Meacham, Elder Joseph, xviii, 5, 10, 102
Meagrath, Dr., 131
Meats and Fish, 169-170
baked fish, tomato sauce, 170
sausage, 170
savory meat, 170
Medical Flora, 24, 210
Medical practices, 101-114
Medicines and Medicinal Wines, 189-194
blackberry wine, 190
cough candy, 191-192
cough syrup, 192
currant wine, 191
dog bites, 194
falling womb, 193
homemade grape wine, 191
nail wound, 193
rheumatism, 193
rose syrup, 190
snake bites, 194
toothache, 192
Millennial Laws, xix, 115, 157
Miller, Amy Bess, 55
Miller, Chauncey, 122-124, 136, 211
Miller, David, 121, 124, 136
Moore, George, 129
Mother Siegel's Syrup, 135
Mott, Valentine, 141
Mount Lebanon (formerly New Lebanon), xxi-xxiii
re-created herb gardens, 56-57
Myrick, Elisha, 25-27, 205
Myrick, Susan K., 122

National Druggist, 148
New Guide to Health, A, 105
New Lebanon, New York, xviii-xxi, xxiv, 2, 3
catalogs, 204, 207, 210, 215, 217, 225-226, 231-232
location, 6
physic gardens, 29
seat of Lead Ministry, 7
seed business, 36, 38-39, 41, 43

Niskeyuna, New York (later called Watervliet), 5
Norcoossee, Florida, xxi, xxiv
North Union, Ohio, xix, xxiv, 15
  seed business, 36
Norwood, Wesley C., 135
Norwood's Tincture of Veratrum Viride, xxi

Parent Ministry, 12
Parker, David, 108, 126, 128, 140, 145, 205, 211
Partridge, J., 126
Philadelphia Centennial, 145
Physicians and Nurses, The Order of, xix, 103, 114-115, 117, 122
Pierce, Franklin, 126
Pleasant Hill, Kentucky, xviii, xxii, xxiv, 13
  medicines, 30
  re-created herb gardens, 57-58
  seed business, 38, 43
  wartime, 15
Pope, Debbie Larkin, 57
Potpourris, 187-189
  organdy sachets, 189
  potpourri, 189
  rose jar, 187-188
Prentiss, Ephraim, 158
Prescott, William, 125
Pure Food and Drug Act, 154

Rand, Eleazer, 8
Rafinesque, Professor Constantine Samuel, 210
Re-created herb gardens, 45-62
  See also Canterbury, New Hampshire; Enfield, New Hampshire; Hancock, Massachusetts; Mount Lebanon, New York; Pleasant Hill, Kentucky; Sabbathday Lake, Maine; South Union, Kentucky
Rose cultivation, 177-179

Rural Home, 111

Sabbathday Lake, Maine, xv, xviii-xix, xxi-xxii, xxiv
  catalogs, 213, 226
  herb business, 30
  manufacturing, 14
  re-created herb gardens, 59-62
  size, 12
  springs, 108
Sage, 97-98
Saratoga Springs, 111-112
Sarsaparilla, 139
  advertisement of syrup, 144-146
  distribution, 144-145, 148
  manufacture of syrup, 142-144
  See also Corbett
Savory, 98
Savoy, Massachusetts, xix, xxiv
Sawyer, Otis, 213-214
Scherer, Kitty, 54
Seven Barks, 135
Shaker Almanac, 151
Shaker Anodyne, 151, 153, 215
Shakers' Manual, xx, 146-148, 151, 153
Shane, John, 58
Shirley, Massachusetts, xviii, xxiv, 8
  catalogs, 232-233
  seed business, 30, 36, 38, 40
Sleeper, Nathaniel, 33
Smith, Eldress Betsy, 107-108
Smith, Caroline, 46
Salads and Dressings, 168-169
  potato salad, 168
  shelled bean salad, 168-169
  tarragon dressing, 169
Soaps and Candles, 186-187
  Bullard's oil soap, 186
  candles durable, 187
  shaving soap, 186-187
  toilet soap, 186
Sodus Bay, New York, xx, xxiv, 16
Soule, Eldress Gertrude, ix, xxii, xxiii

Sources and supplies, 198-201
  botanical drugs and spices, 200
  dye references, 201
  dyeing supplies, 200
  herb plants, 198-199
  labels, 200
  organizations, 199
  potpourri supplies, dried botanics, essential oils, fragrances, 199-200
  rose plants, 198
South Union, Kentucky, xix, xxii, xxiv
  catalogs, 233-234
  re-created herb gardens, 58-59
  seed business, 36, 38, 103
  size, 13
Stevens, Levi, 112
Stevens, Ruth, 112
Stevens, Zaccheus, 102
Stickney, Elizabeth, 130
Stickney, Prudence, 173
Stuart, Philemon, 108
Sweet marjoram, 99

Tamar laxative, 214
Tenney, Richard P. J., 125, 129-130, 141
Tenney, William, 118
Thompson, John, 8
Thomson, Samuel, 104-106
Thomsonian School of Medicine, 104
Thomsonian Materia Medica, 33, 105-106
Thyme, 99
Tincture of Veratrum Viride, 135, 154
Tripure, William, 20, 119, 126-127
Trusses, 118, 211
Tyringham, Massachusetts, xviii, xxiv
  catalogs, 234
  seed business, 31
  size, 8

U.S. Pure Food and Drug Act, xxii
Union Village, Ohio, xviii-xx, xxiv
  catalogs, 205-206, 208, 211, 227
  physic gardens, 29

prosperity, 15
seed business, 36
size, 15
United Society of
  Believers in Christ's
  Second Appearing
  (Shakers), xiii, xvii

Vegetables, 170-171
  baked beans, 170-171
  potato cakes, 171
  savory green beans, 171
  stewed beets, 171
Vining, Charles, 213

Wall, Miriam, 51
Walsh and Cummings,
  149
Wardley, Jane and James,
  xvii
Warren, Benjamin, xix,
  113, 119-120
Watervliet, New York,
  xvii-xviii, xx, xxiv, 2
  catalogs, 204-205, 207-
  208, 211-212, 216, 227-
  228, 234

physic gardens, 29
seed business, 30, 35, 39
size, 5
Watervliet, Ohio, xxiv, 15
Weeks and Potter, xxi,
  146, 148, 161
Weldon, Tom, 56
Wells, Mildred, ix, 45, 48-
  52, 189
West Gloucester
  (formerly New
  Gloucester), 12
West Union (Busro),
  Indiana, xix, xxiv,
  12-13
Whitcher, Benjamin, 8
Whitcher, Mary, 162-163
*Mary Whitcher's Shaker
  House-Keeper*, xxi,
  146, 161-162, 166, 170
Whitcher, John, 145, 211
White, A. J., xxi, 149, 151,
  214
White, Elder Freeman,
  192
White, Jefferson, 216

White Oak, Georgia, xxii,
  xxiv
Whitewater, Ohio, xix,
  xxiv, 15, 43, 228, 234
Whiting, George B., 25-26
Whittaker, Father James,
  xviii, 10
Wiggins, Chase, 8
Wiggins, Martha, 117
Wilson, Josephine, xxii
Winkley, Francis, 36-37,
  39
Witch Hazel
  (*Hamamelis*), 149
Wood, Daniel, 128
Wood, Jonathan, 108, 121
Woods, Sarah S., 161, 165,
  171
Wright, Grove, 113
Wright, Jesse, 118
Wright, Lucy, xviii

Youngs, Benjamin, 102,
  156
Youngs, Isaac N., 101-102

Galen Beale and Mary Rose Boswell.

About the Authors

Galen Beale worked for seven years at Canterbury Shaker Village as herbalist and crafts coordinator. She has published numerous articles on shaker herbs and crafts and is a garden consultant.

Mary Rose Boswell has written on a wide range of topics in the field of preservation and the decorative arts. She was the curator of collections for the Association for the Preservation of Virginia Antiquities, exhibits curator for the New Hampshire Historical Society, curator of collections for Canterbury Shaker Village, and is now Director of the Belknap Mill Society in Laconia, New Hampshire. While employed at Canterbury Shaker Village she edited *Seasoned with Grace* by the late Eldress Bertha Lindsay. In 1990 she received a national award from the American Association of State and Local Histories for this work.